Hat of Candles

Essays
2008-2019

Hat of Candles

Essays
2008-2019

Richard Wirick

Ekstasis Editions

Copyright © Richard Wirick 2021
Cover art: Francisco de Goya, *Self Portrait at an Easel*, 1790-95
Author photo: Amelia Wirick

Published in 2021 by:
Ekstasis Editions America

Ekstasis Editions Ltd. (Canada)
Box 8474, Main Postal Outlet
Victoria, BC V8W 3S1

All rights reserved. No part of this book may be reproduced in any form without the written permission of the publisher, with the exception of brief passages in reviews. Any request for photocopying or other reproduction of any part of this book should be directed in writing to the publisher.

Hardcover ISBN 9781952339028
Paperback ISBN 9781952339035
Ebook ISBN 9781952339042

Contents

I. OPEN WINDOW [PLACES]

CHINESE LETTERS
i.   Tree Of Blue Rivers   13
ii. The Goddess Of Democracy   19

MIDWEST IN THE SIXTIES
i.   In Christ There Is No East or West   19
ii. Green, Whale-Back Mountain (Letter from Appalachia)   35

BLUE HIGHWAYS
i.   Man in Black Again   46
ii. The First Sam Sheppard   53
iii The Teacher's Sermon (Letter from India)   57
iv. Deep Play (Letter from Indonesia)   64
v.   Chechens in the Capital (Letter from Moscow)   72
vi. Prisons of the King (Letter from the Chiapas Rebellion)   75
vii The Ground Game (Letter from Nevada)   83

II. BIOGRAPH [PEOPLE]

i.   Encomium: Ann Ackerman   95
ii.   The Persistence of Desire [John Updike]   99
iii. Worlds We Have [Saul Bellow]   105
iv.   Never A More Honest Man Lived (John Cheever)   106
v.   Whatever Is Moving [James Schuyler]   112

vi.   Chilly Buddha Hall [Phillip Whalen, Allen Ginsberg,
      Gary Snyder, 1973]   117
vii. Kazin, Perambulating [Alfred Kazin]   121
viii. C.K. Williams   124
ix.   Brains, Bats and Implanted Thoughts [Philip K. Dick]   128
x.   Boss Cupid [Thom Gunn]   135
xi.   Who Was Phillip Roth?   141

III. THE LIBRARY OF BABEL [BOOKS AND WRITING]

Flim Flam, Flum [David Samuels: *The Runner*]   149
Naming and Necessity [Adam Thirwell: *The Delighted States*]   153
Coming Through Slaughter [Kathryn Harrison: *While They Slept*] 157
Devil in My Beehive [Joyce Carol Oates: *Journal 1973-82*]   161
Juxtapositions [James Tate: *The Ghost Soldiers*]   164
Poets Writing Letters [*The Letters of Ted Hughes*,
    *Words in Air: The Complete Correspondence between
    Elizabeth Bishop and Robert Lowell*]   168
A Writer's Life [Carol Sklenicka: *Raymond Carver*]   175
Days Are to Be Happy In [Roger Rosenblatt: *Making Toast*]   180
Racine on the Prairie [Richard Ford: *Canada*]   183
Eros, Builder of Cities [Eric Berkowitz: *Sex & Punishment*]   186
Under the Overpass [Russell Banks: *Lost Memory of Skin*]   190
The Duke of Self Regard [Norman Mailer: *Selected Letters*]   193
Modernist, Downhill Racer [Ian MacNiven: *Litterchoor Is
    My Beat: A Life of James Laughlin*]   197
Lucia Berlin: *A Manual for Cleaning Women*   201
The Captive Sylph [Ruth Franklin: *Shirley Jackson*]   205
Barque of Hobbes [Ian McGuire: *The North Water*]   208

Blood Soaked Plain [David Grann: *Killers of the Flower-Moon*]   211
Spies and Prophets [Max Boot: *The Road Not Taken*]   214
The Mind Makes Up the World [Daniel C. Dennett:
   From Bacteria to Bach & Back]   217
A Pugilist at the Riots [Norman Mailer: *Four Books of the Sixties*]   220
Where the Days Go [Carlo Rovelli: *The Order of Time*]   224
The Shadow in the Garden [James Atlas: *The Shadow in the
   Garden: A Biographer's Tale*]   228
Audacity and Distraction [William Giraldi: *American Audacities*
   Joshua Cohen: *Attention*   230
The Master's Farewell Gift [William Trevor: *Lost Stories*]   235
Writers and Horseraces [Gerald Murnane: *Stream System*]   238
Wake of the Flood [Curtis Sittenfeld: *You Think It, I'll Say It*]   242
Love Is the Crooked Thing [Julian Barnes: *The Only Story*]   244
Men Without Women [Joseph O'Neill: *Good Trouble*]   246
River of Dreams [Vanda Krefft: *The Man Who Made the Movies*]   248
Righting the Brain [Anne Harrington: *The Mind Fixers*]   251
Who Was the Shining Path? [Starn & La Sterna: *The Shining Path*]   254
The Supreme Court and the Illusion of Voter Fraud
   [Carol Anderson: *One Person, No Vote*]   258
From Langley to Lahore [Steve Coll: *Directorate S*]   262
A Trial Lawyer's Book of Days [Ben Fountain:
   Beautiful Country, Burn Again]   266
Vincent Katz (ed.): *Black Moutain College: Experiment in Art*   270
Meltdown [Adam Higginbotham: *Midnight in Chernobyl*]   274
West with the Sun [Carrie Gibson: *El Norte*]   278
In'Shallah [Tim Macintosh-Smith: *Arabs: a 3,000 Year History*]   282
Till Death Do Us Part [Susan Gubar: *Late Life Love*]   286
The Halt and the Blind [Richard Gergel: *Unexampled Courage*]   290

Prisons of the King [Alan Ryan: *On Politics*] 294
Two Quiet Giants [Sean B. Carroll: *Brave Genius*] 297
Sadness and Happiness [Scott Stossel: *My Age of Anxiety*] 300
Ethnology's Rivers & Tributaries [Charles King:
   Gods of the Upper Air] 303
Mean, Mean Streets [Alex Koltowitz: *An American Summer*] 308
Anat Crit [A.O. Scott: *Better Living Through Criticism*] 311
Rose of Mississippi [Charles Frazier: *Varina*] 315
Nature and Verse [Robert Hass: *Summer Snow*] 319
The Shimmer's End [Shaun Prescott: *The Town*] 324
Lured by the Wolf [Jessica Stern: *My War Criminal*] 328
Fathers and Writing Sons [Colm Toibin: *Mad, Bad &*
   Dangerous to Know] 332
Big Brother, 2020 and 2.0 [Gish Jen: *The Resisters*] 336
Robert Stone's Fiery America [Robert Stone: *Three Novels*] 340
Break Time [Emily Guendelsberger: *On the Clock*] 345
Interconnections [Deborah Levy: *The Man Who Saw Everything*] 348
The Pandemic's Cassandra [Emily St. John Mandel:
   Station Eleven] 351
The Bow Tie Justice [John Paul Stevens: *The Making of a Justice*] 356
Razor and Silk [Vivian Gornick: *Unfinished Business*] 360
Strout, Again [Elizabeth Strout: *Olive, Again*] 364
A Gay Rights Prophet [Eric Cervini: *The Deviant's War*] 367
Out on the High Wires [David Means: *Instructions for a Funeral*] 371
The Traveling Chair [Elizabeth Winthrop: *The Mercy Seat*] 375

To The Memory of My Father
Gene Arlen Wirick
(1932—2020)
Who tended toward the 'non-ficticious'

And to the editors: Richard Olafson, Laura Mazer, Mitch Albert,
Andrew Tonkovich, S.L. Wisenberg, and Anthony Robinson
at Beacon Editorial

Whose idea this was

If Socrates leaves his house today he will find the sage seated on his doorstep. If Judas go forth tonight it is to Judas his steps will tend. Every life is many days, day after day. We walk through ourselves, meeting robbers, ghosts, giants, old men, young men, wives, widows, brothers-in-law. But always meeting ourselves.

> ~ Maeterlinck
> *Wisdom and Destiny*

When you can assume that your audience holds the same beliefs as you, you can relax and use more normal means of talking to it; when you have to assume that it does not, then you have to make your vision apparent by shock—to the hard of hearing you shout, and for the almost-blind you draw large and startling figures.

> ~ Flannery O'Connor
> *The Habit of Being*

Open Window

(Places)

Tree of Blue Rivers

If President Xi's new-found, perpetual hold on power has any effect on the average Chinese citizen, it is not obvious in the evening strollers on the Bund, Shanghai's great financial district laying along the barge-flecked Huang-pu River. It has long been the third largest in the world (after Wall Street and London), and if my economic consultant is correct that China will essentially rule the world by 2050, it will have moved to first place sometime long before that. The breezes from the night river make this a perfect walking promenade, and as you look across its waters to the new trading district of Pudong, sheer visual wonder is hard to contain. The towers look like several Manhattans strung together, and the highest, like the sinewy Shanghai Financial Center at over two thousand feet, the world's second-tallest, perfect what Dallas design-builder Anthony Robinson has called the Vertical City. There is nowhere to look but up; if you look down, the swift, obsidian water mirrors back the long parade of shifting, glassy fire.

The wise political prediction money saw Xi's ascent as not inevitable, but certainly not too surprising. Though Xi was placed in posts that that established him as the Chinese Communist Party's future dynamo, he went a step further and ensured he could have no possible successor. The late winter suspension of term limits thus indicate that he intends to emulate Mao and stay on into old age (he is only 65), a state of affairs unheard of in the post-Deng era. Xi has taken the chair of numerous economic and graft-watchdog committees, posts that the heir apparent for them, Li Keqiang, seemed destined to fill. But Xi has pushed to the forefront his theory of the "three represents," authored by new politburo member Wang Huning. The Three Represents is a hodgepodge of "new authoritarianism," aversion to Western democracy, and, as if to guarantee lesser freedoms will operate cleanly, the ever-present zeal for anti-corruption measures, sometimes created on the fly like some sort of Trumpian overnight publicity gesture.

Wang Huning is a fascinating figure. He is gaunt and tall—most un-Chinese—contrasting with Xi's stalwart and straightforward blandness. Wang did not seek out his power. He is the type of intellectual that many leaders opportunistically foreground to legitimize blunt policy moves. Wang is from here in Shanghai, a young professor at the prestigious Fudan University. He has the deep historical-intellectual bent of a Kissingerian academic: aloof, detached, a "mere scholar" who nevertheless keeps a sharp lookout for moments of effective policy influence. His anti-Western bent should work well with Xi's new policies, though the latter involves the union of state-owned enterprises with (often) foreign and privately-owned service sectors. Xi has long promised economic reform in the style of Deng Xiaoping, but he has yet to deliver.

But Xi is first and foremost a figure of power, of control over the media and the police-repressive apparatus of government militias and intelligence services. Xi has made himself the head of committees on foreign affairs and national security. And while the presidency gives the nation's leaders equal footing with foreign diplomatic representatives, the cold, hard truth of chairmanship is a very anti-Western control of the military. After all, the People's Liberation Army belongs to the party, not the nation. This makes China unlike almost all other great nations of the world, even Russia. And it all goes back to Mao's first axiom of realpolitik, that "all power grows out of the barrel of a gun."

If the foregoing gives the equivalent of a macro view of things as we see in physics, the population builds itself incrementally, in a granular manner, at what might resemble a subatomic level of progress. Learning new, practically effective mundanities is a slow and bumbling process. But Chinese tenacity is a model for the human spirit, and nowhere is this more obvious than in the mastery of Western practical habits. The skill set most dramatically acquired in the last two decades is best chronicled by my compatriot Peter Hessler, the Beijing bureau chief for *The New Yorker*. It amounts to driving an automobile, to gaining that most precious of inland grants of freedom—the driver's license.

We don't get to see the slapstick of this in coastal cities. But China, not unlike the United States, amounts to a large geographical mass that must be traversed by the internal combustion engine. And do not even dream of alternatives to fossil fuel transportation. If my own governor, Jerry Brown, dreams of an emissionless future of electric vehicles and bullet trains, his nightmare is the Chinese future, where coal burn-off and photochemical smog make the capital of Beijing look like a toxic fog chamber. My hairdresser describes Shanghai as the world's "sexiest" city, referring mainly to fashion. If it has crept inland to the capital we need to start with D & G and Tom Ford facemasks, bright and necessary flecks in the haze that gives you only a one or two-block visual range.

So let's stick with the sub-atomic for awhile and apply for a Chinese driver's license. The exam questions are often like something out of a Marx Brothers movie, and are punctuated by simple edicts one might not even think of, like "In taxi, is fine to carry a small amount of explosive material." Translations of the booklets are difficult, but you get plenty of zaniness and a constant theme of aggression:

China did not become the Asian dynamo by tolerating the word for traffic jam, largely untranslatable save for the phrase "a go-slow." The rules for passing another vehicle are what gives the Western taxi passenger, and driver license student, the willies:

> 80: If, while preparing to pass a car, you notice that it is turning left, making a U-turn, or passing another vehicle, you should:
> a) pass on the right
> b) not pass
> c) honk, accelerate, and pass on the left.

I have been impressed with the safety-consciousness of motorbike and trishaw taxis in Shanghai. But in the interior, the pedestrian, oddly, is not the king, and "the formation of aggressive skills" translates into "passing the test with the examiner."

117: When approaching a marked pedestrian crossing, you should:
   a) slow down and stop if there are pedestrians;
   b) accelerate in order to catch up with the car directly in front of you, and then cross closely behind him;
   c) drive straight through, because pedestrians should give vehicles the right of way.

The courtesy of fair warning has been at least internalized by downtown Shanghai drivers, who would do well in short stints as instructors in the countryside. Who said there was a shortage of jobs for new college graduates? There are crashes galore all over the interior here, from Chengdu to Yunnan. But as is often the case with progress, forgiveness is more easily dispensed than permission.

353. When passing an elderly person or a child, you should
   a) slow down and make sure you pass safely;
   b) continue at the same speed;
   c) honk the horn to tell them to watch out.
269: When you enter a tunnel, you should, you should:
   a) honk and accelerate;
   b) slow down and turn on your lights;
   c) honk and maintain speed.
335. When driving through a residential area, you should:
   a) honk like normal;
   b) honk more than normal, in order to alert residents;
   c) lean arm on horn to notify residents you have arrived.

Again, my affection for my fellow Angelinos notwithstanding, I would grant, had I President Xi's authority, the equivalent of a Ph.D in Chinese Driver Education to each of the four million motorists in the greater L.A. Basin. The horn is obviously key here, even in the smaller, mid-country cities. Hessler describes it as an essentially neurological extension of the body, something that channels the driver's reflexes. He compares it deftly with the difficulties of acquiring their language, and shows that subtleties of pitch and deliverance can make all the difference.

Chinese is tonal, which means that a single sound like *ma* has different meanings depending on whether it is flat, rising, falling and rising, or falling sharply. A single Chinese horn, on the other hand, can mean at least ten distinct things. A solid hoooonnnnkkkk is intended to attract attention. A double sound—hoooonnnnkkkk hoooonnnnkkkk —indicates irritation. There's a particularly long hooooonnnnnkkkkk that means that the driver is stuck in bad traffic, has exhausted curb-sneaking options, and would like everyone else on the road to disappear. A responding hoooooooonnnnnnnnkkkkkkkk proves that the recipient isn't going anywhere. There's a stuttering, staggering honk honk hnk hnk that represents pure panic. There's the afterthought honk—the one that rookie drivers make if they were too slow to hit the button before the situation resolved itself. And there's a short basic honk that simply says: My hands are still on the wheel, and this horn still serves as an extension of my nervous system.

The passage is not only accurate but is quintessential Hessler. If, as Wittgenstein said, reality is the shadow of grammar, then linguistic tonality is the mirror of the Nanking Road's essential, incessant clamor—a signal that the microcosmic, coral-like granules of civilization have arrived and are beginning to assemble themselves.

The night music of the Bund has no such discordance. I walk along it with my son, a banker, who notices it also. The walkers' faces are awash with the peace of economic stability. To be rich is glorious, and by the standards of much of Asia the urban Chinese are rich indeed. They do not put their money in their wardrobes or driveways, but in their childrens' educations, in American real estate, in the ever-burgeoning companies whose stunning, flickering ads make the Pudong towers resemble something out of Blade Runner's sensory overload. Only calmer, less menacing.

For now, the Chinese populace is willing, like Russia's, to lean in to old autocratic models to keep this equilibrium of prosperity. The psyche of the individual Chinese citizen—that mixture of conformity with brash self-reliance—will probably remain an enigma to Western sociologists. But physical well-being is growing, fanning out like the budding "blue rivers" of the ancient scroll painters. Xi has been described, not without some queasiness, as the new Sun King. But as the old proverb goes, "The sky is high and the Emperor is far away." For now, for this moment, the Bund walkers are blessed with calm waters and soft breezes.

The Goddess of Democracy

When you walk into Tienanmen Square you are stunned—there's no other word for it—by its vast emptiness. It is a great concave crater of grey stone, the identical governmental buildings framing its silence and small bundles of trees bending in thatches around the wide doors of its federal ministries. But above all, the haze and the dead air and sheer acreage bespeak emptiness, vacuity, a soundless void. It is like one of those flag-flecked DeChirico paintings, calling attention to its geometric forms that somehow became, for some unknown reason, empty of everything human.

So it is essentially an unpeopled place. It may have been a place of the people in 1949, when Mao, whose face gazes Oz-like from the balcony of the Forbidden City, announced the new regime after decades on the Long March. And it became a place of the people for a short historical moment in 1989, but more about that in a minute.

That weekend I was at the medical school graduation of one of my best friends. In the days before the ceremony, we watched the TV footage of crowds gathering on the capital's boulevards and subway platforms, people of every conceivable stripe: college students, municipal workers, seniors in wheelchairs, gymnastic instructors who led the great bends and stretches of the pre-office national exercises, sometimes there in the Party's otherwise sedate *sanctum sanctorum*. All we could see on the TV screens was a sea of banners, the great marked sheets fluttering waves through which bobbed tens of thousands of smiling, self-surprised faces.

By the time we emerged from the med school auditorium, out into the already torpid Dallas sunshine, things had grown more menacing in that other ceremony 9,000 miles away. I had never heard the Hippocratic Oath recited by new clinical graduates, and my ears were still happily ringing with it, with the first lines Galen and Herophilos had uttered to their own teachers: "First, do no harm."

In the preceding days, there seemed little chance that harm

would come to the Chinese multitudes calling for democracy. The army had allowed them to pitch tents in the square, drive vehicles around in a normal ped-only zone. There was an exuberance on the faces of both the marchers and the soldiers, a dreamlike wonder at the unfamiliar, the sheer happy oddity of the newly, suddenly allowed. The soldiers had no weapons and looked more like cheerful traffic cops. And the demonstrators were respectful, conversant with the militia, bowing in the ancient, Confucian gesture of mutual "honoring."

What we couldn't see was the pain of autocratic history floating in the crowd, a sense of zero-sum or either/or: their happiness either stood for real traction toward Deng's promised liberties, or it was baseless intoxication. They were delirious, but was it well-founded hope based on reforms, or, like religious novices, were they simply giddy with delusion? As for signage and symbols, the crowds also were not pushing it. They folded their banners and stowed them away each night. They didn't surround their tents with junk. The one exception to their humility, their mutedness, was a thirty foot tall Styrofoam replica—the resemblance was denied but unmistakable—of the Statue of Liberty: her backside was too big, she gripped her torch with two hands, like desperately catching a runaway pet, and there was a kind of grimace in the look she cast out over the multitudes. But here she was: The Goddess of Democracy. A Beijing University student pointed to it and told Orville Schell, whose *To Be Rich Is Glorious* chronicled Deng's reforms: "There's no way the party will ever get things back into the old bottle; just look around us—history is sweeping them away!"

Not so fast, the Owl of Minerva might have said. He was forgetting the old Confucian adage that one "Can reach for the heavens, but must not forget to keep yourself on the earth." As with a lot of events seen from afar, what we couldn't see on our TV in the Texas hotel was setting up the framework of a catastrophe. The demonstrators were not just occupying the Square, arguably a benign nothing to the leadership. Several regiments of the Red Army had been dispatched to keep the Square peaceful. But they were on their way from a garrison, walking, riding in jeeps and armed personnel carriers (APCs).

This is where the students upped the ante. Several *hundred thousand* of them blocked the soldiers on the entry roads. As the putative people's army was being stopped by the people themselves, the focus shifted to a who-blinks-first blockade of the surrounding streets. Premier Li Peng had already appeared on TV May 19th to declare martial law, and Deng, informed of the blockage, grew furious in the presidential palace. Zhao Ziyang was secretary general of the Communist Party and basically sympathized with the plight of both marchers and their unprecedented, powerful new media outlets. Finally, in the late afternoon of June 3rd, the loudspeakers around the square thundered with Deng's usually avuncular baritone: "For many days now, the Liberation Army has exercised restraint, but now it must absolutely counteract the rebellion."

And that was it. The soldiers suddenly had guns, the tank and APC turrets suddenly had shells in their huge magazines. The infantry fired volleys into the crowd, then fired at the medical students—I remember my new doctor's gasps—who came to treat them on the ground or get them onto evacuation gurneys. (It was eerily like the Mexico City Olympic riots in 1968, when the medical students saved scores of people wounded by Echeveria's rifles.) When the dust cleared the morning of June 4th, bodies were still being carried away. As with the armed response of many such regimes, there was a humiliating sadism in the treatment of the dead. Morgues were told by the government to refuse refrigeration of bodies, and the most vivid memory of some was how their friends were placed in the sun until their bodies were bloated with maggots.

The U.S. had become so dazzled with Deng's small, clumsy steps toward capitalism that President George H.W. Bush did not raise his voice too loudly. He was more concerned with balance of power, Kissingerian calculus, than with individual human rights. He mumbled about tyrants from "Baghdad to Beijing," but never got more specific about what we all saw, iconically, in the single protestor standing before the long barreled Soviet tank, the "Tank Man" who simultaneously walked into the history of photography and human suffering—the futile, lone pilgrim staring down an 80 millimeter cannon with his mixture of goofiness and stunning defiance.

Bush was so concerned about keeping the lines open with Deng that he dispatched his National Security Advisor, Brent Scowcroft, to secretly placate the Middle Kingdom's leader, who had finally showed his true colors. Clinton also was unforgivingly flabby with China on human rights, not only facilitating its entrance into most-favored-nation status but fast tracking its entry into the World Trade Organization. China's slow road to new freedoms soon got eclipsed by more vivid, more media-drenched [with the advent of 24-hour cable news] episodes of state and tribal savagery. First the now Tito-less, fragmenting Balkans fulfilled their prophesy of bloodbaths, and the Rwandan genocide was a mere four years away. Human rights got muffled under geopolitical priorities like land borders, Mideast skirmishes, oil, eco-catastrophes, and the disastrously necessary boom-bust cycle of financial capitalism.

Since 1989, the opening of new reforms has been maddeningly incremental. Wang Dan, one of the Tienanmen leaders, had helped organize the enormous music festival on May 27th, where Chinese pop stars were clamoring for invitations to play. Wang was to address the crowd as he had the previous week (most photos of the dais have him at the microphone) and he was racing down the Yangtze River in a hydrofoil, dictating a speech in a barber's chair, to get to the June 3-4th demonstrations. He was too late, and though he missed the actual massacre, was jailed twice with long prison terms after he was finally caught about a month later. He commented recently:

> Our movement failed 30 years ago because we lacked support and experience in promoting democratic change. Many of us pinned our hopes on the liberal factions of the Communist Party leadership to initiate changes from within the system, but we underestimated the power of the party elders. The massacre shattered our illusions, helping us to see the brutality of one-party rule.
> ~ *New York Times* 6/2/19

Much of this sounds like cliché, but you know what they say about cliché. How far has a democratic China come since 1989, and if the foregone answer is "not much", what are the reasons? They are essentially two-fold: economic prosperity and the technological surveillance state. Maya Wang of Human Rights Watch said this year's crackdown before the anniversary had been harsher than usual, with house arrests less common than direct custody by intelligence services. But the first issue of economic security and a rising standard of living has taken young peoples' minds off the police-repressive apparatus that so dramatically came down on their old siblings and parents. Rises in mean income and the standard of living have led to less concern about freedom of the press and assembly. Deng's economic reforms led to vast advances in the tech sector, and almost any Chinese university graduate is guaranteed an upwardly mobile employment model, something that never existed in the decades before 1990.

With the rise of securities trading and finance capitalism, the standard of living provided by the "banking world" and its symbiosis with Hong Kong and the West has created tiers of status within the young populace, and climbing its rungs is no longer shameful, even if it is not demonstrably sought after. President Xi has also sent the unmistakable message that the benefits of money and an easier life come with a necessary nationalism that eschews comparisons and copying of Western "freedoms." Chinese migrants no longer seek refuge from upheavals at home by building new lives in Southeast Asia. They can get all the benefits of living in Hong Kong or Singapore by simply staying in their home cities. Opportunities and the New Nationalism have led to an apathy that disheartens artists, filmmakers, writers and political commentators.

A second reason insurgencies cannot reach decision speed is the laser-speed advance in technological surveillance. The country is perfecting a vast network of digital espionage as a means of social control. China is a society in which trustworthiness, i.e. fealty to the Party, partakes of a rating system. Wherever you go, your "citizen score" follows you. Imagine we were back in the 50s, and everything Joe McCarthy had on you was somewhere on a hard drive that all authorities—federal, provincial, city and academic—could access with lightning speed. Everyone carries a National ID, and all of your actions in the world outside your door are swept into an information dragnet from the video cameras mounted on every vertical structure, including all the hundreds of light fixtures in Tienanmen Square. However small your crime, say jaywalking or shoplifting, facial recognition algorithms match the camera-gathered footage of your face to the photo on your national badge.

For we hapless writers, there is a content-filtering Great Firewall that prohibits foreign internet sites including Google, Facebook, and *The New York Times*. This writer tried to file copy on a story with a simple word attachment to an e-mail. We were in Shanghai and the hotel proprietor explained this impossibility with a humiliated but dignified embarrassment. Finally my son—at great insistence from me because he is a basketball fan and the fresh story was the U.S. NCAA shoplifters who made off with (Vuiton?) sunglasses until Trump freed them—took screen shots of the seven pages and flitted them across the ocean to my editor in Vancouver. But the hotelier, who could face substantial fines for harboring a Western rule-breaker, warned me with trembling hands and wet eyes: don't experiment too much. Don't send out anything about the Xi regime good or bad. Don't swim on the devil's lake in this country. The intelligence services are a step ahead of however far ahead of them you think you are.

* * *

I finally stood with my son on the Square early last year, on our last day in Beijing before heading to the Sodom the Xi government brands Westernized Hong Kong. A millennial, he is very much a visualist. A good reader and editor, he nevertheless knows how effectively the image reigns. I pulled up the picture of Tank Man, which he had never really seen even in Santa Monica High School history class. He was transfixed by it. He magnified the man, magnified the tank barrel, the periscopes, the other tanks waiting in line behind the first one. He looked up at me and asked with his eyes "Here?", pointing to the ground. Before I could say yes, a soldier came up behind us and looked with reticent approval at the photo, the picture and the event that existed before either he or my son were alive. Then he gave his obligatory warning, in perfect English, that photography was not allowed.

But the picture that mattered had already been taken. It was almost Soviet in its mixture of the valiant and the quotidian. A single student had walked the hero's path by simply, seemingly doing nothing but just standing there, swinging around two white garbage bags. One man, one boy younger than yesterday, his white shirt flickering before the oncoming, deadly night like a candle in Babylon.

In Christ There Is No East or West

We were playing ping-pong in the basement when my father noticed that the barber had taken off so little of my hair. For years he'd done my haircuts himself, a horrible ritual where he would pull and tear at the spaces over my ears with an old Sears electric trimmer, sitting me up on a chair mounted beside the nail-filled jars of his workbench. So he was cutting me a break letting me go to the barber now, and he had his idea of what the man should have done, how I should have properly instructed him.

He put his paddle over the ball and laid them on the table and came around and grabbed me by the collar, slamming me up against the wall of concrete blocks. He pulled his fist back like a barroom fighter and suddenly, out of nowhere, told me that I should take a swing at him, that we needed to really get this kind of thing finished between us. I pissed my pants a little, wondering how far the thin saws and axes were back in the other room, the place of the old hair cuttings. He had hit and slapped me through the years, but this was taking things to a whole other level. It was the high, fearsome ground of tavern brawlers, hockey parents smashing each others' faces, fathers and sons whose bourbon at their deer camp cabin had one of them leaving barely alive, the other with a new heart stained crimson with demons.

Above us at the top of the stairs my mother opened the door. "OK down there?" she called. He let go of my collar and backed away. He shook his head and started to lift his finger when she spoke again. "Guys?"

"We're good," he said.

The back of my head had hit the wall hard. The swelling started and I could feel the trickle starting under my still too-long hair. The warm circle of pain spread out around the welt. He figured there was something back there so he handed me one of his red bandanna work handkerchiefs. We stared at one another like uncertain, terrible animals as I dabbed myself with the cloth. He made a give-me-back motion with his hand, not wanting her to see anything in the laundry of what the rag had become.

Things were different now. We had walked into a strange new land of unlikeness, unwelcome. We had crossed over to the place where there was room for only one of us in the house, where only one could be free of danger and only one would be left to cower, to circle or run.

The name for midgets now is little people. This seems much better, more appropriate and fair. Midget had taken on a grimy adjectival life: politicians using it to describe their opponents; nations taunting one another with size as an arbiter of what a state can be. Truth to tell it had become a flat-out insult. You described your competition or enemy as such. The new phrase was made of good, unblemished words. And the second word of it was "people."

I once had my life saved by a little person. It would have been something to have had him back in the basement, playing ping-pong with my father. This tiny, muscular man appeared out of a group of shuffling teenage boys who had surrounded me in Crawford Market in Bombay. I was older, around forty, stringing for a London magazine into neighborhoods taken over then by the PJB gangs. He was simply, suddenly in front of me, dividing me from them with something they respected. Maybe cold steel. Maybe people he knew. Some sufficient evil.

To avoid going home at nights in the small town where we lived, I would stand in the phone booth on the square, talking to my girlfriend. And when I could get away for a whole day and evening, I would hitch hike the hour's ride south to Columbus. The state fair was there. It seemed, especially with its entertainers, to bring the wide world that was out there into our benighted grassland. Bob Hope, the Bee Gees. Johnny Cash would sing with his new bride June Carter, and her whole dynastic country family would be there with their clear, bright-water voices, dobros and autoharps and other Appalachian instruments I didn't know the name of.

The fair was always hazy, the dust rising up around the stringed lights until their own light turned yellow. This made the dark into a sea of phosphorescence. Tents grew up around you like mushrooms as you walked. The ground was straw-stamped, black packed soil that smelled of animals. Arches stretched overhead made out of red elm planks or ears of wired together Indian corn. Blasts and wheels of color came out of everywhere, banging and stinking and unravelling, lighting up the thickening air like fireworks.

I avoided the Bob Hope show. My politics then would not permit it. I was out on the edge of the SDS and Student Mobilization Committee, trying to bring the high school into their orbits. The principal and vice-principal—both of whom had just hired my mother as a teacher—could not stand the sight of me. The Democratic Convention had just taken place in Chicago, the Mayday actions had closed the commuter bridges in Washington. Leary and Eldridge Cleaver were in exile in North Africa. Everybody was on the lam, taking up guns. Walking along past the livestock barns, I hummed the great Country Joe McDonald song 'Air Algiers': *Hopped on a plane/Oakland—New York/Oakland—New York/New York to Marseilles/ Hopped on a plane/One-way on Air Algiers/Stay down in the Casbah/Cool it for a couple of years.* It was my inspiration hymn to get away.

On the way to the freak show tents I passed an enormously muscled man in a striped, strapped T-shirt, lifting a nine pound hammer behind him so far it touched the loose fasteners of the truss he wore. He stayed still like that for so long I thought maybe the hammer would pull him backwards into the dust, like a weightlifter needing a spotter. He was still as a statue, two minutes, three minutes. When he brought the hammer down on the tilting plank the ball flew up the column so fast I couldn't see it, and when it hit the bell the cloud of dust at the top shimmered outward in perfect, circular waves.

The freak shows were what I had come for, remembering them from past years when my father put me on a quota of only two or three. Many shows in these smaller pavilions were not people but animals, like the capybara rodent from Central America whose size was greatly exaggerated and who did not, as the sign said, eat human flesh, but rather shoots of what looked like shriveled rhubarb. In other tents were trees that had grown in odd shapes—dinosaurs or Bible figures, or a Saturn with broad rings of peeling bark.

But the true freak shows, in tents whose door flaps were left teasingly open, were usually little people. Sometimes the man at the front selling tickets was one also. The illustrations above the tents were on sagging, bright-colored canvases, paintings whose color was off signature and had no perspective. The lighter hues had faded in the many years of traveling. The eyes of the picture of the bearded lady were brown with dirt, and the mirror she held, so badly drawn it could have been a club, had gone from silver to a dark, smudged gray.

I saw the Crab Man first, whose sign promised a crab son I couldn't spot anywhere on the stage. He held in his pincer cones of fingers photographs of his ancestors, all with crab limbs, all with turbans fronted with crests and jewels. He put the pictures down and picked up the microphone and described the swamped kowloons he had grown up in, and how his hands had kept him from becoming a fisherman. The other pincher hand reached forward, picking up and replacing a cigarette on the small square speaker box.

Much of what he said was unintelligible.

I walked out, rubbing the welt on the back of my head. It had scabbed over, and I wished I had a bandage to keep myself from picking at it.

The Amoeba Girl was the first one that really impressed me. It was like God had decided to use her as some kind of joke. The bottom of her—her legs—were joined together at each end like a pretzel. Her waist was so thin it looked like she was a woman who had been cut into two pieces, and above her waist, reams of fruit and peacock feather tattoos went up her stomach and under her bathing suit top, curling like liquid whips around her neck bone and shoulders. She looked at me. I rubbed the back of my hair again. My hand dropped to my right back pocket, where I had Lenin's *Eighteenth Brumaire*.

Walking back onto the fairway I looked down into pages I had marked. Lenin said that when the revolution was perfected it would fit the future inside of itself and create its own past. There would be an eternal present, where people would study and gauge where the next phases of a classless society would take them. It had a spiritual sound to it. Timelessness, directionlessness were the anchors in the center that held everything from drifting away.

The bearded lady was disappointing. The canvas painting out front had made her look like the real nickel—flaming orange hair and two bowed bone-white tusks. The light was bad inside, two bulbs under old, mildewing lamps. She was just a lady with some kind of brownish rash or one of those giant birthmarks, a hemangioma, which did grow up a patch or two of sickly hair. She didn't say anything about herself, never looked out at us. She looked in a mirror and smoothed her cheeks, which seemed to me to be smooth as a cue ball.

Next was Lord Puffin and Princess Wee-Wee. Lord Puffin weighed 708 pounds and had to be hoisted, he said, with a flatbed of pulleys. He could eat ten entire chickens in a single sitting. Princess Wee-Wee sat in an immense velvet covered divan. She sent her urine out through a system of tubes shaped into glass-blown, whirling circles and little catafalques. The effect was a sort of uric ballet, something sharp giving the softness of what it carried a pattern, a beauty. Nobody spoke or laughed or sang. Neither had mics. Both of these monsters ("It's who we are," the Captain said) let their arms hang down at their sides.

The stick man was wonderful, very real and delicate. His joints were appropriately fragile and bulgy where they met, like the walking stick insect whose green and brown versions I'd seen beyond the bent screen of my bedroom window. He had enormous, soft, leaflike eyelids that slowly rose and shut like the blinds of a house, and when he answered questions with a microphone his arm whipped up quickly to wipe the bottom of one of his eyes. His other arm steadied himself—if he took it away he would fall backwards down onto the wooden stand.

Next was a woman that did not seem so much deformed or freakish, but was fused to a pole that she twirled with, colored ribbons wrapping around one another as their ends were carried in circles by tiny marching dogs. She was beautiful, with a halo of golden frizzy hair like Glinda, the good witch in the Wizard of Oz. She didn't speak but if she had I imagined it would, like Glinda, be polite and high and delicately ghostly.

It may have been her twin sister who was at the other end of the tent. She actually looked *more* like Glinda than her sister or Glinda herself. She had a tall, circular hat that looked at first like oversized playing cards, but each of which said 'Article of Faith' across the top. A Biblical exercise or homily or prayer was under the wording of each article. They pictured peaceable, sitting animals, people being pushed in wheelchairs, workers serving long tables of meals to the dispossessed. She reached her hand down in a kind of blessing to those who approached her. She seemed the exact opposite of a freak, the picture of generosity and calm.

The next man was about as big as a medium-size dog, and he lay on his back dressed in clothes from the Revolutionary War period. He had that kind of wig and tricorner hat. But his arms and legs were stumps, little paddles. His skin was like a blanket of dark gray feathers. He held a mike in one of his wings and described how the men of his family had been like this for generations, talking about his six children, winking and saying that he had at least one working appendage. Then couplets came out of his mouth, the second line of each lilting up in a twist.

Carriers, messengers ran back and forth between the tents and within them. One named Max came toward me after he was finished lifting something. He wore a truss. His unshaven face was gold-orange in the light, the black bristles stiffened up and glistening. He looked up at me—six feet of pimply hippie by then.

I'd heard about carnival people, the sex, the few opportunities all of them had and how they took them with one another. There were drugs too, much more serious than the weed I was smoking—liquids and powders, things that needed to be cooked.

It seemed Max took it upon himself to dispel me of this, though I hadn't brought it up, or even said hello to him. He pointed to a room where there was music. The closer we got, the more formal the music sounded. It was sacred music. They were hymns. His tiny, stubby finger jabbed forward.

"Daddy Mention in here," he said. "The preacher." Max's eyebrows were thick and bushy, like the caterpillars that ate leaves.

Daddy Mention sat in his own tent with his back to the entrance, in a green swivel chair seated in front of a stereo console. The records he kept putting on were the hymns we had heard. I remembered some of them from church with my grandmother, she and her garden club ladies singing in high, birdlike, horribly shrill voices that made their adam's apples lurch up and down. They had titles like 'Be Thou My Vision,' 'Rock of Ages,' and 'In Christ There Is No East or West.'

They all had the same story of everything leading up to a point which gave those past events some kind of meaning. Then everything past that point got its significance from that same, still point. It was like the *Brumaire*, where a moment came in which society evaporated and the need to work went away. That point, that instant in time pulsed out in a bright throb backward and forward, like the lamp of a lighthouse.

For my grandmother it was the Crucifixion. That was the tool the minister gave her, and one I never understood.

The only thing I could imagine as an event, something that happened, a moment in time unlike all others, would be one where no one would lift their hand against anyone else. The space would simply be an absence of cruelty. And it would have the force of a revelation, something that transported you and that you transported within yourself, wherever you went. Your heart would be filled with it, like whatever the apostles of the Christians, the followers of the Brumaire carried with them.

I wished for that now, a kind of peace that would infuse me, that would let me cross to safety. I ran my hand along the back of my head, brushing the hair up and down.

Mention kept putting the records on. Max leaned back approvingly, looking at me and then looking at him. He was making a point that his point was made. A sputtering light bulb above him popped and sprayed down in a rain of glass.

Daddy Mention's jacket was green velvet, and he wore a sort of ascot that spilled up out of it like cream from the top of a fountain drink. He seemed wider than he would be tall if he stood up out of the chair. The seat let him swivel and reach, picking through cellophane stacks of discs. But he didn't turn around. Only his pigtail was there, wagging below a bald spot. He had an earring here, long before men wore them. The short clean fingers of his hands were delicate as spiders, moving the black, flat food of the music on and off the uneven turntable.

Max motioned me up, as if he would introduce us. But I realized I was supposed to make that overture myself, to interrupt him with my supposed importance. I couldn't do it, couldn't interrupt this man who seemed to be controlling everything.

I moved over to the side so I could see more of his face. He winced with the concentration of his work. A long knife scar ran down the side of his jaw like a thunderbolt.

There was a coat or a cloak that covered his lap, hanging down to the floor. Something was under it. In the dim light of what the one bulb left there were what looked like pedals on a piano's bottom. But when I stepped forward they became feet. The feet were not his— they pointed away from the cloak bottom—and if I squinted hard I could see they were wearing women's heels. They were bent with the work of whatever the woman was doing, moving, twitching slowly. Then I could see. It was a girl's legs, dark skinned and with dark stockings in wide squares like a fishnet.

Max was smiling. He motioned me down, cupping his hands around his mouth like he was going to whisper. But he had to speak sharply in the noise, almost a shout.

"The weasel," he said, dragging out the first syllable. "She greasea the weasel." He backed away, winking, stretching his arm out and putting his other fist down into its crook until the lower half of it sprang up straight.

I couldn't breathe. I looked toward the tent entrance and down into the grocery bag I carried things in when I travelled.

I ran out. Down through the outer rings of the fairground, out through the wide swales of the campus, I saw the afterprint of Mention and the legs as surely as if I had tripped over them or run into their joined bodies.

An afterprint. A black negative with clarifying, silvering figures.

Out on the 270 I spread my feet in the gravel and put out my thumb. I was more impatient now than frightened. The welt was still there, but the scab that covered it was hard. I put one of my Mother's valiums under my tongue. All around me the high grasses of the fields waved like a moonlit underbed of down—a dry, shaking ocean.

An eighteen-wheeler pulled over. The peace I wanted now, as the tranq bloomed up in my limbs, was just to sit back in the cab, watching the town lights that curved up out of the long miles of dark earth.

It would be an hour, an hour and a half until I got back to the house. Back to the other world, where I knew my father would be sleeping.

Green, Whale-Back Mountain
(Letter From Appalachia)

The phone woke him up. He heard the greeting, and then heard a deep, accented voice crackling from across the river in West Virginia. It seemed now that was where the calls always came from.

"Your advertisement. The Kohans. We will come to arrive at four o'clock."

He pulled himself up and looked out the window. The Appalachian foothills were filled with morning sunshine. Great bands of shade grew through their hollows, a slow but still moving darkness that he had always imagined to be the only visible movement of time. These small green mountains ran the length of Hocking county, holding the river of the same name that swelled with rain and raced away East into the silent, brown Ohio—the river they called Leviathan—at the towns of Belpre and New Willow Temple.

He looked at their mailbox across the road. "Haroupia" it said. The final "a" was hidden by an elderberry branch.

"Approximately," the phone message went on. "To four o'clock." Philip's stomach turned at the sound of the voice signing off.

"Thank you." It was the same accent, the accent of the Hoowan people that had come the last time to buy one of their horses and who had seemed at first like any of the other buyers who traveled in from the small towns around Parkersburg, the sprawling and hazy city on the River's other side. His father had told him about the Hoowan. They were hill tribes from a country over near Vietnam, though his father had never seen them when he was fighting the war there. They were traders, shopkeepers, farmers. There had been stories about them in the Cincinnati and Athens papers. They had struggled to leave the country whose government had grown up around their ancient villages, and whose army had chased them out through mountains much like these, shooting men, mothers, even children as they ran toward the Thai border.

The other Hoowan family had come only a month ago with a borrowed horse trailer without a top. The car they drove was nice enough. After Philip's father and the man had done the paperwork and the barn hand had marched the horse up the plank, seemed as normal as any other sale.

Then the father had started to get in the driver's side but brought something out of the cab. Before Philip and his father and mother and his sister could do anything, before any of them could even think, the man lifted a rifle to the horse's head and pulled the trigger. The horse dropped down in a great spray of blood. The trailer bed sagged as if a load of rocks had been poured into it.

His mother and Irin had run screaming into the house, and Philip had crouched when he heard the shot. The man got in the truck and drove away quickly. His father called animal control, and two officers came out to make a report.

It was then that they learned that the Hoowan killed horses for meat, or at least had eaten them back in their native land. There was nothing anybody could do now because the Hoowan man had paid for the horse. It was his property. The officers made his father sign the sheet on the clipboard and separated out a yellow copy and handed it to him.

In the days and weeks that followed, there was little talk about what had happened. It was mentioned in a tiny box story in the Athens paper, stating that the man had been cited for discharging a firearm on someone else's property. Philip's mother decided the time might be right to go with Irin to see relatives in Armenia; they had not been there since the earthquake in 1986.

His father had cleaned the horse's skull and brain fragments from the corral posts. In the ghostly kind of non-speech that families talk in around the house and dinner table, it became understood—at least by Philip—that no more horses would be sold to anybody south of the state line.

In the barn his father built after making what he called the "pig money" in construction, Philip looked down on the horses each day from his perch in the feed stalls. The older man wandered on ahead, speaking to the animals in the snappy salesman's speech he had learned from his father, the first to live in America. Philip simply watched the great brown chewing heads, waiting for them to throw their mouths in the air when he re-filled their buckets of oats.

In the shop corner of the barn Philip found a mower blade his father had stuffed in a box to go to the dump. Philip picked it out, and for no reason he could think of other than the sadness he still felt at such a large animal's death, he began wrapping one end of the blade with adhesive tape, sticky and soft, white and thick and hanging with threads. Later he brought it upstairs to his room. It went under some loose ash floorboards his mother had not yet discovered.

As summer was ending, his mother's postcards stacked up on his desk, Philip suspected his father would try to sell horses again, though the boy figured he would be more careful. Philip almost had a premonition about new ads the man might place, new rumors he would be spreading through the feed stores and lumberyards. Philip felt his father's horror at what they had witnessed together as deeply as his own, as a sort of different note in his family's single chord of grief. If he could put a sound to his own feelings, it would be harsher than his father's: the crack and stretch of tape ripping off a roll, being wound around and around the swing blade's handle.

But Philip was also, he thought, uncovering something about the will of the Haroupian men. Horse trading was what his father *did* now that he was retired, and he would have to get back in the game sooner or later. His father only knew by doing. "Action is the machinery of faith:" the Armenian proverb was quoted to him and his sister until they learned to roll their eyes, and then it was recited to them even more.

Doing, not thinking so much, was the way the man learned and tried to teach them all to learn. Surely thinking things through from every direction lessened the chances of error. But sometimes just getting up and moving, *moving* could do it too, his father would say. For him just opening the door wider chased the waiting mistakes away, the sun sending the rats back into the hay.

His father had given him the morning off and the two of them knew what was in the works. When the truck came up their road he saw a man with a moustache driving. Next to him was a six or seven-year-old boy. An older son, thin and very tall, stood at the rail sides of the plain flatbed trailer. The breeze blew his tattered Bengals T-shirt against his chest.

Philip was relieved of even having to entertain the boys. The barn hands would take them into the kitchen and give them lemonade and cookies. Philip stayed up in his room. He had taken the swing blade out. He folded his hand into the spongy grooves his squeezing hand had given it, like the grip on an arcade game handle, the grip of a pistol.

As the buyer passed with his father through the hallway on the way to the office, and before Philip could see them, he heard the two men stopping by the gun case. What was his father doing, Philip wondered, looking at a whole trove of displayed and pampered weapons? It would have been the least he could do to bring him in through the garage.

"You like Savages!" the buyer said. "Yes," said his father.

"Good gun!" said the buyer. "Not jamming like the Thai gun, the Chinese made."

"Good guns, good guns," his father said. "Especially the shotguns. Little recoil." After a silence his father said. "No kick."

"No kick! I like," the man said. "'Better for you here," he said, his hand patting the fabric of his shoulder.

"Let's bring you down…" His father's voice trailed off in a cough as they descended the stairs.

Philip could see them now. His father sat behind his desk while the man pulled up his trouser legs, setting into the guest chair.

"Mr.…?"

"Bo-ween," said the buyer.

"Mr. Boween, I want to show you a few things I've.…" His father looked around the office, at the plaques and awards, the certificates on the walls.

"I want to show you what I've been able to do. To get myself started on something new."

Boween coughed.

"But I'd like to tell you first that, well, you could sell that horse, you know. Sell it at a profit."

"'Scuse me?" Philip could see Boween's face clearer than his father's. The man was confused.

"I mean, you can re-sell it to someone else, for their kids, to have a horse. That's how good a price I'm giving you."

Boween dropped his head and looked straight at Philip's father. "Six hundred."

"Six hundred. But you could re-sell it at a thousand, easy. I just can't go down cross river to do it now."

"But my children, they like the horse. We have a room," he said, twirling his finger in the air. *"The room,"* he said. "Enough."

Philip's father leaned forward the way he always saw him do when making a deal, or trying to extract somebody's word on something. "Don't tell it to one of your people, though, if you do sell."

"No. I will not," said Boween. "I could not explain presently. The reason. But no sale to my neighbors."

"Good," said his father. He leaned back and looked around himself again.

"That guy runnin' the country your people are living in? He's horrible."

Boween nodded. "A nut."

"The man is a nut," his father repeated.

"Not even a good nut," said Boween. "He just a try-to-be nut."

Philip's father pointed. "There's a lot of building going on down where you are. You ever do any carpentry?"

"Carpen?" asked Boween.

"There are things. There are programs."

"Pogroms," Boween said flatly.

"Programs," his father said, a little loudly. "There must be someone in your group there. Well, I *know* there is. People who could get you on track."

Boween drummed his fingers.

"Computers," his father said, looking each way with excitement and then straight back at him. "That's everything now. Computers are the world."

"Bill Gates the world. We just live in," Boween said, slapping his checked, pulled-up pants. He gave a short, sharp laugh, as if someone were striking him.

Philip saw his father rocking slowly, truly or not-so-truly trying to hold back all-out laughter. Philip had seen it many times on deals. "The Closer Laugh," his father called it. You recognized the teller and acknowledged the quality of the joke. But you did not lose yourself. You kept control.

"We build," said Boween, "the lost drives. We bring them back."

"You rebuild hard drives?"

"We image them. They see the image. They build themselves little pieces, by little pieces, until they are whole."

"I'll be *damned*," his father said. "I cannot, I repeat I *cannot* turn one of those sons of bitches on." He shook his head.

"New world," said Boween. "I can teach you turn on."

Philip's father was still looking at Boween, sizing him up, Philip knew. They were in different occupations, different *areas*, his father would say.

His father put his hands on his knees.

"You won't sell the horse there on your street."

"I will not."

"Promise."

"Promise, to cross my heart."

Then they looked at each other through the silence of the hot, thick air. Philip heard Rory's tail flicking, shooing flies from his hide.

"You know," his father said. "My people sucked mud." Boween raised his eyebrows, brought his hand up to his mouth.

"The Turks. Made them march. Marched and marched them, till they died."

Boween nodded. "I have heard."

"So we started here too," his father went on. He coughed again. "We came with nothing."

His father pointed to a portrait of children standing before a building's steps with a kneeling man.

"All dead." His father swept the entire picture with his hand. "My grandparents' school class."

Boween ran his hands back and forth on his calves, and said, "Tragedy."

"Who killed them? You want to know who killed them?"

His father pointed to the half-kneeling man, whose head bore a small round cap.

"Their teacher. Him."

Boween's eyes were wide now as he exhaled.

"He was a Turk. Once the fighting started, he marched them. He marched them and then he killed them."

Boween turned his hand back and forth slowly, looking at it as his father sat back down.

His father sat and stared at Boween. It seemed like forever to Philip. Boween smiled and frowned in an erratic way, shifting from one side of the chair to the next with an artificial energy, as if posing for pictures.

"I guess what I am trying to say here, Boween "

Boween waited.

"Your hard drive business sounds great. Can't go wrong with it." Bowen nodded, reaching around, patting for his checkbook.

Philip's father came up out of his seat and then sat down. He had never taken his eye off Boween.

"Trust is what we have here, my people," said his father. "We trust here, in America. We learned we could do that."

"Truss," said Boween.

"What happened with the school? All that? Not here. That's for the other place."

His father pointed away, past the pictures. "That's for the other world."

Boween blinked, nodded.

Philip could tell his father was through when he broke the stare.

But he still looked at the man when he brought the receipt ledger up out of his desk drawer. He took the check from Bowen and put it under the thick glass paperweight. The sound of the writing pen could be heard in the silence, and the rip of the receipt from its perforated stub.

Philip rearranged himself on the floor. He still did not like the look on Boween's face. He satisfied himself that it wasn't anything about them, these people, which would be prejudiced. But still. There was a dark sparkle, an eagerness in his eyes.

The two men went up the stairs to get the boys. The four of them walked out the door and up to the high point of the driveway in front of the dinner bell. The fathers stood talking and the younger boy got in the back jump seat of the long cab. The older brother put down the gate and pulled out the ramp as the barn hand walked Rory out. Rory put his head down, stamping a little, just before he walked up. The brother settled him in and put a blanket around him and gave him an apple.

Just before the brother got into the cab, Philip saw him lift a shoe tree out of the truck bed to make more room, and three or four horseshoes. The boy also lifted out a can of water and a long leather and sheepskin case, putting them up in the cab beside his little brother.

A swath of fire rankled down Philip's chest. He sat up abruptly.

Another long, sick wave went like warm milk through his lungs as he watched his father and Boween shaking hands.

He reached for the swing blade. He knew how he would do it, like he'd seen it done in some action films. He wouldn't ask Boween and the boys for the gun at all. He would just walk quickly *to* one of the trailer's rear tires, making a tap punch along the siding. Then he could wedge the blade in and lean on it, pushing all of his weight until the tire blew out. Once the tire was flat, there would be nothing to talk about. He would be done.

Philip stood up in front of the door. He could not open it. He tightened his grip on the blade. He watched the men shaking hands, Boween walking around and getting behind the wheel, the two boys waving. He could not open the door.

Philip sat back on the bed. He raised the blade as far back behind his head as he could, bringing it down into the floor. It made a long crack in one of the ash planks that he knew his father would see. And Philip would see it forever as the clear and constant proof of his cowardice.

At the dinner table, two hours later, his father could see the tears in Philip's eyes.

"He's different," his father said.

"You don't know that," Philip said, refusing to meet his father's glance. The burning had subsided after he came downstairs, but he was still furious. He looked at the salt and pepper shakers. He thought of what he could do now. Refuse to work the horses. Open the pens and let them go.

"I think I made an impression on the man," his father said.

He would open the corral and all of the doors of the barn and let them out. He would shoo them away with the *big* sombrero the one hand, Fero, had brought him from Mexico.

Philip pushed his plate away. "I'd like to be excused."

"That's fine," the man said. "We got a feed stop tomorrow. Just a little to do."

Philip stood in front of him. The burning was coming back to him, back around his eyes, the bottom of his hair. He would have a few hours to read before it got dark. He would not come back down to sit with his father in front of the fire. He knew his father would not ask him to.

When he got to his room the clouds were bunching along the mountain ridge, the heather purple on their slopes, the road white. Cars were coming. Both the cars turned onto side roads and started climbing the hills. The third was a pick-up with a trailer, and Philip heard his father's cell phone ring.

Philip saw the truck with the trailer and Rory in it starting up their drive. The screen door slammed and his father walked out and waited in the yard When Boween got out of the truck he motioned for the boys to stay inside and walked with Philip's father back into the house. They were standing in the kitchen where Philip couldn't see them.

"Problem?" Philip's father asked. Boween was silent.

"You were selling to a neighbor? It was going to a family, wasn't it?"

Boween let out a breath and said, "No."

"I have called the bank," Boween said, "As I suspected, there *is* no sufficient money for the funds. Not now."

"Well," his father said.

"Maybe next month. I was wrong to come."

"No problem. No problem at all, Boween. I'll hold the... "

"Next month much problem too. Bills from doctors."
His father sighed.

"New lease for pasture," Boween went on. Philip heard Boween reach in his pocket and pull out the check. He heard a rip, then a sudden lurch to his father's voice, trying to stop him.

"Come with," said Boween.

Outside, Boween motioned to the older boy, who seemed to have the long leather case ready to hand out the passenger side. Boween took it and unzipped the back and pulled the long brown gun out of the sheepskin.

His father turned it around, looking at the finish on the wood. He lifted it up into an aim and sighted across the field. His father nestled the stock on the ridge of his waist, thinking.

"A Savage," said Boween.

The older brother turned around in the cab and sat hunched over. He ran his hands through his hair and shook his head. The men went around to the driver's door and shook hands. His father set the gun across his shoulders and rested each of his arms on it. Before the engine started, Philip thought he heard Boween say something to his father in another language.

Philip leaned back on his bed. At first he didn't think anything at all, but then he started thinking about the next day. He could not hug his father or really even thank him too strongly, as Philip was just becoming fourteen. And they were men. His mother would be back soon with Irin, and there would be time for such things.

Philip was tired. He shut his eyes. Before he passed into sleep, or even before he got to the filmy place he traveled through to get to where the true, black slumber would pull him down, he looked at the four walls around him. Around those walls were the walls of the hall, and around those the four sides of the house, and around those the square lines of their lot containing the house and the yard. And around their lot were the fields and around those the sharp squares of townships, and outside of them the long surveyors' lines that marked away the counties, patches and patches of them lined up along the valley like foundation stones the rest of the state rose up from.

Down in the corner of one of the squares, as if he were looking from an airplane, he saw the truck with the trailer beginning to pass over the bridge into Parkersburg. The three men were not speaking to one another in the cab and Rory was back in the trailer, chewing, blanket covered, unmindful of men or their danger, looking out through the high, silver girders arching up over the river in the sunlight.

Man in Black Again

Johnny Cash: The Life
Robert Hilburn
Little, Brown, 469 pages

Lucian Freud, whose sensibility was as far from an Arkansas country singer's as could be imagined, was obsessed with the Johnny Cash song "Chicken In Black." It was one of the singer's most forgettable creations, embarrassing him so much in later life that he tried to get Columbia Records to pull the recording. But Freud saw in it [at least according to Greig's new bio, *Breakfast With Lucian Freud*] a sort of comic montage of our deepest fears: death, abandonment, physical deterioration, loss and interposition of others' personalities. To Freud, Cash's chicken was the Chaplin Animal, scaring us into titters as it twirled its head like a cane, walking the high wire of identity shifts above the abyss.

Cash was the sun at the center of many orbits. ['Johnny was the North Star—you could set your compass by him,' said Bob Dylan.] Freud may have been the Pluto of that lot, the cold, outer periphery. As one moved toward the singer, the influences made more sense and fell into place. All of country-western appeared to be infused with his dark, gritty testaments to restraint, to temptation resisted and succumbed to. 'I Walk The Line' topped the charts in 1956, a hymn to fidelity that could only have been penned by a philanderer. Cash created duets and foursomes as fast as a square dance caller, and the ballroom floor was the very laboratory of 50s and 60s popular music and talking-blues storytelling. It had the diversity that stunned Greil Marcus when he heard Dylan's 'Basement Tapes' or Nash's Smithsonian Archive—it was that 'Old, Weird America,' an 'Invisible Republic' populated by the (always singing) drowned and saved.

Cash's first collaboration—collaboration! From that most isolated self-portraitist!—was that of his family back in cotton country

Arkansas. Daddy sang bass, Mama sang tenor, and all "the children would join right in there." But he saw a largeness to his life, a feeling it belonged to the world, and so he moved to Nashville and L.A., past crossroads as divergent as gospel, country, folk and rockabilly. The first family of Christian music, the Reverend and Mother Maybelle Carter, would eventually take him in by way of a daughter to be his second wife. But he first had to weather the Hercules tasks of a serviceman's ennui, Tin Pan Alley's gatekeepers, and amphetamine addiction that made him feel 'like the wad of powder wrapped around a cannonball.'

Collaboration by happenstance, by accident, was one of the Man in Black's specialties. Probably the best known was the 1956 evening in (his first producer) Sam Phillips's Sun Studios in Memphis, when Phillips's other artists and recording aspirants wandered in and strapped on instruments: Carl Perkins of 'Blue Suede Shoes' fame, Elvis Presley, and Jerry Lee Lewis, a contentious young bird-dogger with a head of blond curls like Shirley Temple's. It was called the Million Dollar Quartet, and while bootlegs of it circulated for years, it was Floyd Mutrux (full disclosure: my friend and client) who made it all cohere in his stage play of that name, now running in nearly every theater district in the world.

Cash saw collaboration's two poles in the cesspool of captivity (fox holes, prisoners) and the bright nimbus of the newly blessed (he was baptized perhaps three times). He was fascinated by incarcerated populations, and in his legendary 60s prison shows both took song fragments inmates had scratched out on napkins, and brought them numbers he'd especially written for the occasion. ['16 Minutes To Go' was a Villonesque gallows ballad, and 'Wanted Man,' one of many collaborations with Dylan, were standouts from the San Quentin concert.] His voice carried a deep, somnolent anger, and burglars and murderers saw him as their twang-tongued Orpheus. The night before Utah's Gary Gilmore was the first man to be executed in decades in the U.S., back channels arranged a phone call between the condemned man and his idol. 'Is this the real Johnny Cash,' the prisoner asked. When the great voice assented, the murderer, only hours from the firing squad, replied 'Well, this is the real Gary Gilmore.'

* * *

I first saw Cash, in the flesh, in the presence of his almost-in-laws, the evangelical caliphate of Border Radio's Carter Family. I was high up in the bleachers at the Ohio State Fair. The stage lights were dim, and the figures they were trained on melded into a yellowish, pulsing ball. Dust from the cattle barns drifted over us: church people having seen him at Billy Graham crusades, fans waiting for Bob Hope's show, pimpled hippies like me in green velvet pants and tennis shoes.

Now *this* was collaboration, with the man in black walking around like a demon among angels. Mother Maybelle, June and Carolyn sang in steady trios, hovering over the flow of the old woman's autoharp. Johnny's voice was the anchor that kept the ship from drifting off. His baritone throbbed all the way through 'Keep On The Sunny Side,' 'Pickin' Time,' 'Wreck of the Old 97,' and 'Five Feet High And Rising.' Thinking back on my father's vinyl collection, I remembered Cash would do a few of these in rounds or echoey step-downs with the sisters backing him. He sang 'Were You There (When They Crucified My Lord?),' and when he recited the last verse-line of 'SOME-times it causes me to tremble,' each of the sisters would take it into the bridge with pair-notes calling out '[T]remble, tremble . . . . . tremble.' Then he would come back with a final, authoritative 'TREM-BLE,' and their voices closed around his like a winding shroud.

But there was rocking to be done that August night in '71. We youngsters demanded he step out with 'Mystery Train,' 'Get Rhythm,' or 'The Rebel (Johnny Yuma).' Only he and his shadow filled the spotlight then, the boom-chicka-boom of the Tennessee Two replaced now by the harmonies of his sisters-in-law. He sang 'Giving Good Weight,' where the truck-driving narrator fools the truck scales reader with an inventory of low-tariff goods like eggs and livestock, plastic and beans. When he drives off the scales he leans out the window and strums louder and faster and confesses his true cargo of 'pig iron, pig iron, I got aaa . . llllll pig iron.' 'Thou shalt not lie' was not a commandment, and the narrator was an addled man trying to feed his family, so the women behind him just giggled, swaying and snapping their fingers. The final flourish had to have no holiness whatever, invoking just a single sinner, male type. It was 'Big River,' which Bob Weir of the Grateful Dead would later cover in over 1,500 performances. The narrator chases the same skirt from St. Paul to the Louisiana Delta, coaxed southward through the maze of waters by her 'long Southern drawl.'

* * *

After the demise of his ABC television show [featuring first TV performances by recluses like Dylan and Joni Mitchell], and through numerous bouts of addiction in the 70s and 80, Cash's chances for pairing up with other musicians seemed to evaporate. By 1982, The Blasters and the Stray Cats, along with a host of British bands from Birmingham, gave listeners all the hillbilly rock it wanted. JC was beginning to take on the weathered patina of a relic. There were tours with Waylon Jennings, Willie Nelson and Kris Kristofferson, under the banner of The Highwaymen. They were a potent foursome, with especially effective duets by Cash and Jennings, a musician who, like Merle Haggard (among the *inmates* at the San Quentin shows), probably never would have existed except in the penumbra of the man who stood behind him.

But as time wore on and a new generation of country-rock performers—one being his daughter Roseanne—were on the ascent, Cash seemed lost. His managers and agents fished for large venues. But he traveled in lesser domains, mainly in the Upper South and Sunbelt. They were small clubs, dinner theater, obscure festivals that let him rest on his laurels for 50-something nostalgiacs. Columbia dropped him. His wife fought off increasing bouts of illness, and so did he. Cash couldn't sell out even the most modest of auditoriums, and not even forty miles from his home in Nashville.

Then came Rick Rubin, the rock producer who looked like a cross between Zeus and ZZ Top's Billy Gibbons. Against all advice, Rubin hatched a plan to commit Cash to a series of studio dates that would consolidate into a smorgasbord of new songs and covers.

Against all advice, Rubin wanted to do it in his home studio outside Los Angeles. Rubin proffered the idea in a tremulous call to Tennessee, wondering if Cash would even take it or know who Rubin was. Cash's wife June was making movies by then, and the singer had shaken off his years of resentment at how badly he had been treated when he lived in the San Fernando Valley in the late 50s and, like Elvis, was trying to break into film himself. As T.S. Eliot said, 'You only abandon yourself to a new faith when you've got nothing else to lose.' Cash was not objectively at that point yet, but he felt the industry to which he'd given his talent was so preoccupied with new acts that he may never again have the chance Rubin offered with his ingenious archive-new work hybrid.

Early meetings were promising, and as Robert Hilburn notes in his new biography, *Cash: The Life*, Cash drew a parallel between Rubin's patient manner and Sam Phillips's easygoing approach in the tiny Sun Studios a generation before. Rubin wanted to go back and mine Cash's more sinister side, the messenger of dark forces that made him so attractive to criminals, exiles, and young rockers. 'Delia's Gone,' a song this writer heard on his father's Sears hi-fi hundreds of times, was an old standard re-written by Cash in the 60s, a somber, Dostoyevskian study of violence and remorse. This was the hook Rubin wanted, the vehicle that would return Cash to the shadowy place he occupied before he became a symbol of goodness and family in the 70s.

It's opening has the prisoner singing to his block guard:

Delia, oh Delia, Delia all my life
        If I hadn't have shot poor Delia
I'd have had her for my wife
Delia's gone one more round, Delia's gone.

First time I shot her
I shot her in the side
Hard to watch her suffer
But with the second shot she died
But jailer, oh jailer

> Jailer, I can't sleep
> 'Cause all around my bedside
> I hear the patter of Delia's feet
> Delia's gone, one more round, Delia's gone.

As Hilburn has it, the song had all the zest and confidence that allowed Cash to push musical and cultural boundaries for decades, the "maverick tradition of his best fifties and sixties recordings." Cash brought out songs he had written during his post-Columbia, Mercury records days that he had kept hidden until he could get them into the right hands. Rubin said "I wasn't looking for songs that would 'connect' Cash to a younger audience. I was just trying to find songs that really made sense for his voice. By that I don't mean baritone; I mean resonate with his character so he could sing the words and have them feel like he wrote them." Over several days, Rubin and Cash had nearly three dozen songs, and the producer felt he'd gotten just what he wanted. Cash left for a Branson, Missouri concert series with Wayne Newton, despondent at having to open for Newton before an audience of unappreciative blue-haired retirees.

The American Recording series of CDs turned out to be one of the greatest Second Acts of an American musical giant. Rubin had Cash lay down primitive treatments of new and earlier penned compositions, revival numbers he had sung on Graham crusades, and, most ingeniously and importantly, somber tunes from rockers that Cash could cover as if his own. He sang Leonard Cohen's 'Bird On A Wire,' and Neil Young's bittersweet 'Heart of Gold.' When Rubin suggested Steve Earle's 'Devil's Right Hand,' Cash became ecstatic at the first few bars. Earle was one of dozens of young acolytes who saw Cash's TV show as the high water mark of the early 70s. Again, the prison angle presented itself: when Earle spent time on the inside for cocaine and weapons possession in the mid-90s, Cash had been—along with Emmylou Harris and Waylon Jennings—one of the few people who had written to him.

On and on the sessions went. The albums were described by Rubin as '[S]tarting from scratch and introducing a new recording artist.' As Cash's daughter Roseanne said, "Rick came along at exactly the right time, because before him, Dad was depressed, discouraged, and it was a powerful thing that happened between them, and Dad was completely revitalized and back to his old enthusiastic self." She went on: "I think Rick saved his life at that moment." 'Endless Highway' and 'The Man Comes Around,' along with the final 'Cash,' emblazoned with a shadowy toddler picture of Johnny from the thirties, were immensely surprising, gratefully received masterpieces. Indeed, packaging was part of Rubin's brilliance. 'American Recordings' cover was a black and white image of a prophet, shot by the Dutch photographer Anton Corbin, who did U2's 'Joshua Tree' album. Cash stands in a high desert landscape in a ragged funeral coat and cane, two dogs on leashes beside him. Randy Lewis wrote in the L.A. Times that '[C]ash has collected 13 songs that peer into the dark corners of the American soul. In that respect, it's akin to Clint Eastwood's 'Unforgiven,' both in its valedictory, folklore-rich tone and its wealth of characters who embody good and evil in varying proportions."

These "aery populations" that had filtered out of Cash's early records, into those of Jennings, Ry Cooder, Dylan, Dave Alvin and others, had come full circle back to the master who had conjured them. As Cash's painful ailments increased, the final 'Ain't No Grave' CD is filled with eerie, spectral short pieces like the Hawaiian dirge 'Aloha Oe,' much of it sung a cappella. It is the voice and shifting register of a man looking to cross the bar, to return to the Great Artist who had sent him. When that happened, he gave new meaning, crippled as he was, to "finishing strong." He finished mightily, beautifully, in songs that will be listened to, like Stephen Foster's, a hundred years from now.

The First Sam Sheppard

Mr. Peanut
Adam Ross
Knopf, 352 pages

When I was growing up outside of Cleveland, the Sam Sheppard murder trials galvanized not just our sleepy news cycle, but all of the Upper Midwest and the rest of the country. Sheppard, scion of a family of osteopaths, was accused of killing his trophy wife Marilyn in their elegant Bay Village mansion, and after an initial conviction resulting in a ten-year prison term, was retried with F. Lee Bailey at the defense and eventually acquitted. Sheppard's case was the basis of the '60s hit television series *The Fugitive*, and sympathies for the parties broke down along class lines with a special vengeance. In working-class Northern Ohio, almost everyone thought this admittedly philandering doctor was guilty. I remember how much my father, a tire salesman, detested Sheppard, a contempt that was shared throughout the factory towns and farm villages by the male heads of most families. Not only were most fathers jealous of a doctor's income, but in those days the small-town physician had an involuntary one up on his fellow, mere mortal males: he got to see everyone's wife naked. In fact, in the words of a doctor-writer friend of mine, he saw everyone's wife '*more* than naked.' And the arrogance of the defendant and his carpetbagging, swaggering defense lawyer didn't help any.

The Great American Sam Sheppard novel has finally been written by Adam Ross, a relatively new writer from Nashville. But in his *Mr. Peanut,* what could have been a straightforward, serious literary thriller (and a lot more in terms of traditional writing) has much more going on with it, specifically a set of postmodern devices that surround it like a rickety Rube Goldberg mousetrap. *Mr. Peanut* actually starts with the alleged spousal murder by one David Pepin, a computer game designer and would-be novelist, accused of force-feeding or sneaking into a side dish a lethal peanut, to which he knows his wife reacts with hives, seizures, and eventual closing of the throat. Commencing with David's endless fantasies about killing his pathetic, obese, bed-ridden spouse, we are suddenly confronted with her corpse and the truly open question of whether the cause in fact was her husband's malice aforethought, his negligence, a third party's foul play, the wife's disposition to suicide, or her simply reaching into the wrong snack tin.

When the police show up to investigate, the novel takes its strange, superstructural turn—the investigating detectives have marital difficulties that mirror Pepin's, and the first gumshoe is named Ward Hastroll. His wife is an almost cartoonishly exaggerated version of Pepin's, someone so depressive and overweight that she has not been out of bed for five months. Hastroll, too, has vivid fantasies of murder, or of his (also Pepin's constant daydream) better half's death by natural causes such as lightning or drowning or the glutton's sometimes inevitable *Selbstmord*: choking on the last allergic handful of snacks.

It is the other detective whose name is Sam Sheppard. His wife has more complexities than mood disorders and surplus poundage, specifically yearnings—again like Alice Pepin's—of a creative, vagabonding life engendering the couple's 'true' potential for a rich and fulfilling existence, much like the deluded spouse of the protagonist in Richard Yates's *Revolutionary Road* (its influence on Ross here is palpable and undisguised). Sheppard's Marilyn does inflate and deflate with the ferocity of the frantic dieter, but she also dreams of the adulterer's instant, new-made identity; the traveler's plangently constant race against boredom; and the wealthy matron's sense of material privilege being both a kind of immunity from sadness while at the same time an ever-tightening prison. The Sheppard narrative at this point takes over and the book, after its first roller-coaster drops and twists, begins to even out and settle into itself as a plausible, entertaining story. The detectives focus on a suspect named Mobius, the counterpart to the 'one-armed man' that the TV fugitive and real-life Sheppard fingered as the true killer, and whose hair and flesh samples were keys to Bailey's winning an acquittal long before the days of O.J.-era, exonerating DNA.

Both within the outer, framing stories and the more conventional Sheppard tale, the true brilliance of Ross's writing is its exploration of the toxic paradoxes of marriage. As Stephen King said of this book, it may well be the greatest exploration of domestic strife since *Who's Afraid Of Virginia Woolf?* The book never flinches in its focus on matrimony's funhouse mirrors of dissatisfaction, ennui, contentedness, and occasional bliss. Like Albee and Yates, Ross has a staggering gift (especially in such a young writer) for portraying marriage as the most universal and yet mysterious, sometimes unfathomable of relationships. Attention will be paid (to paraphrase another eternal husband, Willy Loman) to this author's brilliance at tracking a husband and wife's simultaneous search for fulfillment in the other while holding that same person responsible for every unhappiness and disappointment.

But even more than in Yates, and somewhat less but more fascinatingly than in Albee, Ross's Sheppard and Marilyn (and David and Alice and Ward and Hannah) demonstrate a self-knowledge, an awareness of their groping struggles with one another and an appreciation of their inherence in the institution they occupy. Here is Marilyn Sheppard driving the Bay Shore highway along Lake Erie, wondering exactly who she observes is as curious as Karenina, or herself:

> She could go anywhere now because she was operating under '(Sam's) presumptions.' She drove down Lake Road, studying the drivers in the oncoming lane. Where were these men and women off to? Did their husbands or wives know? Were they where they were supposed to be or was everyone sneaking around? She had, if anything, greater latitude than Sam, and if she chose she could afford even more convenient forms of deception because in the past he'd predicated his deceptions on her absences...

The six-person, three-pair characters' inner worlds of longing, wondering, and fantasizing are rendered without a false moment, without so much as a single misplaced recognition. The jagged graph of marriage's modulations, peaks of ecstasy and stagnant, bewildering troughs of oblivion, all take place in tremendously realistic interior concentrations like Marilyn's drive here to the Sheppard clinic.' For all its attempts to foster stability, marriage is life and fate's persistently unpredictable microcosm: '[N]o guaranteed gifts for the good or punishments for the bad, no fairness in what the Lord giveth and taketh away, except for the undeniable fact of corporeality, and thus one's own death.' We run from loneliness only to see that companionship entails the same dice throw, the same black, unreadable map.

Relationship insights notwithstanding, one ends up wishing Ross had tagged less filigree onto the fine, central story where most of these insights come to the doctor and his frustrated Scheherazade. The Sheppard material is so solid and well-realized, its characters so inherently believable, that the Pepin/Hastroll/Narrator's wraparounds seem unworkable and contrived. One wants to carve away the fact that Pepin's secret book also has the same opening as Ross's, the fact that competing tales and alternate endings—drawing droll attention to themselves—fly off the smooth running central narrative engine like bad timing belts. Can't anyone tell a straight-ahead story anymore? Ross does, but wraps his succulent Cleveland kielbasa in unnecessary bacon strips. Writers of Ross's traditionalist talents might want to stay away from clever devices. They often come across as nothing more than that, and send the reader back to what sustains.

The Teacher's Sermon: Letter from India

There is a specter haunting history, the teaching of history. I saw it first in my eighth grade schoolteacher, Mr. Davis, a stern giant whose spectacles blazed in the window sunlight and whose legs were so long his belt seemed to circle his armpits. He taught us that victory by the North over the Confederacy was not just the product of superior efforts, military hardware, weather and terrain, but was rather the triumph of a Christian abolitionist God who looked, yes, like John Brown, his arms spread and his fists gripping a bright carbine of righteousness.

Mr. Davis, we knew, was also a minister at the Hilltop Non-Denominational Church in Lucas. It was Ohio, 1966. Our parents were laissez-faire in matters of religion, but with the Bomb aimed at us in a possibly godless world, they gave Mr. Davis free reign. When I told my mother some of the things he said, she thought him quaint. It was, after all, a small village, and Davis had been my parents' teacher as well. (In 1947: same subject, same classroom, same bomb.)

I sit now in Delhi with regulars of the RSS, the BJP or Hindu Fundamentalist Party' military branch. In some sectors they have been charged with ensuring instructional comportment with the Hindu "national vision." Though held in check somewhat now by the re-election of the Congress Party and its backlash against Hindu-centrism, my lunch mates were directing book confiscations in schools less than two years ago, and still wield an intimidating power over the upturned faces of tens of millions of children. They are sort of a Mr. Davis writ large, pacing in front of the class with high-buckled pants and wagging pointers.

The state and the church always insist on a role in teaching history, and the true student of the discipline appropriately resists. "Being left with what has happened," as Robert Lowell called it, can never have an ulterior agenda. But recently, both religious and secular states have sought to advance their goals behind the objective mask of historical instruction. Those who steer off course can be called into the hallway for a caning. Bush and company tout the historicism of the Pakistani and Saudi religious schools—madrassas—as terror instruction, and the truth of this must be measured by the agenda that administration is advancing at the moment, who it wishes to invade or isolate. But an equally menacing form has surfaced in other places, including France, where philosophers warn of the state's desire to "discipline and punish." Some French members of parliament advanced a bill early this year that reads: "School courses should recognize in particular the positive role of the French colonial presence overseas, notably in North Africa." Vraiment? A thousand historians, writers and intellectuals signed a petition demanding a repeal of the law, stating that it imposes "an official lie on massacres that at times went as far as genocide in the slave trade, and on the racism France has inherited."

Authorities elsewhere are dictating to teachers the contents of their lessons. In Japan, the only history texts allowed are ones that minimize aggression in the Sino-Japanese War. Nanking and related incidents were preventive, prophylactic measures, according to this view. The French petition's critics, notably the historian Pierre Vidal-Naquet, cite the Japanese trend as one France should avoid before it's too late. "If this country wants to be that way," he told Liberation magazine recently, "it's going the right way about it .... dictating lesson plan contents to teachers."

Even in England, history texts have been proposed that would rehabilitate the Empire, recasting the crimes of John Bull. In the wake of 9/11 and Blair's hip-joinder with Bush, British historians such as Niall Ferguson, Andrew Roberts, and Gordon Brown have attempted to downplay English atrocities in Kenya's Mau-Mau rebellion, where deaths in colonial camps are now thought to exceed 100,000. See Caroline Elkins's *Britain's Gulag* (Faber 2005).

Here in India, authorities should be especially mindful of the atrocities of power, and the grave danger of glossing that is part and parcel of any nationalism. It was here that 30 million died in *fin de siècle* famines as British administrators insisted on the export of grain (repeat Ireland), British courts ordered 80,000 floggings a year, and the English militia stood aside during the avoidable Bengal famine of 1943. British and Indian history texts are empty of such references, Master and Slave seeming to conspire to wipe memory clean.

But the Indian Hindu fundamentalists who skirt in and out of power here are embarked on an oddly myopic memory and textbook cleansing of their own. The BJP, which ruled here from 1999 until its ouster in May 2004, is the moderate political body of the much more radical group of men I have been spending my mornings with. The ideological fulcrum of both BJP and RSS is that India is a Hindu nation, and minorities such as Muslims may live here only to the extent they accept Hindu directives and govern their lives accordingly. RSS is known in particular for its enforcement enthusiasms, and the inspiration it takes from classic 20th Century fascist organizations. Yes, they have guns. And yes, their shirts are brown.

RSS leaders I met with unabashedly approve of the "educational cleansing" that started in 1980, when BJP-ruled schools issued textbooks that revised years of tolerance toward Muslims. The new history primers demonized "Mohammedism" as a reckless invader, working to internally topple Mother India from the 14th Century Muslim "invasion" to the present day. RSS would, when it deemed necessary, police the schools and make sure the Vedic-centered party line was foregrounded. Teachers who didn't thump the Hindu tub were warned, and more than a few times, sacked outright.

This ideological sea-change cannot be overemphasized. The Congress Party that ruled India for decades, and which is back in power now, stressed what is written in the Indian Constitution: though settled by Aryan "Hindus," several millennia ago, the country is populated by a single, ethnically homogenous people. Muslims and Hindus mingled together for so many centuries that that their racial distinctions fused, with religious differences becoming more muted.

RSS and MJP drink from different wells. Their intellectual forefathers are writers like Madar Golwalker, the "Guru" who first fashioned the "Hindu Version" of history. For the Guru, Hinduism is not just a religious faith, with its differences fanned by religious flames of divide and rule. Muslims were savages and invaders, desecraters and polluters of the national bloodstream. Golwalker drew sustenance from racial purification agendas of Nazi philosophers, tossing out boomerangs like the following: "Ever since the day when Muslims first landed in Hindustan, right up to the present moment, the Hindu nation has been fighting to shake off the despoilers."

You can sit here on a late spring morning with the RSS men, planted on bags of flour, sucking cheroots and pipes filled with cheap tobacco dust. Around them, the buildings their party sought to restore—the "new miracle of BJP public works"—are tatty and stained and flaking. The men grimace as they inhale, looking triumphant in the soft, steady rain of paint peelings.

More than anywhere else outside the Middle East, the militants' belief in ascendancy is not just tied to a past imperial reign, but one whose essential nature is military, in this case guerilla. The holy books of Hinduism, the Vedas, contain armies and generals, trumpets and standards and the renunciation of surrender. Gods and warriors are indistinguishable: one is a holy mirror of the other, which is a caste and is pedestalized as an ethnic tradition. The holiest cities are thus the most militant. Of the six urban centers sacred to Shiva, two have erupted in anti-Muslim violence in the past fifteen years. The Ayodha disturbances involved the destruction of a mosque "built over" one of Rama's ancient temples, supported after the fact with archeological justifications. (One thinks of Arafat, Netanyahu, and the potshard debates over the temple mount that tanked the Oslo accords.) Most recent and most horrifying were the Gujarat pogroms of Summer 2002, in which several thousand Muslims were blamed for a train fire, then hunted down and butchered by the BJP and its media toadies.

An RSS driver takes me around sections of the Hindu temples pushing in upon the suffocating, shrinking squares of mosques, their towers being shortened by BJP councilmen because of the "noise pollution" of Islamic muezzin prayers. Vivek is an RSS "minister of information." At the last corner of government buildings we turn before heading into the old city, and he gestures toward the wide British malls and arches and says something remarkable for an Indian, utterly without irony.

"British came, they occupied. Their, how are you saying, Golden

Age. It was their time."

We head into the narrow *gallis,* where Islamic establishments have been driven out in the BJP's "five strong years." "But never did British tear monuments down," Vivek goes on. "Never destroy." We come to Alimumbayah Mosque, among the oldest and largest in India. "Only Muslim people," he says, waving a finger. "Only Muslims. Only mullahs tearing down and killing."

The same wince on the smoking guards' faces as Vivek's as we go by the Mosque's front entrance, where a rally proceeds behind a long white banner proclaiming the Three Great Terrorists: Bush, Blair, Sharon." The mosque's great central dome seems strangely human, splayed, wearing only the vestiges of its former confidence. It is like Gulliver waking to find everyone smaller than himself, but still having staked his arms and legs to the ground.

To Vivek, to the RSS, and to even the most moderate of the BJP "tolerants," the Hindu restoration is a slow, incremental occupation of time itself. The Vedic faith suffered for centuries under the Muslim Mughals (Vivek compares Eastern Orthodox countries, Serbia, Macedonia ruled by the Ottomans), but the triumph of Shiva's many-diety system is inevitable, implacable: as old as Asia itself, and thus older than Europe.

In or out of power, it is along these stress lines that BJP and its military branch sets the earth rumbling. Vivek does not support the recent "sweeps" that have struck a Third Reich note in Hindu-centrist strongholds like Pune, an outlying suburb of Mumbai. I ask him about the RSS goons' dust-up of a history research library earlier this year simply simply because of its appearance in a book positing the illegitimacy of a Hindu national hero, the 17th century anti-Muslim guerilla Shivaji Dhousle. "No book burning," he says. "No police knocking on the midnight door."

But the more he explains, the more I realize he is not so much against this violence as indifferent to it. Such actions are self-purification of an already acceptable national curriculum. The violence is, to him, of no consequence, because it is redundant and unnecessary. Any didact will show moments of insecurity, like the nervous Ph.d candidate repeating the themes of her dissertation. But these are mere hiccups, nothing to get upset about.

The violence he speaks of is, if anything, calculated in Goldwalker's words, to "shake off the despoilers." He justifies it with the long centuries of perceived Muslim captivity. "My family," he says, "before anyone can remember. Generations back." Overpopulation is perceived as another tool of Islamic weaponization. When we are at stoplights and beggar children tap their cups on our window, he shoos them off and tells me to button my wallet pocket. "Every Muslim family, four or five children. Six, seven, eight children." He shakes his head. "In China not allowed."

All historical "corrections" come alive now in Vivek's gestures, his rising tone. Such campaigns are restorative, exorcistic and thus pre-rational undertakings, even if revision of books, coldly rational revisions, are one of their goals. And corrections are lines drawn in the sand. They amount to minding the gate against the swarm of "four or five children" multiplied by 200 million Muslims, twenty percent of the nation's population. Like Israeli views of the Fertile Palestinian, it is like the Mongol horde rising from within, walking into what Barthes called "the living room of one's freedom."

There is one other thing building toward these future explosions. It is the lag time of the written word (and certainly the historical text) behind electronic, digital media. The mullahs' exhortations are in the distance now, their loudspeaker crackle submerged in the market din as Vivek steers us into New Delhi, Hindu Delhi. He turns up his radio, turned all to the Star stations that told tens of millions of Hindus to revenge the Gujarat fires, to hunt down Muslims wherever they were, to drag them out of their living rooms. (It was the Hutus, remember, leaning by their radios in Rwanda, before even before one machete was lifted.)

And if this were any doubt that this were a true war, all this about what has happened and will happen, the telling of what has happened and will happen, I simply ask Vivek who wins. "Who wins?" he repeats. He points to the Shiva on his dashboard.

"And why?"

"It is predicted," he says, and smiles. I remember Mr. Davis only smiling once in the Civil War class. He was trying to explain how the

North had won, and was lifting his pointer toward a Union powder boy. The pointer's tip came to rest on the young, wounded and frightened soldier's satchel, on the very center of which was really an explosive of prophecy. It was a cross, gold and smudged with fingerprints, etched on the tattered leather.

Mumbai, May 2005

Deep Play: Letter from Indonesia

Fellas, imagine being able to take off Mr. Happy, let it walk around, air irself out a little. Maybe get into conversation with other, similarly situated members, take a constitutional, show off the plumage for an hour or two. Maybe, in the midst of all the preening, let it get into, *encourage* it to get into, a scrape, a fight with another perambulating wiener. And if it wins that fight, let it fight another, and another, and so on. Not since Chris Starling took a photo of his unit in my high school circa 1972, with a Polaroid camera (still a novelty to us in rural Ohio) and put it in the trophy case have I been this focused on dislocation and the lower urological quadrant. Not until I came to Bali.

Now imagine a stand-in for the anatomically impossible: a creature, a bird so infused with penile identity as to be a complete equivalent in almost all aspects of a man's life. In a decade of field work here, the anthropologist Clifford Geertz found that the "deep psychological identification of Balinese men with their cocks is unmistakable." All double entendres with "man" and "cock" are intended, and fit perfectly with the Balinese conception of the body as a set of separately animated parts. Geertz's predecessors in this over-studied ethnology, mainly Margaret Mead and her husband Gregory Bateson, saw fighting roosters as separable, autonomous penises, genitalia with their own strengths, moods, and varying tempers. In the dirt combat circles of Balinese villages, Geertz confirmed that fighting cocks are "masculine symbols par excellence, about as indubitable and, to the Balinese, about as evident, as the fact that water runs downhill."

The equivalence goes back centuries, with inscriptions from the tenth century using the term "cock" metaphorically to mean "hero," "warrior," "champion," "man of parts," "political candidate," "bachelor," "dandy," "lady-killer" or "tough guy." Each sequence of male existence is fleshed out (sorry) with the metaphor. An eligible bachelor is a "fighting cock caged for the first time." Parsimoniousness is described as a cock held by the tail, lunging, unable to engage in truly tough, risk-laden, genuine commerce. A desperate gambler—one who has lost all the "deep play" we shall discuss below—is likened to a wounded cock in his death throes, upside down, claws twitching above his bloody feathers. Wars, inheritance disputes, streetfights—all are compared to the wingy flash of two crazed, well-trained bantams.

Cocks are displayed, but in a bashful sort of nonchalance. Rows of men squat in the shade, always more than half holding a docile, mollified rooster. Others walk the streets with the great girth of the birds under their crooked arms, the rooster's red, anxious head poking in and out of the hole of its owner's arm. The birds are groomed more than any pet, and sometimes any child. They are given a special diet, their cages moved from room to room in high viddas to gain the optimum track of sun and shade.

At its outer symbolic extremity, the cock is regarded as a patchwork of dark power, not just the penis but the id that is its vital engine. Animality is feared and loathed in Balinese culture. Eating, defecation, perspiration—because of their perceived animality—are accomplished quickly, and are universally detested. So a man's identification with his bird is not just with his penis and its control, but also with frightening forces, things that must also be carried but thereby confined, kept down. The perfect animal—one minute docile and the next combustible—is chosen to embody both sides of the male psyche. What is controlled and most valued is also a portal of evil an omen of explosive destruction.

It is in the fight itself that the explosion arrives. "Man and beast," Geertz writes, "good and evil, ego and id, the creative power of aroused masculinity . . . .all fuse into a bloody drama of hatred, cruelty, violence and death." The winner of the cockfight is infused with moral satisfaction and testicular glee. Heaven is described in the tenth century chronicles as a man whose cock has been victorious; hell is the loser, the limp body of the dead bird, the Mariner's albatross.

I had heard of the actual fights in Ubud, the tony hideaway of the rich up in the Central Highlands. Nothing as course and revealing as a cockfight would be allowed within the city's high walls. But just outside, in the yard of an abandoned gas station, the men stand in line with their birds while other men write down names and wagers in thick-columned grids.

None of the fights are related to one another. There are no statistics or common goals or tournaments. There is no sense of consolidating progress in the life of even the most victorious cock. Rather, as each fight ends, six or eight or ten men slip slowly into the ring with their bird and scour the landscape for a plausible opponent. The cock-keepers do it all with an indirect, sidelong attention, feigning only partial awareness of the coming destruction. Like anywhere else in the wagering world, the truly deft bettor is the cool-headed one, parading his rooster's prowess but conveying his full ability to absorb a loss.

My driver takes me down into the cockfight or *sabungan* area, out beyond the markets and filtration plant, on a shaded side street blocked off at each end by a canopied mini pick-up. I have watched from a distance for days, and now have come after a match has been made and the chosen birds have their spurs (*tadji*) attached. These razor-sharp, pointed steel swords, four or five inches long, are fastened by a process as guarded as a trade secret. Only a half-dozen or so men know how to do it in my village. (The spur-attacher, the *tadjigan*, is also the maker of the spurs, but his compensation is never monetary. If the rooster he assists wins, he is awarded the spur-leg of the victim.)

Besides the elaborate betting patterns, spur affixing is the most delicate and specialized of tasks. The *tadjigan* winds a long length of string around the foot of the spur, a little ridge, and then widens the circle of his wrapping around the cracked yellow claws and curved nails of the waiting bird. With the exception of negligible, small-bet fights, the owner never fixes the spur. In the normal scenario where spur fixers and cock handlers are not the owners, they are almost always a close relative—a brother, a male cousin, sometimes simply a close friend. These owner-handler-affixer triads are amazingly impenetrable, though individuals within them can change roles, slowly developing the skill sets of all three.

My driver explains the basic betting patterns, the use of even money betting and odds on the side grow into formulas so complex that different Hindu gods are said to watch the notations and markers. There is a single, axial bet between the principals at the center, the *toh ketangah*. Around this fixed point are the innumerable peripheral bets placed by the ever thickening ring of audience, the *toh kesasi*. The axial bet is, without exception, always for even money; the peripheral bets are never without odds. As Geertz famously put it, "What is fair coin at the center is a biased one on the side."

The center bet is placed by the two owners, or, more properly, the owners and a few beer-besotted compatriots. This *koh katanngai*, more to show honesty and transparency, is very high, for a large amount of currency. The side bets are smaller, dazzlingly rapid, and take place basically in the same way the stock market operated before government controls: a glorified, perilous gambling parlor. The side-bettor who wishes to bet the underdog shouts out a short-side number indicating the odds he wants to be given. If he shouts "five," he wants the underdog at five-to-one. The backers of the favorite, i.e. those in a position to give odds if they are short enough, demonstrate their choice by calling out the color-type of plumage markings of the incumbent.

The side bets rise in a crescendo of underdog-backers offering their proposals to any takers, the favorite-backers shouting out the color of that bird over and over—each repetition of the name a rejection—until the odds are favorably shortened. It is a mystical, delirious humming. The only thing I have ever heard that is comparable—and again part of what ethnologists call a Buddhist "focused gathering"—is a sutra recited by a theater full of *nichiren shoshu* chanters, all of them on cue, not a single speaker hitting a word outside its preordained, practiced pacing.

Here also the pattern rises into a cacophonous crowd, but is much more varied, and, at least to the novice, disarmingly disorganized. Frenzy doesn't begin to describe it. Right up until the moment the cocks are released, the crowd is like a choir spitting out quarter notes of a Handel operetta. Each of them are unfulfilled bettors desperately searching for last minute opponents at a price they are comfortable with. In the shimmering half-second before the wings beat out of the keepers' folded armsa, the shouts and screams of the echoes trail away, vanishing under the purring and clucking of the birds.

Then they are released.

I nudge forward with my driver, about half way into the outer region of the side-betting circle. Merely watching like this, especially for an outsider, is frowned upon as patronizing and, and, well, ethnographic, which is even worse. So I take out 50-60 *ringgits*, fold them in half lengthways, and bend them around my center and pointer fingers.

The handlers have put the birds down into the ring, facing one another, the swords double-checked by the handlers tapping the bright steel gently with their sandals. The pressure on the weapon also reminds the birds of their mission: unbridled hatred, annihilation, no rest until the opponent is lifeless and lifted away. A bucket of water sits at the favored bird's corner, into which a hollow, holed coconut is placed. It takes twenty-one seconds to sink, a slit gong announcing its arrival at the bottom.

The handlers are not permitted to touch the birds during this period, but the birds *can* commence fighting. If, as often happens, they have not engaged after the drop, the handlers pick them up and stroke, fluff and pull and prod their feathers and crests.

These two fly at each other immediately. The wings arch up like raised human hands, the heads butt one another. Feathers fly off and float in the air above the two of them, each trying to firm their stance enough to raise the armed legs and get in the pivotal first jab. (The key for the first striker is to be lifted away quickly so as not to receive a return blow; two mortally wounded cocks will result in a tie as they hack one another to pieces.)

The underdog raises its sworded leg and drives the first blow home. The crowd roars, hands full of bent bills flying up, some of the men jumping. This is, of course, the most interesting and desired result: odds takers all along the spectrum of two-to-five, sometimes two-to-eight or ten, have become unhinged. They keep their arms in the air and spin around and hug one another, the soon-to-be-fattened flapping in the dust clouds.

The underdog handler lifts his bird away, The handler of the favored bird believes the wound is superficial, and begins to 'palliate' his charge. My driver, who hasn't wagered anything and thus has ten free fingers, makes what first looks like a victory sign, then begins wiggling the two digits. It is the sign for "wait," the spectral bell lull between rounds—the moments in which the referee calculates whether he can count the bird down or not.

The favored cock handler brings in a team with ladles. They dip them into the bucket of dark, woody water, but rather than throw them on the animal itself, each of them drinks a mouthful and sprays a fine mist over the not-yet-bleeding bantam's torso. The spur-fixer, designated specifically for this task, parts the bird's beak and spits in water from between his clenched teeth, a half-second, three-second squirt. When too much goes in, the bird turns its head and the stream hits the side of the cracked yellow beak, the dusty, wagging coxcomb.

The odds-takers are hysterical. They surge forward from behind us. I feel fists and bill edges crawl across my back like insects. Some of them point to where a wound might be; the place they thought they saw the sword land, the places—underbelly or upper neck, wing attachment points—where most of the razors hit their mark. The handlers can't hear above the roar, a sea-surge crashing on rocks. All bets are paid on the spot, in cash, and everyone is hungry for the endgame.

The treatments are over, and the test begins anew with each handler setting his bird down. The coconut is lifted to the top of the pail again and the handlers inch forward. There are two more twenty-one second drops of the coconut, totaling the "decisive minute" as an untranslatable Malay word. During that time, the cock that has delivered the blow must be set down to show it is not visibly bleeding and can stand upright by itself.

During the drop of the third coconut, the wounded one's handler parts the beak again and blows in pure air, waiving away the sub-handlers with waiting mouthfuls of water. Then the handler sticks the bird's entire head in his mouth, takes it out and blows more air, strokes it, closes its mouth again.

Usually a wounded cock's man has a harder time, trying to rouse a final flicker of life into the bird. Usually he is drenched in blood. Usually there are signs of fading hope on his face, waves of his head in a giant, single negation.

The favored cock still has fight in him, and he is placed down as carefully as if he were constructed of crystal. Usually the first blood-taker, flush with its strike and inspired by the rising roar, quickly finishes the other off with a final blow. But such an outcome is by no means certain; if the wounded cock can get a stab in that causes the seeming victor to go down, it is he who prevails, even if he falls over a second or two later.

The coconut watcher signals that the third drop has concluded. The judges want to stop; the owners want to continue. The underdog doesn't disappoint, thrusting its sword into the chest of the stunned favorite. The metal catches in the breastbone for a second, causing the bird to be pulled toward its victim and merge with it for five or six seconds, like prize fighters in head holds waiting to be separated by the referee.

But then he pulls his claw away. Shreds of bright blood and bone chips fly out of the favorite's wound. It turns and starts to walk away toward the ring, then totters, then drops. The crowd's roar completely covers any other sound: the thud of the loser's fall, the screech of the victor-bird.

*   *   *

Bets are paid off as the ring is cleared. All wagers are immediately settled without IOUs, no meeting of minds on credits or calculations. Some of the losers wandering away look especially disconsolate. They are the favorite-bettors who gave high odds and are now having to pay out much more than they foresaw.

My driver lets me know these are the "deep players," the victims of excessive wagers that the Dutch, when they still ran these colonies, tried to regulate out of the public wagering system. The utilitarian philosopher Bentham, who saw the social contract founded on each citizen striving for maximum utility at marginal risk, was utterly stumped by any betting in which either wagerer was in over their heads. He thus saw "deep play," described in *The Theory of Legislation*, as "immoral from first principles, something that should be legally prohibited." He thought such behavior belonged only to "addicts, thieves, children, fools, savages, who only need protection against themselves." (This seems in keeping with what I, who studied Bentham as an undergraduate, remember about him: a nerd, held upside down by fellow students at a high table at university College, London, change rattling out of his pockets. Our professor went on to describe him as a "stiff," quite literally, his body stuffed and standing in a glass case in one of the school's hallways.)

The problem of Deep Play is rampant in Balinese society, and more for the fact that money victories are linked to status far, far more than to the actual lightening of wallets suffered by the losers. The possibility of a single, high status leap by winning a long-odds bet outweighs the possible material losses for the "plunger", or Deep Play bettor. So the symbolism of status change, laying your reputation on the line in the form of one's cock, pushes utilitarianism to one side and makes the bettors symbolists, artists, imposers of form on their social fabric. The bettor becomes the Nietzschean superman who masters, or is mastered by, his society as a result of imaginative constructs.

Still, the plungers are hard to watch, wandering away, sitting on upturned boxes under the eaves of banana sheds. Loaded with beer, they cover their faces with their hands and drift off to sleep. Tomorrow they will be back, or in a week, once they have pawned the remaining acres of their farm or sold a primitive vehicle like a tug-tuk. Hope springs eternal. The cock's vitality will not be dissipated. What starts as private striving is frozen into public, aesthetic form, and whatever its final product, there is no substitute for the force and beauty of its process. Call it the id, the life force, the will to power or some irrational, long-shot rage for form and order. The bottom line is that the bird cannot be put down, cannot be kept from the dusty contest.

Chechens in the Capital (Letter from Moscow)

I went to a Chechen junkyard on the outskirts today to get a carburetor for the diplomat's Lada. The Chechen underworld controls all the used auto-parts markets in Moscow and, some claim, in the entire Russian Federation. After the theater hostage incident in Moscow in 2000, then after the Beslan school massacre in North Ossetia in 2004, the Caucasus natives are a people treated with an almost implacable hatred by many white Russians. As liberal as a group of the latter may appear, the assassination of however compromising a Caucasus Islamic leader is seen always as a victory, an erasure of vermin. I ran into one in his newspaper offices recently. Bedayev was on the run and the two 'black widows' had blown up a pair of planes flying out of Domodedovo, and there had been other suicide bombings. The journalist fancied himself a historian of ideas and had been reading a lot of Erik Erikson. He gave the following account of things, which I offer with no opinion:

The Caucasus Muslims have no nation, or only the most teetering of individual states, states being defined in Hobbesian terms as entities with a degree of infrastructure and a monopoly on the means of violence. Accordingly, the minds of these warriors are consumed with dueling concepts; battles between totalisms or absolutes that one could never imagine in Saudi Arabia or Iran, where the state puts its full force behind the absolute of sexual shame and hiddenness, the negation of sensual pleasure.

In contrast, Caucasus Muslims display all the forces of the sacred and profane *in balance*. The earthly and the pious mix with dazzling attractiveness, and this allure seems to grow the more these people are oppressed. It is what attracted Tolstoy to them, when he was defending against their raids as a young army officer in the 1860s.

Like the ideal human balance envisioned by Martin Luther, the Chechen Muslim encompasses both kinds of 'total states' in the mixture of his personality. The fighter for Allah here is both a total sinner (gambling, smuggling)—but, as long as the mission is *jihad*, always blessed as well as damned, both alive and dead. As Erikson said of Lutherans, the Chechen Muslim cannot strive 'by hook or by crook, to get from one absolute state to another; [he] can only use his God-given organs of awareness in the here and now to encompass the paradoxes of the human condition'.

So the Chechen soldier must accept at the same time his ruffian, outlaw urges and his piety to Allah. Only by holding them in balance can he confirm his identity. What appears to the outsider as religious submission is really mastery of fate; what appears as banditry is actually a weapon against the infidel. There is tremendous free will here —the warrior is the blender, the shaper of his urges, and he can take both enjoyment and a sense of usefulness from them.

When the soldier turns to suicide as a method of battle, he appears to have lost this balance of opposites. The drives that the conscience holds in check overwhelm that conscience. He surrenders to a spirit of non-existence and self-destruction that is simply another biological urge, one of the urges the ego considers as beneath and outside itself at the same time it is mesmerized by them. Suicide as a weapon can be called for by a ruler or commander, but to the true soldier *intentional* self-destruction is futile. No soldier is effective dead, no matter how many of the enemy he takes with him.

To the true soldier, the balancer and shaper, the suicide entreaty should be as repugnant as any of the other unchecked biological instincts. It is just another unbridled portion of what Freud called the *id*, but one far graver than sexual urges or a sense of public recklessness. It is the death instinct, the *spiritus moribund*, boiled down into a single person, a single event, a single travesty. Missions can be advanced by self-sacrifice, but not self-destruction. Suicide is altruism blotting out the self entirely, the mass man occluding the man. (Again, soldiers focus on the here and now: *that* is their spiritual advent, not some notion of Paradise.)

Mindless, commander-ordered battle suicide is a sort of id-intoxication, a poisoning. The self lets the reins drop and lies down on the back of the id-monster's fury.

This is not soldierly. It is most certainly not Chechen.

Control of what would otherwise be wild has always been the

Caucasian hill peoples' watchword. Their power over horses and other beasts of burden was always their very symbol as a people. No Caucasus image or sketch exists in Tolstoy without the horseman and his almost mystical power over the animal. With that came mystical power over all other aspects of life, its preservation in the face of overwhelming odds. The Caucasus warrior 'looks life in the eye, looks the weather and the mountains in the eye', as Tolstoy wrote in *Hadji Murad*. He does not give himself over to them. He does not own them, but they are his companions.

One thinks of the captured Chechens in the longer Tolstoy stories, how their features and qualities draw their jailers in with a hypnotic effect. The prisoner does not sink into misery. He is defiant, his fists on his hips. His features—especially his eyes—could be large and prominent or small and hidden; the eyes are deep, unfathomable. They were never glazed with the sheen of annihilation. The Chechen always fought back. If captured and marked for death, he wouldn't be satisfied with the soldier's usual insistence on a firing squad over hanging. He would fight as they came for him. He would take one of his captors out in the process. He was a hawk, terrible and swift as lightning among the rest of humanity, which rested ledges and ledges below him, mere sparrows.

Prisons of the King (Letter from Chiapas)

Campo Siete is one of those all-night cantinas on the trucking roads that run through the Isthmus of Tehuantepec. These are the blue highways on the map, tiny and mangled, made of the same hand-laid stone the Mayas and Toltecs used for their ghostly altars and pyramids. Coming out of the northern cities, they rise through the scrub-thick, brambled lowlands into the mountain foothills, dipping and twisting until the road breaks down into gravel in the high, cold groves of pinnacle spruce and new-grown juniper. You are only on the peaks a few hours before you begin to loop back their shadowed, southern sides, level by level down again into the warming, hazedraped altitudes. Finally, after hours of stone road again, you come to the great ports the roads were built to feed: Veracruz and Coatzacoalcos, the Caribbean Babylons, their invisible columns of deadly sun and beehives of people tearing away at the jungle's green.

But it wasn't day when we got in. It was a midsummer night, that still, pitch tar spread out with the flashing gravel of the southern constellations. The door to the Campo stood under a single *santas* lamp, the paint rubbed away and the wood worn down by the many hands of impatient drivers. You could hear them inside as you walked up, a muffled explosion of light and noise as the latch gave way.

It had a long bar, like the famous one in Ensenada, but wider, so everyone sitting on the high stools who wanted to and was out of sight of the bartender could bend over when it got to be too much and stretch their stomach and chest along the bottle-dotted wood. The drivers were in front and the locals in back, never the twain meeting, we knew, the drivers seeing the townies as provincials, lazy and backward-Indians stuck here by unshakable lethargy and fecklessness.

But the drivers were only kidding with each other now, the fat one in suspenders in front razzing the others about the weigh stations in the South, how they'd been wasting their time there without bribe money, fools to be stopping and putting up with the oldest and most obvious and transparent of bureaucracies. I could get most of this if I listened carefully, but I needed Mac, whose Spanish was better, to get the rest.

One of the drivers—they called him Suspenders—was going down the line of *campesinos* with his electric box. The grips hung dangling from their wires. Some of the farmers jumped back at the sight of them, as if the box were a vicious dog or a reptile.

The drivers were going for it now, most of them drunk enough to take a few jolts, their backs flattened against the bar and their wide thighs tensed around the stools by the current. We'd seen some of these guys two nights before at the warehouse in Campo Seis, dancing with obviously underage girls in pastel tu-tus and baby-doll pajamas. These outfits had something like bustles, masses of netted fabric that swayed like ghostly, glowing bells. Men like Suspenders danced with them sleepily, clutching the girls' shoulders with hands that looked like the giant, bent fore feet of mantises. Some of the girls had hard, sloping eyes and looked retarded, their hair sprayed into flat, sharp cones and triangles.

The boxes were standard macho regalia for the drivers and for all Mexican men in bars like these. Maybe for all Mexican men, period. It was 1973, the days of the first Chiapas rebellions, what Warren Hinckle was calling the New Time of the Lawless Roads. For all we knew, Echeverria and the cabinet passed them around at state dinners, easing back in their chairs to use them as mettle testers of other Latin dignitaries. I thought for a minute that it may have even been the way the defense minister was "accidentally" electrocuted by his brother in the palace bathtub a few weeks earlier.

These gizmos were simply large, smudged gunmetal boxes, flat hued and thick with prints, lined with rivets, and inside you could see the colored balls of wire and flickering, cobwebbed cathode tubes that lit them. A crude dial was pasted to the top, probably a speedometer or gas gauge from an old tractor, the needle black and the arch of hashes black and numberless.

The box looked heavy but really wasn't, because Suspenders, the guy holding it, would move from stool to stool and customer after customer drunk enough to take it while another man held out the true and actual lightning, the little copper claws at the ends of the wires that looked like jumper cable grips. Box carriers I'd seen in other bars had always, like Suspenders, been short and fat and plastered at the top end with enormous balls of greased and matted hair. And the grip holder, like now, was always taller and dapper and gaunt: the face man, the presenter.

What he presented was electricity, that rarest of tropical juices—the hottest and fastest atoms, the surest maker of men. All maleness here seemed ready to be so measured, and though the very idea of such a thing struck me as boorish and repulsive, I decided to ride with it, to watch it through the clear, clean lens of the anthro-tourist.

After two or three stools, the duo got somebody to take the grips, to fork out the pesos at some *campesino's* egging and lay his drink down long enough to hold the pair of copper jaws. The subject up for inspection now sat very rigid. He held the grips straight out at an angle and gave some kind of unseen signal to Suspenders, who wiped his mouth with the back of his hand and bent over and started twisting the knobs.

The man lurched at first, then hunched and steadied himself, then lurched again and sputtered and shook until the wetted curls of his hair wagged around, growing so runny with sweat that they stuck to his head. There was a lull where the subject breathed quickly—in, out—and the wetness on his stomach and chest spread the length of his shirt. Then the presenter turned the voltage up. But the customer wonderfully, wonderfully *held*, his hair smoothing out and his eyes clinching tighter, maintaining, soaking up the heat of the charge …

The second customer was taller and much more polished, dressed like a *pachuco*, a dandified townie with a moustache and hat. When he was handed the grips, he looked at them skeptically, shaking them and turning them upside down. The men beside him were respectfully silent and ran their hands on the stubble of their chins. When Suspenders tried to return the setting to zero, the *pachuco* waved him off and said, *"este, este"*: He would start at the level the first man had reached.

This man simply rattled. His hair rose like snakes. "I'm reminded," said Mac, "of Frankenstein's monster." But after a few minutes, this man too adapted. He evened, he leveled. A calm came upon him. He was churning cold fire into warm macho fuel.

And on down the line they went, from drinker to drinker. The *campesinos* especially sucked up the volt age like bulbs. I expected them to come away amped up and jittery. But they left the game mollified, like sleepy, fat dogs.

Large, green-dressed men wearing bulky black jackets and belts full of metal and plastic hardware filtered past one of my eyes, blurred more with mescal as the hours wore on. Every two or three people through the doors would be one of them, this squareness of their coats and the long bills of their caps giving them away. Chiapas was far away, and the rebel leader Comrade Marcos hadn't yet come to power. His radiant face had yet to rise from its sea of machetes and maize tents. But the guerillas he would arm had started to gather, here and farther northeast, on the gun running and dynamite highways. Echeverria's vicious army had come early to ferret them out.

With my other eye I could see Mac, watching the box bearers with mockery and envy. How often in those days I misread a face, an attitude, and attributed to people qualities of mind they didn't possess. But I was pretty sure I was right about this new crudeness in him, this strange embrace of some old manly code of values. He'd changed in the two years he'd spent in Carolina since we left our Cleveland high school, I going off to Berkeley and he apprenticing with a scab, cold-weather carpenter crew, a roughshod but meticulous group of fast-working stoners. And he'd changed even more in these four months we had traveled, smoking and snorting, growing inward and cold.

For my money, it was purely the weed he was smoking. It was that and that alone that made him clam up and snap at you when you asked him questions. It was almost impossible to get him, glassy-eyed and paranoid, to ever look at me when we talked. All I ever saw was his riveted profile, the stringy, wet hair falling over scratched glasses. He had the trail-worn look of rock stars back then: Neil Young, the Allman Brothers—full sideburns, flannel shirts. We all looked like that. But he looked it in spades.

I'd had to watch this profile all the way across the country and then down into Mexico for two solid months. He'd been jittery, hunched up over the wheel, staring at the road and lip-synching the Deep Purple songs that came on the radio.

"I could do *this* shit," he said now, stabbing his finger at a glass. He pulled up some pesos. They were new ones, paper singles etched with Aztec pyramids. They shook in his hands, which were bunched into fists that he pounded on his knees.

I must have made a face or something, because he stepped off the stool, pushed my arm aside and turned around to glare at me. 'I'm going to *try* this fucker.' he said, loud, so I could hear him over the music. He slapped the leg of his jeans, which he would drum to songs. He was trying to focus his eyes on me, but all I could see was the scratched glass filmed and whitened with steam.

He whipped his pants again and coughed. A puff of weed smoke came out.

More and more soldiers were coming in now, not obviously through the door, but just appearing in the crowd. After a group of them went by, I saw Mac now at the box.

How quickly Suspenders had gotten to him! *He* fastened hard on the grips. His straight hair had fallen forward and one of his boot heels dug into the rail.

I waited for the first jerk, but I could see that the Mexican had the dial on already. From where I sat the needle looked high, straight up through the numbers at whatever that was, five or six. The last *campesino* hadn't gone any higher than four.

Mac was unfazed. If he was feeling it, he wasn't showing. He looked just as calm as when he'd been doodling on the napkin. Sure, he watched the box, and with something like intent. But it was more the cold stare, the pure, vacant doper's trance. The hooch, the pure, battered wastedness that had drained him. It was fire passing over already-burned ground. The problem was he couldn't drop them. He just stood there holding on. Suspenders just peeled them off his hands, and when the grips fell on the counter, we could see the stripes on Mac's palms. It was then that his shaking started, the faintest tremble when he walked. It was in his upper arms, under the loose denim of his shirt. He came back and settled beside me. He bent his head and closed his eyes. His whole body was moving by then, and somebody must have mentioned the burns.

He put his hands, palms down, very softly on the table, in a dark, bright, and slow-spreading puddle of beer.

I wanted to stay awake with him, but the mescal was strong. It was shutting me down quickly, covering the room with fog. Through it Mac sat with his hands on the table, his teeth chattering as more and more soldiers came in. I blacked out when Suspenders walked toward me with the box.

Mac was gone when I woke up. More of the black-jacketed soldiers were milling around. The *campesino* regulars were thinned out and getting thinner, walking out to their trucks, coffeed-up and starting on the footpaths toward home. The fans were off. The candle lamps were blown out.

I had to piss, bad, and got up and headed for the black tunnel of hallway that wound out to the loading zone and parking lots. The mica sparkled on the tunnel walls and stayed with me in the afterimage as I leaned, eyes closed, in what was essentially a closet, sinkless and mirrorless and roofless, but very tall and quiet and lit only by the moon.

The mescal was still very much with me, because I made a right turn and ended up in the lot, with soldiers suddenly getting up off the packs and boards they were sitting on. They could see I was stumbling, and this is why I could see some of them were scattering or turning their backs, climbing up into the cabs of trucks parked over pools of what looked like oil.

The truck that faced me was filled with stumps or limbs, something wooden and ripped-looking dangling out the end of its covered bed. I had a hard time focusing on it and for a minute was seeing double. Then I took a few steps back and looked again. One man sat on the side rails behind the cab, watching that end of the tarp nervously and taking care to keep it smoothed out. But he couldn't stretch it over everything. Somebody was telling him not to: or, more likely, it was stuck.

There was laughter and then groaning and spitting from the

other trucks. Someone was coughing into the can they drank from.

The more I focused on it, the more one of the wood chunks in the truck looked softer than timber, more pale, somehow, in the light of the kerosene lamp. They had bands of scarring—like I'd seen on Mac—on their bottom sides, and at the end of each were short, spread nubbins or thin, tendril-like dusters, delicately opening. The whole stack of them became pale and clear now as I stared at them, hands open or toes spread, muscles as hard as rows of string in the sparkling dew. All with the stripes, all with the brand, like meat you lift up from the bars of a grill.

Around the back of one of the other trucks I saw them: the metal boxes, stacks and rows of them gleaming in the lamplight. One of them was connected with a bigger wire to some kind of generator. They were exactly the same machines the drunk men had used in the contests. But with the arms and legs I saw in the truck now—some lit by the moon and some half covered by tarps—they had been used differently.

I started nodding finally, swaying. The last of the meal I had eaten in midafternoon was coming up quickly, and I ran toward the bathroom. But there were too many soldiers in the doorway, blocking it to keep the inside safe for whatever they were doing. The long, thick stream came up out of me, burning, spraying across the mounds of gravel.

The only thing I know about the direction I ran in then was that it was away from the trucker's shacks, because they weren't there-only open road running by scrub acres and burning patches of banana groves, with little tar-shingled bus shelters built up next to the curb every several hundred feet. The fumes of the booze were still getting to me, so I laid down under one of them. I spread my arms and moved my head until a glob of pebbles wedged up into a mound under my neck.

I thought of the strangeness of seeing the maggoty side of a people jump up out of nowhere after long weeks and months of their seeming goodness. It took the wind out of you. My mind ranged back through the cities I had come to love, the ones whose very names had lulled me: Guanajuato, San Miguel de Allende, Taxco with its silver basilicas. But even on their streets, in the alleys between the decrepit shops, there had been the dusty windowed coffin stores: scores and scores of baby caskets in frilly white, a world so ready for death's suddenness, for its heavy paw.

I turned my head aside and retched again, but there was nothing in me.

I spread my arms wider, making the motions we used to make as kids making snow angels. The gravel felt good under me: cold, immaculate, and dustless. A wind started blowing, and the tiniest pebbles, as tiny, it seemed, as dust or sand itself, started blowing around me, up through my pants, around my bare head, out over my dampening hands, which I bent down and looked at and opened and closed again as if working a miracle.

It was as cold as snow itself, a heavenly powder. It made a quiet like the quiet of newly fallen drifts on the flanks of mountain roads as you entered their cities again, the deep stillness of their swirled and whitened hillsides.

But before I drifted off, my heart jumped up again, exploding softly, puddling and bubbling its warmth. I was afraid to fall asleep for fear of dreaming again of what I'd seen. And I wanted to know somehow, by some sort of sign, that Mac was all right. I wanted to hear the tread of the old high school boots I had come to expect in the halls of C Building. As much as I hated him now, zoned and stammering and badgering me about some new nothing every day, I had to be sure that whatever I was learning about this place had not made him part of it, and that he would be the one coming back, looking for me.

The Ground Game

Poll Watching, Ballot-Curing, and the Evening Redness in The West

The Landscape

I had agreed with DNC lawyers to serve as a poll monitor north of Las Vegas. I'd watched [just as an observer] elections—especially close elections—for decades, and also actually liked the candidate. I also thought the current president, someone who I not only disliked but sometimes actively detested, was undergoing *some* kind of intensifying mental disorder. The comedian John Mulaney described Trump's management style in 2018 as that of a horse let loose in a hospital: "No one knows what the horse is going to do next, least of all the horse." Through the years of his reign, a period that still exists, I felt less and less safe with him having the nuclear codes, the electronic dam controls of imperiled rivers, the duty to stop an eerie new disease that had covered the earth, killed millions, and trapped ourselves in a frenzied immobility. Friends had monitored polls before, and especially in the last few national vote-counts had expounded on the satisfaction and richness of the experience. If there was any time to do it, it was now. King George III had leapt forward into the young twenty-first century, was spinning dangerously downward, and needed to be stopped. I felt I could make some kind of difference—every person canvassed, every missignatured ballot "cured," was a single rock in a wall against oblivion.

The plan was to meet several days before November 3rd with L.A. Mayor Eric Garcetti's ground teams in the suburb of Henderson, Nevada. I had been invited by my long-time friend Dean, a member of the Young Socialist Alliance whose organizing days went back to Cesar Chavez's farmworker strikes. [I and the rest of our circle sat in our Berkeley dorm rooms reading about Eugene Debs; Dean wanted to *be* Debs, and was out in the fields engaged in the Real Thing.]

Garcetti's city and state were "sure blues," and he said the election for Dems would be won or lost in Arizona and Nevada, something on which he proved exactly correct. That's why he was in Nevada. At DNC headquarters in Henderson, the building was festooned with Biden/Harris signs, which formed a long confetti-like trail from outside windows to the inside walls of this long, chilly space in a strip mall. Enormous online registrations had exhausted me, but the Mayor arrived just before lunch with an inspirational, socially distanced speech, strutting and fretting his hour upon the stage. Garcetti is a machine, polished and skinny, like 1948 Sinatra skinny, and wore an immaculate blazer with a pocket square and pin that said 'JOE-BYE', a play on the first syllable of the Democratic candidate's surname and a caustic farewell to the incumbent. Garcetti's father had been a famous prosecutor, cutting his teeth as a very young lawyer in the Charles Manson case, and ending it after his first lieutenant, Marcia Clarke, lost the O.J. Simpson trial. Both are handsome, Mexican-Jewish men with chiseled features that call to mind Peter O'Toole or the young Gary Cooper. They are solid fixtures in the Democratic dynasties in California: the Pelosis and Feinsteins, the Browns, the Warrens and the Tunneys. The mayor has one métier—politics, and more politics. It was in his sculpted hair, his freckles, down to his lean legs, down to his atoms. However far you were pulling for whatever political cause, he was the one you wanted to be *pushing* behind you. We were driftless barques, and he was the wind.

After endless on-line tutorials about ballot-curing (getting voters to make their own signatures match better), we were driven in a van out to where we would do the actual monitoring. It was an elementary school in the far reaches of Northeast Las Vegas. It was one of those creeping peripheries where certain public edifices, usually airports, were located: far from town, close to freeways, eagerly awaiting a spurt of commercial growth around the anchoring venue. We had canvassed black and Hispanic neighborhoods for days, chatting with laid-off casino workers standing behind broken screen doors. We were finally able to sit down at the actual monitoring, where we traded places with GOP watchers inside of a red-taped box that let us see most of what was going on, and allowed us to make sure no one voted after the court-extended deadline to 8 p.m. A duo of GOP watchers dominated "The Box" for the hour between 7 and 8. They kept standing up and craning their necks, making sure the only people left in the building were registrars, counters, and we Democratic counterparts. One man said he was a miner, and looked at me sourly like the truck stop rednecks looked at Dennis Hopper in 'Easy Rider'.

On a break I went out and sat on the running board of the van and pulled my Browning 9 mm. pistol out of my shoulder holster and laid in on my legs. The magazine was in a pocket of my suit jacket and the safety was on. The slide was not pulled back, but the single-action hammer was retracted and it look ready to fire. The hard cast iron of its chamber and barrel had a "blueing" dye that had been poured into the mold where it had been fashioned in Brussels and Portugal. The walnut stock, or grip, was chiseled with a simple, downward checkering. My father had passed away eight months previously, and this was one of the weapons he left me in his will. There was a beauty to it: say what you wish about the Second Amendment, but certain guns are beautiful works of art. He was a true hunter who butchered everything he shot, but always looked askance at handguns. Pistols were the Other—they belonged to military personnel and law enforcement, and had no real place in his country life of bagging whitetails and black bear in rural Northern Ohio—he'd bought this sidearm as an investment. And a weapon like this, in Santa Monica where I live, certainly amounted to a fish out of water. Friends of mine who knew teased me endlessly about it, asking me if I polished it and the tiny safe it came in with my MAGA hat. My wife dubbed me a "gun person" now that I had inherited the weapons, and threatened me with banishment to the garage couch if our daughter, 16, was ever able to lay eyes on it.

The bigger question, of course, was why, for the first time in memory, poll monitors could be armed. Since Nevada, like many Western and Sunbelt states, was an "open carry" jurisdiction without exceptions, I was permitted to carry it so long as I had the weapon in plain sight, i.e. with my suit jacket off and the gun and holster open to view. Certainly, no one had *told me to* bring the gun, only *that it might be a good idea*. Mayor Garcetti's security detail was armed, but they had gone off to a separate, somehow more important polling place nearer the city. The answer to my question, of course, was the threat of violence from the alt-right. There had been Charlottesville. There had been Kenosha. And before that there had been Ferguson and Minneapolis and all manner of alt-right players showing they were—unlike me—armed in a manner that has startled commentators and those who have nervously shared statehouse steps with the Proud Boys, Boogaloo, and Der Stuhrmer.

I had the gun now because it made me feel safe for myself, Dean, and the rest of the monitors at this poll site. It made me feel safe in the way that the president's people were made to feel safe when he exercised his gun-lobby muscle and equivocated about bad people being on "both sides" of an incendiary protest scenario. This is what we had come to—tribes of people, each of us walled-off Hobbesian laws unto ourselves. Tribes with blue checkered pistols and iPhones watching the peripheries, waiting for mundane or lethal improprieties.

On that running board, looking out beyond the school grounds where we sat, the great shaped rock formations stood in line beside one another under evening drapery of cloud. Behind them were actual mountains, brown scruffy humps forming the foothills of the Eastern Sierra. As undergraduates on cross-country drives out of Berkeley to the East, through Nevada and Utah and Colorado, we would look out the car windows and call the orderly, processional formations the March of the Beasts. They were still here, forty-five years later. They looked finally immobile as the sun declined and relieved them of their shimmer. Their mica patches were still there, thin slits of silver that looked like eyes, watching us, waiting for something to happen.

The Week of Magical Thinking

Dean and I watched the returns until about 2:00 a.m. on Wednesday morning. The lights of the LV Strip blazed like coals outside our enormous picture window. The CNN people were looking very, very grim.

Most of Wisconsin and Michigan seemed red as rubies. But as we slept, county by county, inch by inch, Biden was gaining a lead in the critical urban centers and in a good section of their rural extremities. Nevada, where we'd worked so hard, was still up in the air, as was Arizona. By the time Dean wakened me it was clear that a razor-thin battle was on. No other word for it but battle, and no other description of the process than something razor thin, hideously, intractably sharp. It was happening county by county, which came to feel like street to street, rice paddy by bullet-spotted rice paddy, building by building and room by room. All of Wednesday and Thursday were agony, but the Biden votes grew in those states and then, with agonizing slowness, in both Georgia (!) and Pennsylvania.

Wednesday and Thursday we stayed in the hotel, nail-biting results, with Wisconsin and Michigan bending blue, Trump screeching at each swerve in the road. I could not pull myself away from the hotel television; it was like an Alfred Jarry play interposing itself into what was once a settled, public, and sometimes enjoyable enterprise. "The fraud on the American public," he proclaimed, is "an embarrassment to our country." The people surrounding him, including family members, appeared to be the only ones embarrassed, not by what he was saying but by the fact of his saying it. On Thursday night, he went back to the White House pressroom to claim, again with nothing resembling proof, that he was being "cheated" by a "corrupted system." Harking back to his dismissals of "seven-hundred pound" hackers working from their oversized beds on laptops, he spun out a groundless conspiracy theory concerning corrupt voting officials, a burst pipe (?), and "large pieces of cardboard." No more insane speech had ever been made by an American president, not even Nixon in his hall-wandering Watergate sob-sessions with Kissinger and his chief of staff Alexander Haig.

The only question was whether and how the Republican Party, which Trump had tormented, ravaged, and then marvelously seduced, would begin the necessary disassociation with him that would allow the commencement of transition. You could see in his face the true fulcrum of his undoing: his mishandling of the pandemic, the nearly quarter million lives that lay around his feat like withered leaves. In the final weeks as his (admirably competent) ground game was winding down, he was declaring to rallies full of red-hatted jackals that the virus was vanishing, that he "might" fire Dr. Fauci after the election, and that "this administration, this *great* administration, is not going anywhere."

What this writer realized, not fully until the last, somewhat successful rallies [he brought in 71 million votes] was that while Trump was exiting, Trumpism was not. You saw in his face the certainty that his base was dug in, following his hollow bellowing and promises of walls, a gutted ACA, and revenge upon BLM protestors with whatever repressive apparatus would follow his orders. What Trump could not face was that after a bumbling start, Biden was endearing himself to skeptics with his ordinary decency and respect for bipartisan compromise. Not only was he the necessary anti-Trump (a reason to be elected in and of itself), but he brought with him decades of legislative stewardship and the respect of world leaders he had earned while serving as vice-president. He recognized that the pandemic had revealed the human cost paid by states without safety nets and an underclass without access to medical care until the ventilator beckoned.

Back in Los Angeles by the 7th, I sensed that something arguably final might happen, or start to happen, very early Saturday morning Pacific Time. The rest of the world had, of course, already wakened and had been in front of their televisions, bristling with the same premonition. I drifted in and out of sleep on the long day bed I had pulled in front of the wide-screen. Though CNN wouldn't yet call Arizona, Nevada, or Georgia, it soon became clear that Trump would be unable to maintain Pennsylvania. Even if all remaining Keystone votes came in for the president, it would not be enough for him to outrun the (small) blue waves rippling consistently in from both Philadelphia, Pittsburgh, and their respective suburbs. It was finally over. Trump had attacked science for so many years, and was having his grim future handed to him by science's big brother, arithmetic. I closed my eyes and thought of the Trump family assembled together like Capt. North and the shipbuilder, Victor Garber, in the film 'Titanic.' After Garber points out how the hull's boxed compartments would fill, one by one, like ice trays until they pulled the bow under the water, North asks "But surely it cannot sink?" Garber answers "Oh, it will most certainly sink, as a matter of mathematical necessity."

Legal Challenges, Futility Thereof

Bush v. Gore, though largely limited to its facts, stands for the proposition that federal judicial intervention in a state election process is only justified where there is clear and convincing evidence (a high standard) that that process violates one of the candidates' rights under the Equal Protection Clause. Bush's rights were held to be violated for a very narrow reason. It was not, as some argue, that counting simply had to have an endgame under Florida's election laws. It was that there was a de facto disparity in the counting rules and practices within the state.

The body of the Supreme Court opinion illustrated this by stating that only some batches of ballots were counted by actual election officials. Others were counted by people effectively subcontracted to count them—teams of lawyers, retired judges, county officials, state non-election officials, and even groups of schoolteachers, librarians and whatnot. Where one's polling site's batch would end up was not clear, and there was no way, or no effective way, of telling how competently the non-election "officials" were operating. It was like a maze. One group of counters would require that the chad had to be absent, completely punched through, while another group would count the notorious "hanging" chads, deeming that even though the chad was not punched through, the fact it was hanging showed intent to vote for that candidate.

That kind of disparity among counting personnel has largely been eradicated in the twenty years since "B v. G." It was a tremendous embarrassment for the state of Florida, and no other state wanted to be called out for something similar. These changes have made ballot-counting challenges almost (thank God) obsolete. *See* Cass Sunstein, 'Don't Confuse 2020 with 2000,' The Atlantic, Online, October ___. But there are very few avenues left to judicially challenge ballot-counting, which remains nearly the only way to contest election results.

The remainder of the legal challenges are simply too absurd to even describe, and have immediately turned to dust. If I or one of my law partners were to attempt the loony briefings the Guiliani team proffered, we would be massively sanctioned and possibly thrown in the lock-up. Guiliani has the thinnest thread of a remaining profile that enabled him to avoid such "doomsday" sanctions.

The brick wall that these last suits faced is best explained as follows. The federal courts are very loath to interfere with state government processes, or state officials' roles in a process that eventuates in a federal result like a Presidential election. This reluctance to interfere is called the Abstention Doctrine, and says that once the state process is underway (lots of decisions on when it is "underway"), the federal courts may intervene but invariably choose not to. It began in a Sixties decision, *Younger v. Harris,* involving the draft resistance leader David Harris (then Joan Baez's spouse) and, as defendant, Evelle Younger, the Calif Attorney General who ended up being the fifth name partner in the law firm where I was largely trained. (Younger was a dolt; he had nothing whatsoever, not even a desk, in his office; only numerous American flags on poles (!) and endless pictures of himself with Reagan, who he regarded as the Risen Christ).

Harris, who was eventually convicted in federal court of the felony of refusing to report to the draft board, threw in challenges to the state's draft board review process, as draft boards were a hybrid state-federal animal. The Supreme Court upheld what came to be known as Younger Abstention, which was followed by Colorado River Abstension and three or four other species of the same doctrine. Again, the rule is pretty simple: though the federal courts may have jurisdiction over something very much involving a state's laws and administrative proceedings, prudence and the danger of inconsistent rulings dictates that the federal court should choose not to take the case.

Chief Justice John Roberts, hopped up by the icebox wine of federalism, is a huge fan of abstention. He probably has a T-shirt that he wears at the Supreme Court's basketball court [Kennedy and

Breyer and O'Connor & RBG played there] that says "More Abstention." He is tired of federal court challenges to state processes and he controls the docket ever since the Judicial Economy Act of 1920.

Ten days after the election we were still waiting for the final, *final* result, statutorily triggered in Georgia and Pennsylvania and underway elsewhere as the administration launched theories of phantasmal conspiracies, abandoned ballots, and the time-honored GOP bugaboo of ballot stuffing. A Republican friend sent me the Robert Caro anecdote from one of his LBJ bios that illustrates the old chestnut of Democratic cheating. When ballot-stuffing crews were underway in LBJ's first congressional race, a young aide could not get the name off of a worn headstone in a Perdanales graveyard. The very tall Lyndon grabbed him by the collar and said "Son, you go back and get the name. That man has as much right to vote as anybody in this cemetery."

And so it goes. The Biden pleas for unity seem futile. The president is now the one in the bunker. A national coalition of election officials has described the voting as 'the most secure in American history.' *USA Today*, Nov. 13th. Mike Rappaport runs viral skits of furious Yankee fans telling Trump to "pack up your shit." The memes are as angry as ever and are actually improving. They can and will someday fill a small, perverse museum in TriBeCa. One simply has a sturdy opera soprano with Viking horns and gold breastplates, and the caption "Donald, Donald: she's finally singing." Al Franken described all politics as the ball taking funny bounces (his native state had been ruled by an ex-wrestler). The ball is only dribbling a little now, but it bounced harder and longer than I have ever seen. And it bounced back to us. Now if we can just keep it in our hands.

Biograph

(People)

Encomium: Ann Ackerman (1917-2011)

In W.H. Auden's great poem "Elegy for W.B. Yeats," there are the lines "Time worships language, and forgives/Everyone by whom it lives." Ann read them to me in the book-filled living room of her Markey Street house in Bellville in the Summer of 1971, when I was her student for the last, longest, most luxurious time. I had taken her English and Journalism classes at Lexington High School. I had had that privilege and enjoyed the spell (there is no other word for it) she cast over an assembled group of students. I was among the multitudes who watched her establish the bar for literature and journalism instruction not just for that school and surrounding high schools but also, through her influence, for those of her students who went on to teach these subjects across the country. And many will write about that experience.

But I had something special, which was "Mrs. A" for myself—tutoring me with "Big Red" [Houghton Mifflin's *Major British Writers*]—so that I could leave LHS a year early and be shuffled off, trouble-maker that I was, to Berkeley to begin what she would call (with customary savor when using Latin) my *baccalaureum*.

My Mother had scrounged together two hundred dollars for the fee, and I brought it in a white envelope, wending my way around her son Fritz's disassembled Saabs in her driveway. She counted the twenties one by one, and looked up at me and winked and said "Do I look like Rod Steiger in 'The Pawnbroker'?" Then she squinted like a drill sergeant and said "Are you ready to work harder than you've ever worked in your life?" And before I could answer she ordered me to sit in a straight-backed chair and said "The Greeks. We start with the wrath of Achilles. Dramatic irony. The beginning of the Western canon."

She looked out the window, took a sip of Pepsi, and quoted from Oedipus Rex: "I grieve for the City/For myself and you/And walk/Through endless ways of thought." I can still see the shadows falling over her face. It was electrifying. In the next ten weeks she tugged my eager, often bewildered, always stubborn mind through endless ways of literary expression. She didn't explain how Shakespeare created the first fully-developed personalities with characters like Hamlet; she *showed* how he did by reading the passages that best exemplified his isolation and despair, his constant rumination and resulting moral paralysis. Once she saw that I got it, and that I was a little paralyzed myself with intimidation, with the feeling I couldn't add anything she didn't know already (probably true, maybe not), she broke the tension in what she like to call her Southern Richland County accent and said of the Danish Prince "The boy is just *having a bad day.*"

And onward we trod, she leading me with the torch of her insights—those sparks and flashes!—through Milton, Chaucer, Spenser ("That would be a good middle name for a son," she once said; it is my son's middle name, complete with the second "s"); her beloved Samuel Johnson; her doubly-beloved Coleridge. And then on we went into the late Nineteenth Century (Matthew Arnold, Swinburne and Browning) and up to the current age: Yeats, Auden, D. H. Lawrence and Forster's *Passage To India*. She recited Eliot's problematic, difficult (for a 17-year-old) "Love Song of J. Alfred Prufrock," and showed the difference between meaning and the *sense* of a meaning, between referential as opposed to ornamental language, between words that denote objects and words that create atmosphere. She would go to the kitchen for a Pepsi and come back with I. A. Richards and Lionel Trilling critical tomes laid over her other arm.

Where did she keep those books? How did she have just the passages of criticism ready to illustrate just the effect she was attempting to demonstrate? And if that wasn't enough, she got up on a chair armrest in her black flats and pulled down her Ohio State Master's thesis on the poet Randall Jarrell and threw in one of his couplets or her own commentary to sweeten the stew. Where did she get this energy? She was already fifty-four, but she was delightfully exhausting me. And we still had two and a half weeks to go.

This was something beyond mere pedagogy. This was magic. She was like a genie, a spirit infused with iambic pentameter and the way it "was built" to track English diction not just for the Elizabethans, but for contemporary poets like Berryman and Robert Lowell, whose dog-eared *Life Studies* she just happened to have stuffed under an adjacent easy chair. Her judgment and taste were impeccable—among hundreds of British and American writers, we only disagreed once, over Wordsworth, when I came back from Berkeley starry-eyed and gushing with him. "Flabby infelicities," she said: "Flabby, flabby, flabby. And no normal guy would write that many poems about his sister."

Somewhere in the middle of it all, through the mist of my fatigue and my desire to keep up, the small, spitting wick of fiction writing flamed up in me. She might not have lit the lantern, but she gave it just the right amount of wax and oxygen. The light rose up behind my eyes, deepening and evening. *This is what I want to do,* I said to myself. *This is life,* I realized. Or at least it was the heart of life.

Though her respect for languages (Latin, French, English, and then all the ones she didn't know) insisted on their careful treatment, Ann was never stodgy, never the pure traditionalist. Like any great intellect, she had enormous generosity of spirit, and welcomed new, hybrid forms like experimental narrative and the (then) New Journalism. She knew how very hard it was to write well, and honored the sincere, authentic attempt as much as any student's ultimate success. She buzzed with everything that was going on in fiction and reportage at the time. "Did you see this?" she asked as I walked in her house, holding up the serialization of Norman Mailer's new book in Willie Morris's *Harpers.* Or the newest Doctorow story in *The Kenyon Review* or *The Atlantic.* Or her gold standard: William Shawn's *New Yorker,* which she kept in racks along the back wall of our journalism class, tending to their colorful covers like a steeply banked, secular altar.

In 1989, I sent my first published story to her, and though enthusiastic, she threatened to call the editors over the two typos she found. And when my first book came out, I had the publicists ship it to her with the same trepidation that accompanied review copies going to *The London Times* or *Chicago Tribune.* In a letter, she said I had "gotten" her at about page 37. Though I remembered her admonition to grab readers with first lines, page 37 from her I would take as a compliment. I had succeeded. I had retained at least some of the amber she had poured into this poor vessel.

Ann worshipped language, and, true to Auden, time was good to this constant steward of words. Time put down its scythe and stood like the rest of us, abashed and amazed, and let her live one of the longest lives of anyone I have known. And I don't even know what to call that: literary justice, good living, good karma?

A life well lived is a life well remembered. Like her taste in the written word, her treatment of people, of animals—of any living thing—never fell below a certain level. And with Ann that level was stratospheric. How she ennobled us, pushing us out, reassuringly, firmly, from our humble moorings! I see her now in the eyes of every eager reader, every act of kindness and of love.

The Persistence of Desire: What Updike Meant

This is, of course, the name of one of his stories. In it, a man who has escaped his farm town past, a rustic with urban vanities, nonetheless returns there to visit a trusted dentist. He sees the things that have changed since his childhood visits, the most telling being a digit-based (though not *digital*) clock, its minutes dropping away, as he watches, "into the brimming void."

What has not changed is his passion for a childhood flame who happens to drop by the office, chat him up a bit, blush under his revived attentions, and eventually, almost silently, alludes to the anomies her marriage there has doomed her to. Though his themes are as abundant as Adam's names, persistence is Updike's perpetual character-driver, the life force that animates each form of his characters' transcendence:

> [Janet] arose and came against his chest, and Clyde, included in the close aroma her hair and skin gave off, felt weak and broad and grand, like a declining rose. Janet tucked a folded note into the pocket of his shirt and said conversationally, "He's waiting outside in the car."
>
> The neutral, ominous "he" opened wide a conspiracy Clyde instantly entered. He stayed behind a minute, to give her time to get away. Ringed by judging eyes of the young and old, he felt like an actor snug behind the blinding protection of the footlights; he squinted prolongedly at the speedometer-clock, which, like a letter delivered on the stage, was blank.

And who wrote better about abiding religiosity, the search for faith that Updike saw as essential and unexplainable by reference to historical or social forces? In the story "The Man Who Loved Extinct Animals," the protagonist sees in the joints and hinges of the fossils he assembles the delicate bridges that the mind builds over the abyss.

The brimming void may blind us, he seems to say, but as long as we rivet the beams together, keep busy with the reality or the illusion of building and don't look down, we will be fine for the time being.

Persistence also abides, though less than in other writers, in those characters who shore up some art, or artifact, against their ruin. One of the most powerful of "The Olinger Stories" (Collected in 2004's *Collected Early Stories*), is "The Alligators." An elementary school boy fashions his first illustrations not out of any transcendent wish, but to satirize a classmate whose ostracism is a requirement for popularity. He feels guilt at creating for such a mean and limited purpose, but then, as he shares other, maturing drawings with friends, sees that he has inherited a transfiguring power, and one conferring the consolations of infinity.

What often persists the most could be the most unattractive but necessary of qualities—market ambition, social climbing, the Sinclair Lewis hucksterism that tells us the historical echoes of the "Rabbit" nickname. In the story "The City," a man falls ill while traveling on business, and as he recovers through hallucinations and incisional pain, we think that maybe he will reassess, prioritize, hunger for the stasis of a family and fixed life. But the desire to impress and dazzle is as basic to the organism as eating or breathing, and the brush with death seems to have taught him nothing but the need for reserves of energy stored up by rest. It was always Updike's exploration of ambition that made him that most American of writers. Roth and Bellow approached it brilliantly through urbanized *machers* of immigrant merchant classes, but Updike filtered it through our Rotary Club speakers, the Toyota salesman (*Rabbit Is Rich*) quoting gas mileage stats to us from *Consumer Reports*.

Perhaps the greatest persistence he portrayed was longing itself; yearning, the desire to rise higher and keep hope borne up in one's bearing as the very badge of existence. Like Francis Bacon, Updike believed the world is laid out for us, kindly disposed to our discovery and enjoyment: "Full of Joye and Wondrous Goode." That transporting, almost erotic elixir of exploration runs through the age-sequenced life snapshots of the narrator of "Museums and Women." It first visits him like a spell as he traverses a county reliquary with his mother:

Who she was was a mystery so deep it never formed itself into a question. She had descended to me from thin clouds of preexistent time, enveloped me, and set me moving toward an unseen goal with a vague expectation that in the beginning was more hers than mine. She was not content. I felt that the motion that brought us again and again to the museum was an agitated one, that she was pointing me through these corridors toward a radiant place that she had despaired of reaching . . . . .I was her son and the center of her expectations. I dutifully absorbed the light-struck terror of the hushed high ceilings and went through each doorway with a kind of timid rapacity.

What is sought here—though great—is not as important as the *sensation*, the very texture of seeking: *she was pointing me . . . . toward a radiant place she had despaired of reaching*. Updike owns the luxuriance of The Search more than anyone (perhaps excepting Walker Percy) in modern letters: he invented the theme out of whole cloth and then perfected it in more than fifty books, through hundreds of characters. His perspective on it was tactile, limber, instinctual, breezy, and at the same time solemn, like one of his epistolary clergymen. William Pritchard said of him, reviewing the collection with the above story as its title: "He is a religious writer, he is a comic realist; he knows what everything feels like, how everything works. He is putting together a body of work which, in substantial intelligent creation, will eventually be seen as second to none in our time." Eventually seen? For those in the know, the fathomless depth, and the *dexterity*, was staggeringly obvious from the start. Chip McGrath, in his tribute in *The Times,* posed the question: "If you could write that well by taking a pill, who wouldn't swallow whole fistfulls of them?"

Though we had no way of knowing it, my colleague Victoria Pynchon and I saw him in his very last public appearance, at UCLA's Royce Hall in December. He read a quick passage from *The Widows of Eastwick,* where Alexandra, the aging Rhode Island witch of the Seventies, is now an old woman on a Nile cruise, telempathically electrocuting bats that are flying across her steamer bow and mussing her hair. Everything you could want in establishing a scene is there: the colors of the foul but suddenly clearing river, the Monet hues of the Egyptian twilight, the precisely rendered sound of something we'll never hear but know could sound *only that way* were we to witness it—a bat's fur and rubbery extremities flaming up and then dousing themselves to death in the water.

Wrapped up in this sensuous music—much as with his beloved Proust and Bellow—is the effortless, sudden ranging between third person and first, the immediately recognizable hinges of his free indirect style. It is what hit American readers of *Rabbit, Run* like a thunderbolt in 1959, or like the welcome sun Harry sees on the first page, sliding open the door of his dark, Satanic linotype shop and blinking at the kindly-disposed world, the bright, haphazard gravel under the soles of his basketball hi-tops. It was the same shifts in register and perspective that made you always know but never care which thought was Rabbit's or which was his creator's. He dove like a . . . what? Like a bat—down into everyone's head and hovered there meticulously. He got out of them just what was needed for reality to create their observations and then, with a pirouette Sam Tannenhaus called "pure magic," let his characters' minds in turn press out upon the world their seeing had reconstituted.

He honed this to perfection in the opening scenes of *Rabbit At Rest*, where the narrator jumps inside Rabbit (he's waiting for his wife to get out of the bathroom at the Ft. Myers airport) long enough for us to feel the man's gluttonous elation, then leaps back to look at his character like a Babbitesque, portly clodhopper, chewing and dribbling a candy bar, gazing at his own strange sunstruck extinction:

> While she's in the ladies he cannot resist going into the shop and buying something to nibble, a Planter's Original Peanut Bar, the wrapper says. It was broken in two somewhere in transit and he thinks one half to offer his two grandchildren when they're all in the car heading home. It would make a small hit. But the first half is so good he eats

the second and even dumps the sweet crumbs out of the wrapper into his palm and with his tongue eats them all up like an anteater . . . . . As he tries with his tongue to clean the sticky brittle stuff, the carmelized sugar and corn syrup, from between his teeth—all his still, thank God, and the front ones not even crowned—Rabbit stares out at the big square of sunny afternoon. As the candy settles in his stomach a sense of doom regrows its claws around his heart: little prongs like those that hold a diamond solitaire.

We come finally to the little shadow under the intensity of appetite: its forbiddeness and its premonition of oblivion. You stuff yourself, but with something of your own negation.

Later, even closer to death, Rabbit looks up from his heart bypass operating table and sees on a video screen his own horrific viscera, "the pulsing wet tubes we inherited from the squid." Harry is reassured that his doctor is Jewish, having a

> Gentile prejudice that Jews do everything a little better than other people, something about all those generations crouched over the Talmud and watch-repair tables, they aren't as distracted as other persuasions, they don't expect to have as much fun. They stay off the booze and dope and have a weakness only . . . . for broads.

We get Harry's immediate assessment of his surgeon's vices, but only after we've sailed around the room a little, flitting omnisciently within the purely authorial, purely sociological adumbriation of the character.

At the reading, Updike finally layed down the copper-jacketed book and talked awhile with a writer from the *L.A. Times Book Review*. All his observations were witty, generous, self-deprecating, and in the words of his own epitaph for his beloved editor William Maxwell, "funny and wise and kind and true." He finished with a gush of enthusiasm about the newly-elected Obama, clasping his hands together, appearing to rise up out of his chair like one of his early cartoon whiffenpoofs. Then he took a series of mostly inept audience questions, steering each gracefully toward a cognizable answer. The inevitable what-are-you-working-on eventually arrived, and for once he really didn't have a thought-through response. He shrugged his shoulders, slapped his palms on his knees, and said "I'll only say I intend to stay in this writing business until I drop over dead." And lucky for us, by God, he did.

Worlds We Have: Remembering Saul Bellow

Bellow built narrative through the sheer device of character more than any writer since the nineteeth century. Accordingly, he displayed these extraordinary strokes on stories—long and short—as well as in the more exhaustive firm in which one "gets down to it," as Henry James said, in one's only holy temple of the novel. Just as Tommy Wilhelm, the hero of *Seize the Day*, watches the faces of Wall Street searching, achieving, devouring, grieving, amazing the psychic content of personality—everything revealed in the concentrated visage, we can watch a brilliantly-etched range of souls prance the canvas in the *Collected Stories of Saul Bellow*.

There is the early Mosby, in exile from the Wall Street world, but as with all of the blind, "catching the many flies of ennui" in his tropical hideaway. Mosby is more flatly dimensional than his arguable cousin Henderson the Rain King, also a great rememberer, but Henderson's undirected variousness deprives us of the narrowly focused, the "recollection of passion in tranquility" (Wordsworth) that Mosby gives out so generously through memory's revisions and regrets.

Some characters shimmer with world-historical presence, like the Harold Rosenberg-based hero of "What Kind of Day Did You Have?" (this novella took up nearly the entirety of a single issue of *Vanity Fair*, when some of us held out hope the magazine would amount to something other than pablum). Bellow braces us with the chilly oxygen of these "big idea men," people who form schools and movements with single pen strokes or lectures, new deviations in the *nachraglich*. They are Supermen looking down at the bovine masses from the lofty *viddas* of Michigan Avenue, taking the form of industrialists, lawyers, poets, media moguls, fixers. These stories are jammed with the kind of pure, packed characters Augie March would at the made man's odd-job poolhall that his mother warned him against entering, and where new futures floated above the clatter of scattering balls:

Grandma Lash would have thought that the very worst she had ever said about me let off too light, seeing me in the shoeshine seat above the green tables, in a hat with diamond airholes cut in it and decorated with brass kiss-me pins and Al Smith buttons, in sneakers and a Mohawk sweatshirt, there in the frying jazz and the buzz of baseball broadcasts, the click of markers, butt-thumping of cues, spat-out pollyseed shells and blue chalk crushed underfoot and dust of hand-slickening talcum hung in the air. Along with the blood-smelling swaggerness, recruits for mobs, automobile thieves, stick-up men, sluggers and bouncers... business giants neighborhood cowboys with Jack Holt sideburns down to the jawbone, collegiate, tinhorns...

Each of these stories shows how its protagonist had all of his influences waiting for him and how, notwithstanding the life-force Bellow advocates vociferously, so many fates become the product of sudden turnings, lost passageways, or simple, lethargic will-less gestures—throwing oneself on the tide of events. For Bellow's stories, just like his longer works, are nothing if not event-seas, malleable and protean, populated by "reality instructors, would-be big personalities, destiny molders and heavy water brains, Machiavellis and wizard evildoers, big-wheels and imposers-upon, absolutists."

Indeed, the old Chicago character landscape of these tales is one of almost purely uneducated (or self-educated) business giants, lumbering agents of craftiness or sheer dumb luck who launch sinister brawls, vendettas, intrigues and double crosses of double crosses. Bellow's longstanding fascination with such figures is as Dante's with the Ghibertis and other evil Florentine families of his age: the dark side of the individual is writ large in the bully gesture of the big-town *macher*. Aristotle's mandate of "elevated figures" provides the most powerful snapshot of agents of evil and self-aggrandizement. Bellow's stackers of wheat and players with railroads (Ah! The railyard scenes of *Augie March*!) are our modern equivalent of Shakespeare's spiteful, mendacious kings.

Some of the most delicate pieces are almost crystal-pure memories of the author's early childhood in Montreal, before the heavy work of consciousness formation in underworld Chicago in the forties and fifties, an age of American history Bellow truly owns as a writer. Fathers and uncles, sometimes as simply drawn as Chagall's Russian *schtetelvolk,* propel themselves along as simple peddlers until ambition kindles them into the merchant class, prefiguring the card table deal makers of *Seize the Day* and *Humboldt's Gift.* ("Poetry, art, all that was great," Humboldt told us, "but it doesn't get the oil bit down in the dirt or the jet engine up off the ground.) Dreams rub up against The Real here until the stream of sparks gives us the only light we can see by.

Everywhere—especially in masterpieces like "A Silver Dish" and "Zetland: By A Character Witness"—the characters are perfectly drawn and move with just the right amount of human vividness we expect from them. Especially in stories as abundant with love as "A Silver Dish" (its final pages are heartbreaking; one cannot read them without trembling), the common man's defining episodes are brief and glorious and marvelously complete, their acts flowing—as with "Dish's" dying father—so stubbornly and predictably from who they are. Bellow's people can be good men who cannot make good decisions, whose redemptive reach simply isn't long enough; but more often they are the mixture of good and bad that we most often amount to.

Who they are. Who we are. And who are we Americans? We are Bellow's, made by an Artist slightly more prodigious but not quite as wickedly funny, or as mordant and abundant.

University of Chicago, 2008

Never a More Honest Man Lived: John Cheever

Cheever: A Life
Blake Bailey
Knopf, 784 pp.

What do we make of this man? He lived behind the most respectable and conventional of exteriors, where barbecues and Shetland sweaters and commuter trains assembled themselves against instability, and gave the clapboard inhabitants the promise of peace, the promise of rest. Just how much of it all was a Potemkin village masking tragedy? Quite a bit, and we were given premonitions of it with the publication of John Cheever's journals nearly 20 years ago. Now we see the tragedy spread wide, fanned out on the table like a sad poker hand, in Blake Bailey's biography, written with the Cheever family's assistance and approval.

But if we take the desolation as a given, the more interesting question is whether Cheever universalized it and made of it something valuable, a view into our own gulfs of emptiness and indirection. Was his suffering outwardly directed, the kinked mirror that simultaneously shocked us, let us recognize ourselves, and buoyed us with hope? Or was he an absolutely tragic figure, the kind of creature fitting Joyce Carol Oates' description, after meeting him only once, of John Berryman: "His ... general misery [was] he said, 'The price you pay for an overdeveloped sensibility,' but I always believed him to be underdeveloped, with a very weak sense of others' existences."

The answer is not an easy one. He vacillated between these poles, but as he aged the tug of sadness sometimes seemed to drag away all light with it. Cheever's problems were in his beginnings, and then more in his exaggerations of them. If Heidegger saw the source of our happiness in feeling "as guests in the world," leaving us kindly disposed to it, Cheever was as far from this as possible: "I have *no* biography," he wrote; "I came from nowhere and I don't know where

I'm going." While his older brother Fred was the apple of his parents' eye—growing into a manly, affable, athletically prodigious Yankee—John's arrival came after his parents' marriage was spoiling. He attributed his conception entirely to his mother's having one too many Manhattans one evening: "Otherwise I would have remained unborn on a star." And then there was the abortionist invited to dinner by his father, something Cheever brought up with nervously chuckling constancy and finally wrote into his bewildering, genre-busting novel *Falconer*. He always wondered what was worse, the fact itself or his mother's using the anecdote—as he later wrote in his journals —to "seize the affections of her son." No one asks to be born (Heidegger again), but no one deserves the stamp of misconception, that constant, clammy tang of unwelcome.

Though his father sold shoes in Quincy, John was reminded that his family line was aristocratic, that he was a "Chee-vah," possessing "great destiny, ability, great force and grace and love of the world." Soon enough, Fred was a hockey star at Dartmouth and John was a freshman at the B-list Thayer Academy, from which he was ejected just before selling his first story, at age eighteen, to *The New Republic* (title: "Expelled"). The ante was upped with this play of the prodigy card. His lifelong friendly rival John Updike described the story as, "alarmingly mature, with a touch of the uncanny, as the rare examples of literary precocity—Rimbaud, Chatterton, Henry Green —tend to be."

Soon Cheever was selling stories (eventually 121 of them) to *The New Yorker*, a way in which someone could actually make a modest living then. But the editors turned away as many as they took, and Simon & Schuster insisted on so many changes to his incipient novel that it was disassembled for scrap, its parts used to write "short things, out of financial necessity." In the midst of the Depression, he joined thousands of other writers who lasted out that time courtesy of the Works Progress Administration. Afterward, he began to flourish again at *The New Yorker* under its young fiction editor William Maxwell. But he knew he'd never reach the high ground until he sold a novel. It was an ambition he felt all the more keenly having left his rooms at the Chelsea Hotel, "deciding I was tired of sleeping alone," married Mary Winternitz, and departed to that greatest of famous writers' schools, World War II.

Cheever took forever getting the novel (*The Wapshot Chronicle*) off the ground, and he remained perennially, quite vociferously broke. By 1949, however, he was writing an unbroken series of breathtaking stories for *The New Yorker*, tales in which he perfected his persona as a thwarted but clairvoyant spy among the rich—an anthropologist observing his own people. In "The Sutton Place Story" and "The Enormous Radio," Cheever's narrators notice a neurotic, mercenary bitterness behind the façade of a certain "kind of people," ones who

> strike that satisfactory average of income, endeavor, and respectability that is reached by the statistical reports in college alumni bulletins. They were the parents of two children, they had been married nine years, they lived on the 12th floor of an apartment house near Sutton Place, they went to the theater an average of 10.3 times a year, and they hoped some day to live in Westchester.

Of course, Cheever lived precisely there, in Ossining, though as a renter still cursing the meager *New Yorker* checks and unable to transition to the abiding, long-game player he felt his novels warranted. Perhaps then he realized that the stories would be his legacy, the form in which he found his freedom, and the vehicle that let him push from a free indirect narration into something just this side of magic realism. The couple in "The Enormous Radio" are able to pick up on a Victrola their neighbors' conversations, as if it were a party line telephone, overhearing "demonstrations of indigestion, carnal love, abysmal vanity, faith and despair." But these transmissions also remind the listeners of their own venality, the narrator sitting abashed at his abuse of his wife, whose breezy indifference after a weekend abortion (here it is again) shows her as a fallen, brittle vessel of shallowness.

Cheever's marriage and family life mirrored that of the "Radio" characters. His bitterness over money launched him off the wagon (drinking, for much of his life, a fifth of gin or Scotch a day) and into affairs with Hope Lange, with eavesdropping office girls, with men he'd yearned for ever since imagining himself eventually dying by "being strangled at a urinal by some hairy sailor." By 1979, when his collected stories won piles of accolades and finally made him rich, his children—pestered and scarred and shamed—were leaving home to become, with one exception, writers themselves.

Much of the infernal underside of his life comes to us—and to Bailey, who wisely uses it—from the astonishing journals Cheever kept most of his writing life, portions of which Robert Gottlieb published in installments in *The New Yorker* in 1991-92. These diaries are almost unbearably revealing, but contain some of the best confessional prose in American writing. If genius is, as Fitzgerald said, the ability to keep two contradictory ideas in the mind simultaneously without breaking down, then Cheever was *almost* a genius. The contradictions between the Episcopal Easter communion rail with family and his kneeling for quite another purpose in a men's room stall (often just hours later) were too great, and he could not hold these sternly exclusive worlds together. But the descriptions of his ardor (Lange called him "the horniest man I've ever known") are bracing, and one cannot possibly imagine a man more honest and pitiless with himself, which was all the consolation he was left with when the masks melted away.

In the end, posthumously revealed bisexuality, the redemptive retreat from alcohol, and the tremendously cantilevered hiddenness of it all recede behind the authority ("alarmingly mature") of his stories, which earned him admirers like Nabokov and Bellow. Less than two months before he died in 1982, Cheever's wife escorted him onto the stage of Carnegie Hall to accept the National Medal for Literature. "A page of prose," he declared, "is invincible." Updike would remember the moment in his eulogy: "All the literary acolytes assembled there fell silent, astonished by such faith."

What Is There: James Schuyler

Other Flowers: Uncollected Poems
James Schuyler
Farrar Straus Giroux, 240 pages

James Schuyler was the best of what has come to be called the "New York School" of poets, the most accessible and passionate and direct. John Ashbery was the cerebral conjuror, a radio tower drawing in pop and rococo frequencies from every location, every periphery. Kenneth Koch was straightforward enough, but never entirely fused the pictorial with an inner "felt life." Frank O'Hara was playful, cool, conversational, and unquestionably pictorial—the "poet among painters" as Brad Gooch put it—as he charmed and seduced and walked away with the lonely listener's heart. But Schuyler, "Jimmie" to his friends, was the most American of the New York Poets, the most plain-spoken and universal, the constant hunter and gatherer of the vernacular.

Schuyler always told us exactly what he saw, and dressed it in so thin an art that its presence, though never its effect, was nearly invisible. His lines were "like gold to airy thinness beat," in the words of his beloved Donne. As with Ashbery, the range of his vision was never static—he included, to the extent it built up the little comic frames of his stanzas, "whatever is moving." (The phrase is from an essay on Schuyler by Howard Moss, *The New Yorker's* long-time poetry editor, in a book he so titled.) My mother-in-law, a friend of Moss's, claims he never stopped talking about Jimmie, greeting each new poem with hands in the air, fingers extended, like a blind man given a sudden stroke of vision.

The easiness of his lines and cadences were never trite or contrived. Though he arrived with an offbeat, startled surprise at the described object or situation, his expression was as gripping, elegant, and emotionally layered as any effect created by formalists. As idiomatic and offhand a poem as "A Heavy Boredom" plunges us through the ravaging emotional registers the seasons bestow, suddenly and without pity:

> I had sooner go bare
> than sit pent in a business suit
> O how this chafing burns me!
> not even Johnson's baby powder
> soothes: my soles are creased and my
> pits are cranky and damp and sticky.
> For is Summer come
> the lucky ones are sportive,
> from Maine to Key West
> I like Southampton best
> or perhaps a tourmaline lake
> like a tear in the heart of Vermont.
> Too many skeletons. Scribble,
> the trees grow thin,
> won't winter come, Coppelina?

Another lovely weather poem is a simple quatrain: "The wheeling seasons turn / summers burn / then all fall fallow / in ripe yellow."

Schuyler's emotional resonance roils like smoke across the "collected uncollected" poems of *Other Flowers,* just out from FSG. One commentator, Dan Chiasson, calls him the supreme poet of articulated consciousness, and remarked that Schuyler's "blood brother" Ashbery once said that Jimmie "made sense, dammit": not a virtue in itself (plenty of simple-minded poets "make sense"), but when joined to a mind this multifoliate, subtle, and searching, proves something akin to a miracle. Chiasson saw him as "the poet of ingrown courtesy, gossip in a vacuum, remembered friendship, and the one-on-one encounter."

And it's true. Schuyler reaches out for companionable hearts in order to understand—and portray—the uncertainties and dreads of *any* heart. Like O'Hara, who claimed anything he wanted to do in poetry could be accomplished by picking up the telephone, Schuyler needed to extend his mentalism to someone as flailing and stunned as himself for it to come into focus. And what focus he gives it! The poem "Help Me" (from Vincent Price's *The Fly*?) starts out:

> Help me
> find the paradox I look for:
> the profoundest order is
> in what's most casual, these humped and cat-
> ty cornered cubes, the wind,
> so you're planning to be sad
> or casual
> as a hat
> off a yacht,
> afloat
> in a cove.

If poetry is "emotion reflected in tranquility" (Wordsworth), Schuyler can only reflect with a companionable ventriloquist's dummy on his knee. He is pulling the string of his mind's odd twin, a yammering, downtrodden Chatty Cathy. He was frightening when in his manic swings (see "The Payne Whitney Poems" in the *Collected*), and when ebullient, was inseparable from his valiant but impatient patrons. Incapable of solitude, his verse and his very viscera were an extended, lifelong, late-night set of eerie duets.

Sometimes Schuyler's speaker and his Other switch places, dream-morph into one another, fuse and separate and trick the reciprocal companion, all of it working up a slapstick of droll chatter and passing perceptual traffic:

> 4N
> The hospital's elevator is very slow;
> it stops at every floor. Finally,
> four. You knock on the battered
> metal door of Ward 4N. A nurse
> unlocks it and you ask to see
> your friend. "I don't know if
> he can have visitors today. Sit

here." She vanishes. The shabby
room is all too familiar (I've
been there myself). Time passes.
"Got a light?" a patient asks.
The light is given. Someone is
Running. It's my friend, saying
my name. I call to him: he doesn't
hear. He's trotting, all bent
over. Then he goes back: to his
bed, I suppose. "You see?" the
nurse says "He can't have
visitors today." "Is there any
point in my coming back tomorrow. "You might. He might
snap out of it." She unlocks
the metal door. That damned
elevator takes forever. In
the street it's hot and humid
and I sweat, and people walk
freely; going about their business.

    Articulated consciousness and emotional interiority are here pressed outward onto minimalist characters—like Beckett stage figures—and given enough action to form a stoic comedy.
    Feats like this take us ultimately to Schuler's treatment of inanimate "things-in-themselves," his still lifes, the "natural object" as the only permissible symbol Pound would permit the poet. And here once again, his touch was so delicate and true as to be nearly photographic, hyper-real, letting the seen thing sustain its own textures and hues and substance, irrespective of the knowing subject. The poet's transformation is so subtly detached that the object almost seems to throw it off, making its own claim on time and significance. Like the Christ in the frescoes of Raphael, things seem to say *Nolo me tangere:* I do not require a perceptual field for my sustenance. The poet concedes in "Dandelions":

> Hooray
> for a change
> I'm letting the sky
> stay as it is
> tomorrow the sun may come out
> besides what's wrong
> with gray
> you can almost put it
> and shape it
> smoke and dulled
> lights hovering in it
> like clay

The classic "Schuylerian detail" thus lets things stand almost on their own. Its scrupulousness was a tremendous experiment, a ravishing frontier for poetry to pass into. "No ideas but in things," said William Carlos Williams. Schuyler seems to have it that the thing itself *is* the idea, though the addition of mental constructs adds an elevating, honest sheen, a necessary dimension.

To paraphrase Chiasson, if durable verse could be fashioned from mere flotsam and jetsam, things plain and unadorned, then poetry's potential had become, in a very new way, almost infinite. This poesy of diffidence and near-indifference was groundbreaking. Its tricks of perspective and concern were successful, and beautiful, and will last until time breaks down all things but the beautiful.

Chilly Buddha Hall:
Remembering Philip Whalen

Collected Poems
Philip Whalen
edited by Michael Rothenberg
Wesleyan University Press, 932 pages

I needed a break from the symbolic logic I was studying as a sophmore. It reduced all discourse to truth tables, little grids whose validity depended on the initial premises' truth functions. Berkeley was godawful enough of a place to be in those days, shocked into apathy after the Kent and Jackson State shootings. It was like getting to town after the circus had left. The logic course, a mine-sweeper for the philosophy major, made the curriculum feel monochromatic, trade-schoolish, vocational. I felt like I was studying diesel mechanics or dental hygiene.

And the prof didn't like me. He was the great logician Ernest A_____. My papers veered off into metaphysical implications of logical properties, an area—though I didn't know it yet—called philosophical logic, which happened to be *his* specialty, and which of course he wouldn't tell me about until I stopped getting D's on his quizzes and learned the fundamentals. When I sat across from him and watched him touch the cover of my blue books, I thought of the Holden Caulfield line where the headmaster "[T]urned my paper around and around in his hands like it was some kind of turd or something."

So I needed a break from the quantitative. I needed a Blakean interlude, a genuine surface explosion from the imaginative sun. Of course, Bill himself had had the same revulsion at geometry, homeomorphs and symmetries and undergirdings, rational superstructures and their champions: "The atoms of Democritus/ And Newton's Particles of Light/ Are sands upon the Red Sea shore/ Where Israel's Tents do Shine so Bright." True dat. I needed to grab Dionysus by the horns and get down in the suck.

My roommate had gotten us tickets to a reading at the College of Marin: Ginsberg, Gary Snyder and Philip Whalen, clearly a supergroup of Beat show musicians. The campus had a small chapel in a pine grove off Highway 101, deep in the foothills of Mount Tamalpais. The air in the sanctuary was damp and salty for a place so far inland; it reminded me of the "chilly Buddha halls" and Yukon River roadhouses Snyder had celebrated in his newly released *Regarding Wave*. Though I'd carried the brick-like, unwieldy *On Bear's Head* around in my backpack, Whalen's was the work I knew least. And there he was in front of me, staring at some point in the chapel's rear where the whale-ribbed nave rose up and left dangling above us all kinds of strange detritus: white paper lanterns and bones of mountain rams, dried rattling kelp, glass balls from Asian fishing nets that cornered the knotted hemp and kept it afloat.

The poets, chummy-seeming and circled around a little altar of incense, nevertheless seemed destined by the hosts—the old Panjandrum Press—to go in the order of their fame. Ginsberg started with his majestic, wintry "Open Window On Chicago," his voice an incessant, hypnotic Shaman's drum, and finished with "Please Master," his sado-masochistic plea to his guru to strip off his blue sweat pants and blow him and finger his ass. We were rolling. Our sinuses cleared. Little hash pipes blinked on and off like fireflies.

Snyder went next. He read his merchant marine poems, all seemingly set on the deck of the freighter he took to his Kyoto sabbatical, "digging the earth as playful, cool, and infinitely blank." His voice was the opposite of Ginsberg's—circumscribed and delicate, as modest and composed as his tidy, calligraphic handwriting.

Whalen went last, bald and great-bellied, blazing in his crinkled robes and maize and scarlet sashes. We waited. He swung the mike boom toward his head, spectacled and freckled, wreathed with smoke. We waited, waited. His stare still held on the chapel's rear. Absolutely nothing came out of him. Pure silence.

Then he uttered a few clear, pure syllables, and suddenly, all around us, people joined the chant he had begun. It was a sutra, a Buddhist prayer, its cadences and rhythmic hum as loud and deep and even as a cloud of bees around our heads. And there were only a few of us who *weren't* chanting: the sutra was the calling card here, the ticket to the party. But it struck me as what we called in Christian churches a welcome hymn, or "welcome table"—secret and exclusive in its diction but purely selfless, a gesture of entreaty and inclusion.

He had been so sonorous in his chanting, but the verse he recited was even more stunning: strange and funny and fresh and playful. For someone so rejecting of *maya*, the world of illusion, he wrote almost entirely about the familiar, the stable, the domestic. It was a poetry of whatever came into his field of vision, of Things Presenting Themselves, quotidian-lists as flat and glibly descriptive as anything one found in the overly worldly O'Hara or Koch or Jimmy Schuyler.

Listening to him recite—all clearly from memory—was to hear a holy voice as uncompromising in its spirituality as that of Pierre Emmanuel. But unlike these fellow "religious" poets, Whalen steered away from descriptions of systems, explanations of beatific states or journeys. He was not just a Buddhist but a Zen Buddhist. Which meant wisdom was reached by surprise, that literal truth and recitation of facts alone transcended the spiritual clottedness of facticity. Repetition of minutiae was the cutting tool, the knife that sliced through those same facts lying fallow and undescribed. Such is one of the paradoxes of Zen. Such is the ethical touchstone of Whalen's prosody.

I knew Whalen was a slow-working, exacting craftsman: none of the Ginsbergian "first thought is best thought," spontaneous composition for him. Listening to him reminded me of an earlier formalist (Yeats); more properly, it brought back all formalists' recipe for veiling verse's hard labor behind a cultivated effortlessness, something Auden captured later in a poem title: "The truest poetry is the most feigning." And the way Whalen trilled his hard consonants made me think of Yeats on the old, scratched Caedmon recording; like the Irishman's, the Zen poet's voice cultivated a weariness, as if to stress how only hard work and hard forms can push the ephemeral toward eternity:

I praise those extra Chinamen
Who left me a few words,
Usually a pointless joke or a silly question
A line of poetry drunkenly scrawled on the margin of a quick
    splashed picture—bug, leaf
    caricature of Teacher
on paper held together now by little more than ink
& their own strength brushed momentarily over it

Their world & several others since
Gone to hell in a handbasket, they knew it—
Cheered as it whizzed by—
& conked out among the busted spring rain cherryblossom
winejars
Happy to have saved us all.
                  ["Hymnus Ad Patrem Sinesis"]

The poet delivered his lines like a pugnacious football captain. He was never mythological or symbolic. The voice coming through the incense and flower scent was the straight stuff. But its effects were echoing, mysterious, hallucinatory; as back-lit and off kilter as the "plainest" image in a Magritte painting. Whalen is nothing if not a nature poet, but again, his pastoral is one of fallenness, the eye turning back on itself as the describing spirit, the age-old force of human continuity and permanence.

His intonations said a lot about the world that night, all of it simultaneously. He saw whatever drifted by as goofy and puzzling and worthy of our affection, of our scrupulous, passionate observation. But what his poems "said" is that within all that burns something deeply separate—our own yearning, the mind's longing for release from what it can only see. The animate and inanimate illuminate each other, but for all its radiance the inanimate glides away; "floating and gliding," his old roommate Snyder once said, "sliding by." The animate stays. The longing goes on.

Kazin, Perambulating

"God is simply the name for our wonder." So says Alfred Kazin in a December 1944 journal entry from this new volume edited by Richard M. Cook. I was long ago apprised of the wonder present in *On Native Grounds* and *A Walker In The City*, which met with critical praise unparalleled in epistolary and diaristic writing. But I ignored the entreaties, just as I ignored the reception given *New York Jew*, whose personal score-settling caused such a stir in the 1980s. Kazin was always one of those critics one had to *get* to, like Wilson, Kermode, and Northrop Frye. He was rumored to be the most accessible, the most peculiarly American, the most optimistic and visionary. A transcendentalist, the heir to Emerson.

So finally, after 35 years, Kazin's *Journals* enabled me to see what all the fuss is about. If Montaigne is correct and memoir differs from autobiography by having an outward focus—being *about* others—then the narrative arc of these five decades of notes is definitely toward memoir. Especially during the politically rich 30s, and having been a Marxist true believer, Kazin's prose falcon-sharp and keen, and he calls his paragraphs back to his fist with snapshots of great figures, ominous social movements and counter-movements, sparks and flashes of insight.

Kazin's 1930s are brimming with political theories and their refutations, eclectic conjectures hatched by the mass man, the oppressed woman, the outraged, marginalized and galvanized minority. Appalled by capitalism's brutality, he trusted Lenin's diligent broom, "sweeping, sweeping it all away," and stayed dazzled enough by socialism's "immanence only in action," its "methods, substance and form... encompassing the highest promise of human life." When Stalin's horrors were revealed and huge segments of the American Left ran for cover, Kazin envisioned a "third group" that would retain the doctrine's essential vision while casting off its police-repressive machinery.

But for all of politics' external tensions, there isn't a paragraph here that doesn't reflect on the essential interiority of writing, its bracing challenges, the sometimes morbid insecurity of its practitioners. And at the same time the awareness of that makes for the magnetic, attractive *tone* of the writer, a mantle he sees coating Proust above all others: "The tyranny of *love* in him; it fills all the spaces formerly occupied by custom, law, religion. It is the private man's last expression of his finiteness and longing for the infinite. The irony implicit in his own suffering; his awareness of his suffering, of its intrinsic greatness *and* triviality." Kazin saw the writer's loneliness birthed in infancy, the "obsession with childhood" so foregrounded in Joyce and Proust (and Sherwood Anderson), and which gave Kazin the conception and techniques of "personal history" that would underlie his *Walker in the City* (1951).

The success of *Walker* gave him new confidence in his casual assessments, seeing usefulness in every perception and its notation. "Even the most banal and casual observations have purpose," he wrote; journal composition redeems the long string of "days that die so forgotten," he says—it is "pitiful.... Not to save what is unsaveable, but [which can] define what is peculiarly mine." The diaristic impulse constructs personality, bestows coherence, battles back death.

The beauty of Kazin's judgments are that they do not come with the irritable certainty of, for example, Edmund Wilson, or, as was more common, art critics like Clement Greenberg or John Berger. Kazin had "negative capability," and one sees him questioning his assessments even (like H. James) as he swoops in on a work. His mind is a bird with its wings spread, floating and circling, hovering, questioning its decision; when he settles on his prey the movements of his thought are as subtle as rustling wings.

Yet there is no more forceful personality in the book than the author's, who holds his own with Mailer, Bellow, the young and combative Philip Roth. (All of them craved his approval in the 50s—that tap of his wand, which, in its day, was indispensable to citizenship in the Republic of Letters.) It is his snapshots of these other personalities that are so effortlessly perfect, so balanced and knowing. In his only meeting with T.S. Eliot (a legendary intimidator), Kazin's subject reveals convictions but lets slip pretensions and diffidences, and, once again, that subject's *awareness* of each:

> He was extremely kind, gentle, spoke very slowly and hesitatingly, livened up a bit when I pushed the conversation to literary topics. He looks like a very sensitive question mark—long, winding and bent; Gives the impression his sensibility is in his long, winding nose. He said things which just verged on "You Americans," but I grinned when he spoke of Truman and Missouri and he grinned back! When I gave him [Harvard philosopher] Professor Spencer's regards, he brightened considerably and asked if I was a Harvard man.

If I knew his other work better I would say these diaries are a perfect introduction to them. I'll say it anyway.

Bright & Burning: C.K. Williams (1936-2015)

C. K. Williams died last week in Princeton, where he had for many years been a much-beloved and celebrated University Professor of English. He had won every single major American poetry award, and international acclaim for his translations. None of the accolades distracted him from the great and elusive target that had always consumed him—the ecstasies and burdens of consciousness, and the path between them that makes us most essentially human.

His long, ruminative verse-paragraphs had recently lightened into shorter clause pairings, embodying fleeter thought, quicker conclusions, brighter images. It isn't that the dense, impacted long lines of his earlier books were in any way restrictive. They were rich with detail, observational "sketching" used to set up an argument. But the new short form, counter-intuitively, ranged more into social subjects, and how consciousness best apprehended them. His prominent short-line themes became "How we take the world to us / And make it more/More than we are / More even than itself."

"We are not of the world," Stevens had told Williams when he was a verse-obsessed prep schooler. "And not ourselves," Stevens continued, "And hard it is / In spite of blazoned days." ('Men Made Out of Words'). Williams took this as a challenge rather than a statement of helplessness. What is art if not ameliorative? What are days if not blazoned? If you pour a draft of sadness with sufficient exquisiteness, beauty—maybe even happiness—will sparkle on its surface like soda bubbles.

The *Times*' William Deresiewicz had written of "The Singing": "His poetry proceeds not from a verbal impulse, not from a lyrical impulse, not even from a prophetic of visionary impulse, but from a moral impulse. Everything in his work is held up to the most exacting moral scrutiny, beginning with the poet himself."

This moral impulse, not always breaking through the earlier verse-paragraphs, was in his newer work hovering, tender, almost overbearing. He was always bending over the crib, checking the infant creation's breathing. After teaching at a Hillel Center, his identity as a Jew blossomed with 1968's "A Day For Anne Frank," a fine example of his "rescue-fable" that always pulled up just short of sentimentality:

> The twilight rots
> over the greasy bridges and factories.
> it dissolves
> and the clouds swamp in its rose to nothing.
> I think sometimes the slag heaps by the river
> should be bodies
> and that the pods or moral terror
> men make of their bodies should split
> from their cold, sterile seeds into the tides
>
> like snow
> or ash.

Frank and her sisters, when they arrived at Bergen-Belsen, were told that the only way out was "up the chimney." Williams takes this sentence of the unimaginable, reflected upon later in tranquility, and tries to convey its horror through the undirected winter rubbish and bleakness of the Jersey winter. We cannot comprehend what she faced except through analogy, the evisceration of the nature that had tried to shelter and contain her.

His poems vibrated between two frequencies, the domestic and the strange. He honored the boundaries of each but, like Frost, searched along their tunings for similarities and correspondences. He would often come into an idea through stagey set pieces, shockingly exotic, and then taper down into whatever familiarities we could latch onto to allay discomfort. Often the strangeness came in images and the endings settled into speech. Believable, American speech was his method of conveyance. He dabbled with the colloquial, but eschewed epigram, condensation, abridgements. He takes a truism and turns it around as abruptly as what it is describing, yet falling short of: 'A girl shot by the police: In the beginning was love, right? / No, in the beginning . . . the bullet."

He enters with shock, then wanders in the digressions the American grain gives him—saying what people say in their attempts at truth, saying it to himself, his moral "I." Then he comes to rest back in the domestic, but one that is never free of chaos, of the ungatherable, the clamorous and organic. You don't yourself become a sadist by being mean. Going back to "Anne Frank," the music of speech restores the pitiable in the harm you do, the pity for who you do it to.

> When I was about eight, I once stabbed somebody, another kid,
>   A little girl.
> After argument—argument? Battle, war, harrowing; you need
>   shrieks, moans from the pit—
> After that woman and I anyway stop raking each other with
>   the meat-hooks we've become with each other'
> I fit my forehead into the smudge I've already sweated onto
>   The window with a thousand other exhaustions
> to watch an old man having breakfast out of a pile of bags
>   on my front step.
> ("With Ignorance")

Yes, he sometimes wandered too far in the direction of prose, but the voice always had the buzz of the rarified, the musically charged, the mystically askew—what poetry sends us searching for. *Falling Ill* was his last, appropriate collection, reiterating the deaths surrounding him, the near-death of his son Jed, now a major painter, which he wrote so movingly of in *The Vigil*. And finally his own death, coming around the corner as sure and unsure as the PATH train, taking its own gritty time: "What I think poets tell themselves, either aloud or unconsciously, is that poetry is part of the resonance of the world.

Poetry adds to that, the sense that human beings have that we have some moral meaning that is part of the basis of our identity, no matter what our acts are."

'Brains, Bats and Implanted Thoughts':
The Perpetual Life of Philip K. Dick

Most people know Philip K. Dick for stories that inspired movies such as *Blade Runner* and *The Matrix*, films that defined the language of latter day science fiction cinema and its extraordinary advances in special effects. After writing hundreds of stories, numerous novels, essays and screenplays, Dick joined those writers who turned aside from their work and made an eccentric public life their final art, though his work as a serious writer was never that far from serious readers' attentions.

He died in 1982, broke, decrepit, most probably mentally ill. He had been manhandled by publishers, agents, studios. He loved to quote William Burroughs' definition of the paranoid, applicable to himself then as well as to reams of his characters: "He's the one with all the information."

The premises of many of Dick's stories entailed problems that I and my fellow philosophy students and teachers at Berkeley had wrestled with the decade prior to his death. Two of these questions have occupied the philosophy of mind since at least the Second World War, and have galvanized the attention of philosophers and neuroscientists right in tandem with their hold on the imaginations of filmmaking acolytes throughout the 80s and 90s.

The first question served is the sole vibrating note of *Blade Runner*'s entire narrative tension: do robots, computers or zombies [viz. "Replicants"] in any sense "think" or possess something akin to human consciousness? If so, how could that be tested and what would count as proof or lack of proof for that hypothesis? Lovers of the film will recall Harrison Ford's final decision to scrap his mission and explore the artificial romantic mental states beamed to him by Sean Young. They are compelling enough to make this writer fall in love with her at the time, and leave it to professionals of one or another ilk to distinguish from the real thing.

The second question, explored more in Dick inspirations like the

Matrix series and "Minority Report," is more subtle: even if one grants that *we humans* have consciousness, how do we know it was not something implanted in our brains like a computer program, complete with a false but plausible "memory" and reasonable expectations for a similar future?

The first question is easier to answer than the second. It is fairly clear now that machines—fear not—can in no sense have conscious states similar to those of humans or other sentient animals. The difference between thinking and consciousness is important, and the fact that computers or robots can perform the former, but do not have the latter, is not merely academic or semantic. It is valuable to our understanding of the world and our concept of rights and duties —what we feel is ethically owed by one person to another.

Don't get me wrong: machines, including robotic machines performing computations, can think thousands of times as fast as human brains. They can calculate and retrieve stored data ("memory") far more rapidly than our processes would allow. The ability of machines to perform these mind-like functions has resulted in a great leap forward for human intelligence, and has made life immeasurably better and easier for all of us.

But consciousness has certain features that make it something else, something that can only be *experienced* in a human or animal brain. The object experienced is not what is unique; rather, it is the experiencing process itself. It stands alone in the singularity of its features, and thus has an irreducible quality that cannot be assembled from something else or reproduced. In fact, philosophers of mind have come to call consciousness's objects *qualia*, borrowing from Medieval church philosophers' term for the aspects or characteristics of a thing.

Consciousness cannot be accounted for with most, or perhaps any, descriptions of it. One can explain what causes the brain processes of a bat as it flies along sending out and feeling the return of its radar, but that (in an example given by one philosopher) would not give us the qualitative experience of bat-ness. Our own experience provides material that enables us to *imagine* the consciousness of a bat: we can, however, limited our experience, think of what it would be like to have fur and webbed feet, extremely poor vision, to sleep upside down and eat insects. But this would tell us only what it is like for us to behave like a bat, which is not what we want. We wish to know what it is like for a *bat* to be like a bat. But the limits of *human* experience make this almost impossible.

So the experience of bat consciousness, like the experience of human consciousness, is irreducible, unique and incapable of production. Its most important features, what it would be like to *be that way*, is exactly what is most accessible about it. (We could imagine a computer program that approximates the feelings of consciousness as closely as software designers can get it, and some have come pretty close. But would there be a sense of whether the program is actually conscious, unless we were the computer running the program.) So all the descriptions in the world come up against the bare wall of consciousness irreducibility. The particular feel of bat thoughts and bat sensations? Forget about it. All we can do is pretend. We can never partake.

Now back to Dick and his "Android Sheep" story, and its adaptation in "Blade Runner." For Ford and Young, flying off together at the end of the film, she as slim as a whippet in her lovely red dress and Ms. Marple Replicant hair bun, she can have every conceivable problem-solving and computation ability her creators want to bestow on her. Maybe she can man the aircraft better than Ford. She may be capable of calculating the velocity, altitude and clocked nautical miles of the ship ten times—a hundred times—as well as her human passenger. But without a brain inside her, she in no sense possesses consciousness. Her mental events have every feature of conscious events except the feel of them. She lacks the *qualia* of human-ness.

Ultimately, it may not make that much difference, even if their relationship is meant by its creator to flourish. Young-the-Replicant could perform any conceivable acts of outwardly recognizable love, loyalty and cruelty that mark any relationship. They would simply be performed without the first-order level of awareness that we have characterized as consciousness—the textual vividness that Robert Nozick called consciousness's *felt quality*. Ford would never have to know, and he would have no evidence—short of mangled descriptions of her own thoughts—to suspect she was anything other than human.

None of the above is meant to say that conscious agents cannot act in non-conscious, automatic ways in much of their experience. The drudgeries of daily life, our programmed manner of conducting it, are things that make humans a most fertile field in which to plant the race of Replicants. The Replicants in the movie have sensory motor systems that carry out forms of behavior in a non-conscious way, but only because the Replicants have no consciousness. We, on the other hand, can possess the magic stuff and still operate without it. Many mental processes going on in conscious subjects are entirely non-conscious. Both human and Replicant reach for their keys in the same way, affect certain body postures or run after an object that might get away all in the same manner. The reason conscious agents like humans don't *think* these procedures through is that it would be inefficient to bring the behavior to the level of consciousness. We perform them without being conscious of them, though we could be if we wanted to.

* * *

So machines can't think. Not even computers. But forget for a minute the fact that when machines compute and predict, they do it in a way that doesn't involve the dimensionality and particularity—the *consciousness*—that makes up *our* thoughts. Dick's stories were more interested in having us disprove the second question we asked. What if all of our experience, the totality of our consciousness, were something inserted into our minds like an implant? Such a "consciousness chip" would contain an entire false memory system as rich or bare of experience as could be designed. We would possess reams of experiences we never had but which we accept as our proper history of consciousness, precisely *because* they have the vividness we just described and because we have nothing else to compare them to. In *The Three Stigmata of Palmer Erdrich*, Dick posited earthmen on Mars who ingest a drug that makes them hallucinate an entire life back on earth, "Perky Pat Layouts" containing surfers and Barbie dolls as real to them as the "felt life" they currently experience trying to colonize Mars.

If drugs can induce a *state* of consciousness, why can't software designers do drugs one better, producing vast false histories and personalities built out of them, slide by slide and flash by flash, from the whole cloth of binary instructions?

Philosophers have come up with scenarios that are even chillier. Hilary Putnam and Robert Nozick offer the notion of brains bubbling in vats, capable of selecting this or that experience as though it had been lived by a human containing that brain. We would like to think that we'd rather actually *write* a great novel or actually save some tsunami victims, as opposed to plugging into a canned virtual presentation of our performing these tasks. The moral high ground, the morally attractive choice, is to actually perform the experience we desire rather than just, well, *experience* it by downloading it into ourselves.

So what saves us, really, from the "false" true experiences as opposed to the "true" true experiences? Certainly partaking of either of the two, without standing back with any kind of detachment, makes them seem identical, and identically attractive. Hilary Putnam's Howison Lectures, one of which I attended as a barely conscious undergraduate, offered the essential scenario of the "Matrix" films nearly thirty years ago: brains in a vat hooked up to a program that "gives [them] a collective hallucination, rather than a number of separate hallucinations." What happens is that since semantics derive significance from a community, the vat-brains' reference to, say, climbing the side of a building like Spiderman means simply the image of such Spiderman-like climbing. Their reference is not to the actual behavior of going up a building wall with suction cups or climbing pitons. The vat-brains are speaking with a vat-language entirely different from ours, and who are we to say what they perceive is not as "real" as what we perceive?

The way out of this trap is in several steps. The first is to grant that the *real* consciousness (consciousness with its higher-order reality) comes with several aspects, several indicia of reliability that its creations do not possess. First, we can get a certain common sense assuredness, however, weak, that the imagined matter *flows from* the imagining entity. The thought or vision or creation will seem to *spring from* or *emerge out of* the creating thing, and not the other way around. Again, we have a conviction, an intuition, that the created world issues from an effort we expend, a natural impetus that seems impossible to implant or reproduce. The connection between the two always has this cause and effect relationship, one which never seems to run in the opposite direction even in the most extreme states of intoxication. (There are moments when Ford's instincts show themselves, and appear to be something Replicants do not have, or have only weekly or woodenly.)

Another thing about true conscious states as opposed to nonconscious ones is the feature of *durability* and continuity. A dream, almost by definition, comes to an eventual state of evaporation. The *qualia* of an imagined event seems to peter out, to run down. It cannot run the endurance lap we require of almost all of our experiences in life. We might say, again with Robert Nozick, that the "real" thing is the thing that stays constant through innumerable disruptions, that remains steady through a wave of "Lorentz transformations." Consciousness is invariant through all the variations that make up its perceptions and creations.

So the real thing, the creating thing, has the overall character of invariance that lasts through each of its extrusions. It also has the ability to link each one of its creations to the previous one, not in terms of theme, but certainly in terms of origin. Fireworks, however more beautiful than the ground they rise up from and illuminate, still have to be fired by someone. We never have the slightest notion that the ground rises up out of the pyrotechnics. And this is not just a matter of faith or repetition. It is the most common and reliable feature of experience: it simply happens that way and we have a well-grounded assuredness that it will continue to happen that way.

The ultimate advantage of grounding ourselves in the "real" real thing, the creating thing, is the concept of freedom it brings to us. If consciousness is a creating instrument, one over which we (usually) have control, then we really are free agents with all the responsibility that entails. The mind's products are often erratic, amorphous. Our mental creations run in all directions and seem in danger of taking on their own life. But the creative force itself keeps hold of it and reels it back. The ability to go after our creations, to reign them in and control them, assures us that we have far greater power over our destinies than almost anything else in the world, not just non-conscious objects but non-*self*-conscious sentients like our brother animals. Whatever vats are hooked to one another and whatever drugs ingested, we can always reverse course with a true effort of will. Consciousness is the borderguard against the self's enslavement. If the creating agent can never itself be created, then it can never be constrained.

Consciousness does not need to struggle to free itself, but its objects can seem maddeningly fleeting. Everything it attaches itself to can be ephemera. Pan again to Ford and Young in the cockpit of their hovercraft. Ford is not sure how long he'll have the Replicant, as they all have pre-designated, programmed extinction dates. He looks into her eyes, knowing she'd be a lot, perhaps nearly everything, to lose. He shakes away the thought and accelerates.

Boss Cupid

Thom Gunn: Selected Poems
Edited by August Kleinzahler
Farrar, Straus & Giroux, 102 Pages

1.

The poet Thom Gunn was one of those British ex-pats who moved to the states with extraordinarily mixed results. He did so in a time when poetry's scope was being restricted, when it was suffering a loss of its mid-Century academic and formal spaciousness and becoming something of pinched forms, if not ambitions, something of diminished reach. He rode this constricting arc with some irony, because once he was fully formed there was no stronger lover of formality, no greater practitioner of formalism. But he tightened, he narrowed down. Some would say he lightened in his gravity. But in this they would be wrong. His parsing and trimming yielded miraculous refractions, richly varied directions. As Auden said at Mt. Auburn Cemetery, honoring in some ways Gunn's opposite, Henry James, he was a "master of nuance and scruple."

Gunn arrived on the scene with *Fighting Terms* (1954) and *A Sense of Movement* (1957), the first published while he was still a student at Cambridge. These verses were formal in their loftiness, their removal from the world, their utilization of forms half a millennium old. When writing the latter collection, Gunn had already moved to California and was studying under Yvor Winters at Stanford. Winters worshipped the Elizabethans, particularly their work in lyrics. As Gunn describes, "I had long liked the Elizabethans; I knew Nashe's few poems well, Raleigh's, and even some of Greville's; Donne had been, after Shakespeare, my chief teacher. So I already shared some of Winters' tastes, and though I liked the ornate and the metaphysical I needed no persuading to also like the plain style." ('On a Drying Hill': Yvor Winters, from *Shelf Life*). What all the Gunn-Winters mentors possessed was *intelligence,* the notion that poetry was not just musical speech but required intellectual penetration, a moralist's critique of human behavior. The captive falcon thus reminds the falconer of the latter's perhaps unrealized servitude:

> As formerly, I wheel
> I hover and twist,
> But only want the feel,
> In my possessive thought,
> Of catcher and of caught
> Upon your wrist.
>
> You but half civilize
> Taming me in this way.
> Through having only eyes
> For you I fear to lose,
> I lose to keep, and choose
> Tamer as prey.

'Tamer & Hawk', from *Fighting Terms.* The thinness of semantic demarcation between "choose" and "loose" here, echoed in their internal rhyming, nicely conveys the master-slave relationship theme he mined from both Elizabethans and Jacobins (Jonson, et al.). Whether with humans or animals, brutality has its own dreadful music—the bells of shackles and the clink of chains.

By 1961, in *My Sad Captains*, Gunn was reaching beyond the stringencies that caused critics to lump him with Larkin and Hughes. The move to California loosened something up in him. He addressed the change in a letter to Faber & Faber about a decade later:

> The first half [of the book] is the culmination of my old style —metrical, rational, but maybe starting to get a little more humane. The second half consists of a taking up of that humaner impulse in a series of syllabic poems .. which were really only a way of teaching myself to write free verse ..

In the title poem, we see constraints remaining on the lines, but a fresh, delicate new freedom emerging:

> One by one they appear in
> The darkness: a few friends, and
> a few with historical
> names. How late they start to shine!
> but before they fade they stand
> perfectly embodied, all
>
> the past lapping them like a
> cloak of chaos.

Historical figures he once thought unassailable fall away, as surely and severely as the poetic forms of their ages. They still (both of them) stand "perfectly embodied" and "shining", but no longer the sole, authoritative paradigm. They are just another category in human and poetic taxonomies.

2.

Then came the real break, in 1971, after the Sixties in the Bay Area had washed through Gunn like a cold jolt of morphine. "People make marvelous shifts," Alice Munro wrote in her story "Differently," "but not the changes they imagine." Gunn had come out more openly as a gay man, taken a leave of absence from the Berkeley faculty, had some near-death experiences with hepatitis and some new-life experiences ingesting hallucinogens. What followed was *Moly*, a collection that defies classification and represents his apogee as an influential and quite visible poet, in addition to a merely accomplished one. Drugs had recharged his interest in the Ovidian in nature; reality was process, and all objects were necessarily Protean. *Moly* starts with an unsurpassed Oedipal poem, with the possible exception of Auden's elegy to Freud, which doesn't take any first-person risks. August Kleinzahler rightly judges the piece, "Rights of Passage," as one of "the thrilling moments in twentieth century poetry:"

Something is taking place.
Horns bud bright in my hair.
My feet are turning hoof.
And father, see my face
—Skin that was damp and fair
Is barklike and, feel, rough.

See Greytop how I shine.
I rear, break loose, I neigh
Snuffing the air, and harden
Toward a completion, mine.
And next I make my way
Adventuring through your garden.

My play is earnest now.
I canter to and fro.
My blood, it is like light.
Behind an almond bough,
Horns gaudy with its snow,
I wait live, out of sight.

All planned before my birth
For you, Old Man, no other,
Whom your groin's trembling warns.
I stamp upon the earth
A message to my mother.
And then I lower my horns.

Codes of utterance in conflict, the poem is a dazzling merger of free will and fatedness. The deer-boy is liberated by acting out a genetically predetermined disposition. He is *aware* of it all, haughty but apologetic, mother-pleasing but cognizant that he must eventually buck her wishes as well, flashing his antlers on the air. Transformation continues in the second, title poem, which recalls the herb the pig-men knew would throw off Circe's spell and restore Odysseus's crew to human form. Gunn here gives the nod to his new-found psychedelics, but seems also to be honoring any number of transfiguring processes, for "man cannot bear too much reality:"

> I root and root, you think that it is greed,
> It is, but I seek the plant I need.
>
> Direct me gods, whose changes are all holy,
> To where it flickers deep in grass, the moly:
>
> Cool flesh of magic in each leaf and shoot,
> From milky flower to the black forked root.
>
> From this flat dungeon I could rise to skin
> And human title, putting pig within.
>
> I push my big grey wet snout through the green,
> Dreaming the flower I have never seen.

As Edwin Muir noted, Gunn was "endowed with and plagued by an unusual honesty; his poems are a desperate inquiry, how to live and act in a world perpetually moving."

The critics, especially in Britain, declared his career over with *Moly*. But all that San Fran freedom strengthened the timber of his voice, gave it an urbane, wizened maturity. Granted there is some slackness, traceable to a slack time. One can take or leave "Listening To Jefferson Airplane: Golden Gate Park," a couplet which reads in its entirety: "The music comes and goes in the wind/comes and goes on the brain." But the same lysergics gave him "At The Centre," an LSD description that is as structured a capturing of unstructured experience as "Kubla Khan" or Ginsberg's "Wales Visitation." From a rooftop, peaking on acid, Gunn wonders "What is this steady pouring that/Oh wonder./The blue line bleeds and on the gold one draws./Currents of image widen, braid, and blend/ . . . To one all-river." The brilliant, careful construction of surfaces, the imagistic scene-building are paused, buoyed up and lightened by the sudden

"Oh wonder." He registers a new architecture of reality, then stands in amazement at his own creation of it. The mind makes up the world; the turbocharged mind ascends new scales of the marvelous.

Gunn's late career took on more somber subjects: the brittle calcification of Sixties "freedoms," the plague days of the 80s and 90s AIDS pandemic. He succumbed to the disease himself, but not before following the fates of many a comrade in cycles like *The Man With Night Sweats*. The abyss sucks at the realest thing we have, our physical constitution: "I have to change the bed/But catch myself instead/Stamped upright where I am/Hugging my body to me/As if to shield it from/The pains that will go through me/As if hands were enough/To hold an avalanche off." Hands that gave him the writing life now wrap his lover in medicated sheets, empty bedpans, hold off physical attacks of his charges who change [yes, there are bad as well as good transformations], in an instant, from grateful patients to furies of dementia.

The approach of death enabled Gunn to face things like his mother's suicide, an event he had evaded for decades. In "The Gas Poker," he blends the converse worlds he'd always placed so deftly together: creation and extinction, silence and singing, Orpheus's flute as the tool of self-murder:

> One image from the flow
> Sticks in the stubborn mind:
> A sort of backwards flute.
> The poker that she held up
> Breathed from the holes aligned
> Into her mouth till, filled up
> By its music, she was mute.

This new "Selected" collection has that perfect, jacket pocket-fitting size, little more than a hundred pages. It traces the arc of a career with wisely spaced, representative snapshots. The Kleinzahler intro—who better to summarize the man?—is worth the price of the book alone.

Who Was Phillip Roth?

Phillip Roth: The Biography
Blake Bailey
Norton, 898 Pages

In 1969, in a rural Ohio high school, and probably everywhere, *Portnoy's Complaint* was ubiquitous. Everyone had a copy under their arm and if you lost your own you could find another one immediately, on any cafeteria table, the top of any locker, on a fellow student or a teacher's desk or a car dashboard, or on the floor. The largest selling novel in Random House history had a white cover with green lettering. None of us knew what Random House or Nielsen sales-clocking was, but we had never seen a book whose popularity, and for many of the same reasons, was probably unequaled since *Catcher In The Rye*. Our librarian was also an evangelical minister, not uncommon in such places, so Mr. Shook's shelves were not only empty of the novel, but if you went there for study hall you had to check your copy at the door, like a handgun.

The book's subject, which really cannot be discussed here, had the effect of emboldening all of us. There were war protests, racial and feminist tides rising all around us, all of which strengthened the natural advantages of youth. But Phillip Roth's breakout novel was the literary engine of the Sixties, the rocket you climbed on to obtain insouciance, irreverence, the life-force we reached toward through the thickets of incipient sexuality. After a few pages you started talking like the narrator, laughing at his actions but trying as much as possible to imitate his Eastern moxie, his pugnacious Jersey sass. My lab mate in bio was Jon Sowash, who always got his hands on things like this first. One day, after we'd routed through chapter four and in the arid desert of Mr. Morganstern's lectures on earthworm reproduction, Sowash raised his hand in a Rothian flourish and said we were ready to move on to human sexuality. "Earthworms are great," he said, "but we want to hear about the real nickel."

The reaction to Roth's toxic brilliance was overwhelming. Though a chapter of it, with an unprintable title, had appeared in Partisan Review, it sent the Jewish intelligentsia into an uproar. Gershom Sholem, the president of the Israel academy, called it "[T]he book for which all anti-Semites have been praying."

> *Who will stop this man?* This book will be quoted to us—and how it will be quoted! They will say to us: Here you have the testimony from one of your own artists.... I wonder what price *k'lal Yisrael* [the world Jewish community]—and there is such an entity in the eyes of the Gentiles—is going to pay for this book. Woe to us on that day of reckoning!

Other Jewish critics and writers were dazzled—Bernard Malamud, Saul Bellow ("Go kid!"), Jason Epstein and Brendan Gill. But some qualified their praise with a wary testiness. Alfred Kazin said "The worst thing you could ever do would be to read *Portnoy's Complaint* twice."

The main trope of the novel—Jewish repression versus goyish license—could open doors no one wanted to even think about. "Roth kicked the nice Jewish boy bit" Howard Junker wrote, "the stance of the Jamesian moral intelligence, and unleased his comic, foul-mouthed, sex-obsessed demon; his true self." And no less an envelope-pusher than Erica Jong, cresting the tide of popular feminist literary fiction, said "It's bad for the Jews, and it makes the anti-Semites say, 'See, I told you they were animals.'"

Roth made millions with the book and bought a beloved stone farmhouse in Connecticut. There he turned out a group of increasingly autobiographical novels, all of them nasty, zesty and smart, all of them shimmering with an effortless virtuosity. Real-life girlfriends became subjects for innocent writers chased by harradins, as if the hostile public had been compressed into a parade of jilted shrews. *My Life As A Man* chronicled a long, destructive first marriage with an unbalanced student he met and married at the University of

Chicago. *The Great American Novel* was a self-indulgent jeu *d'esprit*, and Roth admitted as much. But in the farmhouse studio, where he never allowed himself to sit but wrote at a podium on foolscap, the arc of a grand design was being planned. It ended up being two great cycles of novels which, in substantial intelligent creation, would have an effect on comic realism unseen since Mark Twain, Rabelais, and Boccaccio. He knew he had it in him. All he needed was the quiet necessary to construct immense, wonderfully unforeseen and unpredictable explosive devices. The constant theme was man's absurdity, his use of *eros* as transcendence, and his hapless but dignified march toward the silence of death.

The first cycle was the Zuckerman Tetrology. It starts with *The Ghost Writer*, where a young writer, Nathan Zuckerman, peeps into the keyhole of his hero-author's mansion, plotting a way to both learn from and then exceed him. The hero is based on Malamud, and Roth, visiting the elder mentor, had once seen a beautiful assistant going through proofs on his apartment floor. This assistant is mysteriously transfigured into Anne Frank, having escaped the Holocaust and come to literary America. What sounds outlandish becomes, in Roth's hands, attractive in the sheer audacity of its conception, and through the subtle, perfectly-calibrated voice with which Roth enlivens the characters. The theme of writerly usurpation and alternative history, as well as the pain of recognizing our personal, artistic and historical illusions is somber, but the prose bursts out like the high strings of an orchestra. The second book, *Zuckerman Unbound*, unleashes Roth's boundless, refreshing genius for comedy, and features a Roth-like quiz show character, Carnovsky, who is stopped on the street and given thumbs up for the quasi-pornographic novel that launched him. He gets wrapped up in the Van Doren quiz show scandals, and is pilloried and celebrated at every turn. This second installment of his opus is by far the funniest—it is pure laugh-out-loud Roth.

The final book, *The Anatomy Lesson*, was written after Roth suffered illnesses and addictions that send him back into a sort of second childhood, reaching after the idealized Kleinian *Imago* of The Mother, the merciful god who relieves suffering and shapes it away from its nihilistic gravitation. The coda of this series, *The Prague Orgy*, cues us up for the actual work Roth did on bringing East European writers to western translators, agents and publishers. Without Roth we would have never heard of Ivan Klima, Vaclev Havel, or Milan Kundera, at least not when we did. There is no English writer of the twentieth century who did more to grace us with those who wrote within closed societies, what the poet Czezlaw Milosz called 'the countries of the captive mind.'

The second great series, whose effects still mightily reverberate, is The American Trilogy—*American Pastoral, I Married A Communist,* and *The Human Stain*. The first book is in a way an ode to decency, small-town life and bourgeois conventionalism. The two others, also set in Roth's hometown of Weequahic, a Newark suburb, both foreground Jewish assimilation but also concentrates on Gentile figures outside his historical community. *I Married A Communist* delves into the phenomena of political movements, 'crowds and power,' the horrific excesses of the Weather Underground. *The Human Stain*, written during the Clinton impeachment, takes its title both from the apocryphal blue dress and the "summer of sanctimoniousness" in which the entire Starr debacle took place. It deftly wrestles with the excesses of political correctness, especially by a narrator who looks through both sides of its window. Spectacular novels like *Sabbath's Theater* and *The Counterlife*, masterpieces which fit into neither cycle, are given enthusiastic but judicious treatment by this biographer, who cut his teeth on bios of Richard Yates and John Cheever.

The author also shines a needed light on Roth's astounding autobiographical tomes like *The Facts* (anti-Semitism keeping his father out of the New York insurance world); *Deception* (the father's role in teaching genteel nondisclosure); and, finally, *Patrimony*, a chronicle of the author's final, heartbreaking caretaking of that same father.

Bailey's book can be skimmed, and definitely should not be dropped on one's toe (I suspended my New Year's resolution to eschew books of over 500 pages—unless their author's names are Proust or Tolstoy—to accommodate Bailey's very long-awaited encomium to his hero.) Roth was remarkably prolific. He kept taking punches for forty years, rope-a-doping the feminists, the conservative Jewish commentators, the anti-self-indulgentists, and the PC police until they all lay in tatters on the canvas. We *do* see him like Muhammed Ali standing over the flattened Sonny Liston, crying out "I'm a bad man." He would have loved the image. For working writers, we simply stood by, breathless with wonder, anticipating his next challenger. No one was able to knock him down. No one even came close.

The Library of Babel

(Books & Writing)

Flim Flam, Flum

The Runner:
A True Account of the Amazing Lies and Fantastical Adventures of
the Ivy League Impostor James Hogue
David Samuels
The New Press, 173 pages

Something there is in us all that bends our ear to the con man. We like the prospect of a bargain. Unlike most Europeans, Americans tend to tolerate the stranger with a story, even if his narrative is stitched so obviously with entreaty. We trust because we expect others to trust us. As the ethicist Bernard Williams points out, it is fundamental to our image of ourselves that we see others as having the veracity we assume we possess. It is easier to trust, less stressful than suspicion and more conducive to psychic peace. It becomes a habit. Like the dying family pet, we instinctually raise our paw to everyone, even the vet whose glove hides the waiting needle full of pentathol.

The con memoir reached its post-war high tide with Geoffrey Wolff's *Duke of Deception* (1979), the story of Geoffrey and Tobias Wolff's legendary sire-snookerer, a man who faked prep school, military and college records to land himself on the boards of General Electric and ITT. John LeCarre's father was also a celebrated broker of non-existent real estate and thoroughbreds, continuing it on into his childrens' adulthoods by begging them, prostrate, for bail money with hands around their knees and cries of "Not prison again, not at my age." It worked.

Now comes David Samuels's *The Runner*, the story of a brilliant petty thief, James Hogue, who re-tooled himself as the self-educated ranch hand Alexi Indris-Santana. Hogue's cons would classify him as crazy under many sections of the DSM-IV, but to look on his actions that simply would be to miss the fact he latched on to the American Dream and the way it allows, encourages, even decorates the wide latitudes sometimes necessary for self-invention.

The book approaches Hogue through anecdotes of his property theft victims, rich doctor-lawyer ski denizens of Telluride, Colorado who let him manage their real estate deals and chalet refurbishments, only to find themselves short of hundreds of gallons of propane and board-feet of rare Honduran mahogany paneling. Samuels' initial explorations fail here: the swindled grousers, still stunned and remaining at still stratospheric levels of wealth, are full of defensive, shameful cliché and can't give any original insights into Hogue's motivational pathology. Samuels spends the first third of the book poking and poking for a good vein, but simply cannot tap one up.

The Runner gets its momentum when Hogue's schemes become grander and paradoxically victimless, i.e. when he applies as an affirmative action admittee to the Princeton class of 1992. Actually born in 1969 to a self-employed potter and a Mexican sculptress of some success, Hogue's "personal statement" transfigured him into a Plato-reading, physics-obsessed, marathon-running drifter that played into Ivy admissions committees' endless capacity for class guilt and grasping, ill-advised mold-breaking. Here is where the book gets brilliant:

> What 'Santana' offered Princeton was a storybook universe that embodied all the requisite multicultural virtues at the same time as it hearkened back to the mythic virtues of the unspoiled West. What the physicist Feynman (oft-quoted in Hogue's autobiographical essay and who was famous for squiggles and lines simplifying subatomic encounters) did in writing about science, Hogue would do by inventing the character of Alexis Indris-Santana, who could appeal to the prejudices of Ivy admissions officers [with] a fairy tale they might understand: even the most advanced science was a way of approximating and communicating a reality that was actually quite different from what was being described. The most advanced minds, with the most advanced degrees... believed that intellectual life was a sophisticated species of fraud. In conclusion, the applicant wrote, "The best that I can hope for from all of this is to emulate Feyn-

man's attitude that science turns out to be essentially a long history of learning how not to fool ourselves." It was useful advice, which the Princeton admissions office had no intention of taking.

This is a little over-stated, especially its sweeping reduction of intellectualism-as-fraud. But it captures beautifully America's barriers to entry to education and wealth, the last thirty-five years of attempts to level that playing field with new "diversity" boundaries and rules of play, and how the ball takes its funniest bounces when a dishonest, brilliant aspirant comes off the bench to work it all.

Oddly, Hogue is outed when one of his professors, remembering the boy's touting of his Western ruggedness, notices that Hogue is petrified of a minor lightning storm on a hike with fellow students and Boulder outreach staffers in Colorado's San Juan Mountains. After an interview (why exactly 150 questions?) with Princeton's academic ethics staff and further background checks, Hogue is revealed to be an ex-convict from Utah who had jumped his parole and engaged in similar deceptions. The University decides that, despite his straight-A standing and otherwise unblemished disciplinary record, since Hogue applied to the school with false information, his attendance, his very existence at Princeton, had to be completely expunged from its records. He had entered as a fiction, and would leave as a sort of meta-fiction. The next day, New Jersey state detectives asked his surprised geology professor to have him step out of class, handcuffed him, and booked him for extradition to Utah.

Then things got really interesting. Opinion among students and faculty at Princeton was evenly divided between those who thought Hogue guilty of little more than a desire to get a good education, and others who saw him merely as a criminal who should be off the premises. The first school of thought invoked his 1540 SATs, his constant presence on the dean's list, his election to the elite Ivy Club. The latter group saw a homeless drifter's ability to exceed at one of the country's top colleges as beside the point: he could have bettered himself with less fanfare, entirely legitimately, at a lesser caliber university. Hogue's attorney, Robert Obler, hoped to put Princeton on trial before a jury and show the boy as a young long distance runner who had tried simply to better himself in the best way he could imagine. Instead, Hogue appeared before a Mercer County judge and pled guilty to undisclosed counts of theft by deception.

More layers of the onion unpeeled. Justin Harmin, the sprightly Princeton PR spokesman charged with saving the face of academe, continued pointing out that 'Santana' was a model applicant in every respect except "for the fact he was a fictional character." (I am not making this up.) Upon his expulsion, and from recommendations by that geology professor, he became a sub-curator at Harvard's museum of precious minerals and gems. Soon more than $40,000 worth of precious stones would be found in Hogue's room, with Princeton getting a good laugh at Harvard's expense. And it turned out Hogue grew up not in Utah or Colorado, but in Kansas. Its official state motto, *Ad astra per aspera* (through adversity, toward the stars), was often invoked by the Latin-fluent felon. To struggle is fine, and to lie is very much a part of the social contract's elastic. "You can fib a little bit," as the Talking Heads song goes, "but not too much."

Naming and Necessity

The Delighted States
Adam Thirlwell
Farrar, Straus, and Giroux, 2008, 592 pages

Back in the days before deconstruction and its silly tyrannies, books of literary criticism tended to be highly structured, fortified citadels. They were like those very, very expensive watches you see advertised in magazines for the wealthy—their interior mechanics seamlessly humming, their exteriors unassailable, the whole package offered on a take-it-if-you-can-handle-it basis. I.A. Richards' *Practical Criticism* and Northrop Frye's *Anatomy of Criticism* [the English grad student's dreaded 'Anat-Crit'] brooked no bend or stretch: straight-backed as Prussian soldiers, these books gave all the orders, asked all the questions, and then slowly, didactically answered them.

Imagine instead a single, coherent critical study as breezy and casual as open house, with other people wandering the rooms, speaking other languages, the broker a B-level translator (slightly) misinforming buyers about the rooms' functions, so that everyone leaves with a different view of the dwelling's configuration. But everybody wants the place. This describes both Adam Thirlwell's book and its central thesis, which is that (slight) mistranslations are the key to the novel's evolving majesties.

Thirlwell looks about twelve years old on the flyleaf, so English burlesque he exactly resembles the Oliver Twist that Fagin sent up the dumbwaiters to burgle Marlybone houses in the 60s movie. But he is supposed to have graduated from Oxford and have one novel, *Politics*, under his belt. His misshapen, utterly comfortable book rests upon two axioms. The first is that precise literary denotation is infinitely important, because of that original language's "uncanny specificity." (The reason you cannot "speak" a language until you are "thinking in it.") The second axiom is that novels not only survive, but flourish and are sometimes improved, by the well-intentioned errors that naturally result from Axiom #1.

I like contradiction as much as the next fellow, but was very skeptical from the opening pages. Thirlwell harmonizes a native word's "uncanny specificity" and its amazing ease of migration not with any coherent theory, presumably because he imagines this to be the work of more dignified but less delightful academic critics. Rather, he "reasons by example," as Edward Levi said all good (at least juridical) judges must. His specimens (he worships Nabokov and his Lepidoptera) are breathless, acrobatic digressions, adopting as their historical template Lawrence Sterne's *Tristram Shandy*: "If all is digression, then there can be no digression; all is to the point."

As an example, the author shows that while all the associations with the name of the hero of Gogol's *Overcoat*, Akaky Akakievich, can only resonate in Russian, its basic stuttering sound and similarity to universal slang for shit can travel into a new tongue. This primes the reader to drop his expectations of living with a character who can make anything decent out of a decent sort of living. At other times, Thirlwell seems to abandon his "uncanny specificity" concept altogether with deconstructionist notions that details aren't as important when there is an obvious subtext. Flaubert's agonies in his letters to George Sand about Louise Colet—all that *mot juste* stuff—is really just subterfuge for the fact that he doesn't want to marry the girl.

But at moments his examples hit you with the force of a revelation, like the great shifts of a new movement in a symphony. In translating Kafka's name 'Josef K' into Polish, one gets 'Jurek K.' The gray anonymity of the name is retained, but the new, beautifully ironic notion of "justice" for one trying (through the entire book) to find out the charges against him is a wonderful expansion, a "deepening by the slightest shift or error" as a result of the new language's inability to take the original's equivalent. Thirlwell's commentaries on Diderot are ingenious, and fine expositions on the mechanics of modernism (3 centuries early):

> Diderot's *This Is Not A Story* is not quite literally true; it is a game with ideas of fiction and truth. It is true in other

ways. At the beginning, Diderot announces that he is going to make up a surrogate reader within the story, who can play the part of the reader outside the story. This reader, in Diderot's head, turns out to be a cantankerous, recalcitrant man whose theory is that all stories say the same thing—that both man and woman are immoral animals. . . . The essence of Diderot's story that isn't a story is to agree with this cantankerous statement, and then make it irrelevant.

But Thirlwell also misses things, sometimes big things, in his readings. While 'Josef K' is—as just stated—trying to find out what particulars are on his criminal bill, he also spends a lot of time denying charges he never wishes to have any knowledge of. This exhibits something deeper, more psychologically idiosyncratic than the situation that confronts him, and is likely anchored in notions of shame and individual diminishment associated with the German *recht* or *Reich* (state or kingdom/prosecuting authority).

While the author's style is sometimes too haphazard, too meandering and diffuse, it is in keeping with his own deft aphorisms on style itself: "A style is a *quality* of vision; There is no need for a style to have a single style." And truest of all—"A style is as much a quirk of emotion, or of theological belief, as it is a quirk of language."

Armed with all this anti-structural structure, Thirlwell himself takes on the queasy, quantum exercise of a difficult, unexplored translation. When you turn the book over you see a different cover: Nabokov's short story "Mademoiselle O," rendered into English by one Adam Thirlwell. [The translator sets no small task for himself, as "O" later became the fifth chapter of *Speak, Memory*, one of the greatest memoirs, in any language, written in the last century.]

The critic's exercise goes some distance in proving his point. Thirlwell's version swings and echoes like a (somewhat broken) bell in the steep-staired tower of Volodya's crescending tale. And though Nabokov's English version brings across indispensable richness, Thirlwell's is more than adequate; it possesses its own vibrant, thriving life. (The translation is not from the Russian but from the French, in which Nabokov wrote many of his Berlin-era 'exile' stories.)

One of the problems of *The Delighted States* may be that it unwittingly bites off on what it purports to dispel, that for all its "digression-as-truth" mantra it may adopt what Frye, Richards and others seemed unable to shake off: literary criticism as positivistic, measurable, something akin to a hard science.

One gets around these problems by doing Thirlwell one better and embracing Ezra Pound's notion of translation giving the widest of latitudes, of being not a rendering but its own stand-alone work, retaining only the barest skeleton of the original. Still, word-for-word correspondence is a good departure point for even this broader view. As they said of Picasso, only the craftsman capable of rendering the real figure gets to go and play Mr. Potato Head with it. My Russian tutor, a Khazankan native speaker and my daughter's *au pair*, was giving me solid Bs until I made the same error that sank Jimmy Carter's Polish translator at the height of Carter's already doomed presidency. I translated something that should have been akin to "We welcome you to our home" into something akin to "I express the warmth I feel in anally copulating with your father." Translation, as Virgil knew, can form whole nations, and bloopers will never bring them down. Language is forgiving, but *en face* equivalence is the soundest of springboards. Accuracy isn't necessarily unimaginative.

Coming Through Slaughter

While They Slept
An Inquiry into the Murder of a Family
Kathryn Harrison
Random House, 275 pages

When the American child abuse prevention and foster care system succeeds, it can seem to work miracles of rare device. But when it fails, it fails utterly. Its charges do not simply fall through cracks, but descend into chasms and emerge as dangerous changelings. The most recent scandals involved bloated pay-per-kid schemes in New Jersey where parents allowed some of their brood to nearly starve. And in tightening the tap of Russian immigration, Putin not long ago cited the fact that of eleven post-Soviet orphans dying under suspicious circumstances, some had filtered, through neglect or misplaced good intentions, into the foster care circle of musical chairs that occupies an odd central position in American child welfare policy.

Kathryn Harrison is a writer who draws a lot of eye-rolling. Not least among the reasons is her memoir *The Kiss*, which chronicled incest with her father commencing in her twentieth year and concluding when he departed to re-establish his fundamentalist congregation somewhere in the Bible Belt. In tackling an intra-family murder growing out of prolonged child abuse in rural Oregon, Harrison quite consciously intends to inherit the mantle of the Truman Capote of *In Cold Blood* and the Norman Mailer of *The Executioner's Song*. But she doesn't have the former's hyper-objective detective eye, and does not even approach the "true life voices" ventriloquism that made the latter a completely unique masterpiece. If anything, she brings to mind the Texas memoirist and novelist Beverly Lowry, whose genre-bending *Crossing Over* re-created the killings that made Carla Faye Tucker America's first woman (and, by the way, first born-again Christian) to walk to the gurney at Huntsville Compound.

In April of 1984, Billy Gilley took a baseball bat and went downstairs to his parents' room, smashing the skull of both his mother and father and awakening his two sisters, Jody and Becky. After comforting Becky and warning her not to enter the room, he used the same bat to open holes in her skull so large that brain matter and bone chips extruded, causing her to die hours later in an ER wing slippery with gore.

Billy's ostensive goal and ultimate defense was that he was spiriting Jody away from their father's horrific molestations, and was himself ending years of uncontroverted, savage beatings and verbal abuse. He was convicted and sentenced to life without parole at 19, and has spent a quarter century in various prisons, now inhabiting the Snake River Detention Facility near the Idaho border, where Harrison goes for their queasy, laconic, sometimes sexually-charged interviews.

But these facts of the crime—three dead, a history of belt whippings by a sociopathic father—are the stepping off point for what dissolves into confusing, contradictory motives by Billy, Jody, and the relatives who adopted the only surviving sibling. Immediately after the incident, sixteen-year-old Jody claimed that though father and son went at one another with hot tongs, Billy Senior's sexual overtures to her were largely verbal and almost certainly unconsummated. Prosecutors assuage what they see as Harrison's misplaced sympathies for Billy, detailing his degree of premeditation, the meticulous way in which he carried out repeatedly avowed threats.

Psychiatric experts concur that Billy had an incestuous fixation on Jody; he put her in the car immediately after the murders and got as far as the nearest roadblock. During his incarceration, Jody did not respond to his letters, and in extensive interviews before trial he was unable to explain his own early tendency to fall asleep in the back seat of the family car with his own open hand on Jody's crotch.

Astoundingly, with great dexterity, Harrison leaves the reader sufficient sympathy for Billy to be cast as something other than a one-dimensional killing machine. He went to social services early and complained of his and his sister's abuse. The caseworker betrayed their confidence and reported the reports back to the parents, which resulted in the father adding the passive, enabling mother to his targets. Some commentators tell Harrison that Billy is the classical parricide in a society whose social services net often leaves the most urgent cries unheard. Murder is chosen as the only way to escape atrocities society won't recognize or measure, let alone remedy, and the perpetrator chooses the only available method to live with dignity, to restore their autonomy, to "re-process" the shards of personality blasted apart by the drawers of first blood.

Much of Harrison's fascinating work was done for her already by Jody Gilley, who went on to graduate from Georgetown with a thesis describing the events from the perspective of the brother she testified against, and whose guilt she sometimes paradoxically assumes. This closeness formed in early childhood either ripened into an exploratory, cerebral, reciprocal incest fantasy, or into a rage at the parents that rose to the point of merging her and Billy's personalities, or both:

> Identifying the murders as the event that "triggered" her re-birth, Jody [in her thesis] could voice a fear that they represented a consummation between her and her brother: a bloody consummation of hatred rather than of love, but a generative force nonetheless. To own her new life, she had to own the act that gave it to her, taking her place not just beside her brother—that wasn't enough—but *inside* her brother, slipping for a moment into his silhouette, trying on his history, his burdens, his fears. Or maybe it had been her violence, an emotion she'd entrusted to him.
>
> For Jody, so invested in control, the idea of exploring the most disastrous outcome of controlled rage must have been—I was going to say horrible, but perhaps it was irresistible—necessary. A way to both own and disown what she felt. A way to explore on the page what she couldn't allow into her life. Hidden behind the mask of Billy, in defense of his murders and her anger, Jody could reveal her anxiety about being judged herself, and express compassion for her brother, as she hadn't been able to do in the courtroom.

So this tale, wobbly and at times stretching its conceits, becomes a saga of brothers and sisters as much as parents and sons, a sort of reverse-Electra myth. You may or may not buy Harrison's subtext that Billy may have gotten a raw deal (at least in sentencing) by being tried before the development of the "abuse defense." But *While They Slept* shows at least how family homicides are rife with false transparencies, hiding deep shadow plays of anger, revenge, and redemption.

Devil in My Beehive

Journal 1973-82
Joyce Carol Oates
HarperCollins Canada
ECCO (U.S.), 435 pages

"The novelist is an empiricist, an observer of facts.... objective and subjective 'reality'... he must guard against the demonic idea of imagining that he possesses or even can possess ultimate truth. In this way he is like a scientist, an ideal scientist. Humble, striving for what he does not yet know, wanting to discover it, not to impose a pre-imagined dogma on reality. The novel as discovery. Fiction as constant discovery, revelation. The person who completes a novel is not the person who began it.... When one believes he has the truth, he is no longer an artist. When we finish a great work we should realize that we *know* less than we did before we began, in a sense; we are bewildered, confused, disturbed, filled with questions... unsettled by mystery."

So reads J.C. Oates's journal entry of March 1975, after she had sent off the Byronic, devil-drenched manuscript of *Son of the Morning*. The personality lying behind her prodigious creations—logorrhea, some have called it—is on amazing display in the first volume of her journals, running from dismal mid-decade to mid-decade as she wove together her *Bellefleur* romances. And if that personality is nothing more than the roving Monad-eye she flashed at me once from under her synaptic, squiggly perm—describing how a poem should "never, ever be larger than a postage stamp," though a rectangular one, stood on its end—then it is more accessible than most, more robustly and fearlessly displayed here than in any contemporary writer's diary since John Cheever's.

From someone who attacked probing biographers' "pathographies" and who said she "could not create an admirable character" (at a reading for *Broke Down Heart*), Oates's journals reveal surprisingly normal and disciplined work habits: placid mornings at the Selectric and name-dropper, dream dinner parties at her Princeton and Ontario homes. [The black and white snapshots of these are alone worth the price of the book.] So how did the vapors get into the McKeesport "burb girl" and Berlind Distinguished Professor? How did she get so good at knowing how maniacs "think", how it felt to stand with her high school girlfriends on boulders in the Detroit River while boys they wanted to date shot cans off their heads with 22s?

Reading, for one. She breakfasts on obsessive Russians ("tragic, or just *a realistic,* view of life?"); opium-addled French Symbolists; Romanian murderers who strangle their landladies like Roskolnikov and then really *do* hide the money under a flat rock. Secondly, it sounds like she made the pycholanalysis rounds in those days, though I may be pathographizing:

> As in [my] *Wonderland* Jesse's earlier memories are closer to him, more definitely imbedded *(sic)* than anything experienced as an adult... so this must be true of all of us... The earliest sights... rooms, playgrounds and backyards and the houses of relatives... fix themselves in the brain far more powerfully than anything afterward... [and]... we deceive ourselves if we believe otherwise...

Or these indecisive, shape-shifting double visions of herself, questioning even the writer's authenticity and sincerity:

> "Happiness" and its variants—contentment, well-being, optimism—are exasperating when they are pushed down our throats. When I read an interview with myself—which, I confess—I find hard to do—for good reason—I'm annoyed at the statements I make as I'd be annoyed at a stranger making them: who cares about normality, about things going right or well, about "Joyce Carol Oates" enjoying her writing? I should say that I find it torture and don't know why I do it.

Ontologies of identity lie under these surfaces like shredding shark's teeth—her novellas aren't by accident called things like *I Am No One You Know* and *Where Is Here?* ("Who Am 'I'" or "Who Is The 'I'" is the irradiating subtext of these 'day books.')

Ultimately and not surprisingly, it is biography and friendships that furnish her most vivid and dangerous material. Many major writers spot character sources in their fellow craftsmen, but nobody vivisects them like the Jeffrey Dahmer-obsessed Oates. There are Alfred Kazin's facial tics bubbling up like tar out of the "deepest loneliness," and "probable resentment of those who are not as unhappy as he." (Beautiful.) There is John Updike's "gentle, sly, immensely attractive modesty," his disbelief of and "slight guilt over his early and easy success." Anne Sexton amazes the diarist with her "final, feverish, death-directed work," compendious and ferocious, but "self-pitying, self-contemptuous, self-despising." Ditto John Berryman: "His alchoholism and general misery were, he said, 'the price you pay for an overdeveloped sensibility,' but I always believed him to be *underdeveloped*, with a very weak sense of others' existences . . . he seemed already dead—an inert, clayey substance, so chilling . . . ."

So while souls prove frivolous, deceptive, rotten or dauntingly saintly, Oates's respite becomes the natural world. It remains a vast, impersonal, spark-lit galaxy kaleidescopically settling and resetting itself: "Sleet storm, blizzard, bits of ice thrown against the windows, crackling tinkling noises, small explosions," and a Jersey countryside filled with "Blue juncots, cardinals and sparrows in the berry bushes . . . vast Siberian lakes, snow so thick the river invisible." For Oates, like for her beloved Lawrence, the "wilde wood" pours out its mystical rhythms to leapers and lepers alike, freeing the author from the world of people and from the institution's mandarin confines. One forgets, before going back through these pages, that for all the vermin in Oates's festering logs there is a surface of sweet bark, sweet leaves— the world becoming its own bright book of life.

Juxtapostions

The Ghost Soldiers
James Tate
HarperCollins Canada, ECCO (U.S.), 215 pages

Is there an American poet more unique and immune to classification than James Tate? He began with searching lyrics like 'So this is the dark street/ Where only an angel lives/ I never saw anything like it,' and moved through less formal, personal structures to the diffuse prose poems of the last few books. The narrative itself—squirrelly as it always is—is the driving force in these pieces. But not only is the narrator unreliable, he sometimes seems to have, say, no molecular structure. As Charles Simic says of these vignettes: "A poem out of nothing . . . is Tate's genius . . . just about anything can happen next in this kind of poetry and that is its attraction." In *Ghost Soldiers*, Tate's newest and largest group, he may have finally moved the form up onto the high, open ground of greatness.

Part of what Tate does on this ground, and hence his singularity, is to solo-face and plant by himself the Surrealist flag in American verse. (Others have preceded and followed, but, as we shall see, brought their own treatments to the "waking dreamscape".) From 1916 to the period between the wars, Surrealism moved from the plastic arts into literature with a vengeance. From Breton's Paris to Latin America's Vallejo (and even in stodgy England), poetry especially embraced Surrealism's unsettling objects, human grotesques, and menacing features of nature. Not so in America. Man Ray was from Brooklyn, but no Man Ray—nothing at all like him—showed up in the New World's poetic landscape.

Maybe this was because America had its own kind of Modernism and was already overloaded with experimentation. There was Eliot's "senses of meaning" as opposed to meaning itself; Faulkner's ornate but dreamless associational segues; Pound's montages of divergent histories and languages; and Stevens' atmospherics of pure, sometimes senseless sound (or sense from pure sound). Who needed a Tristan Tzara or a Mayakovsky in America's homespun, already bustling hothouse?

After World War II, and in the midst of the academics like Lowell, Berryman and Bishop, I count three Surrealists tiptoeing out onto the domestic stage. The Canadian Mark Strand and Serbian-born Charles Simic threw up a host of Surrealist props, but all buffed them with a polished sheen, the odd and unsettling ambered over with formalist shellacks. (In fact, Tate's first collection, *The Lost Pilot*, awarded the 1965 Yale Younger Poets Prize when he was still at the Iowa Writers Workshop [!], fits squarely into this 'formalist Surrealism'.)

But then Tate, who wasn't just American-born but was from the heart of the heart of the country—Kansas City—let loose with a whole new stage full of squeaky, squawking, shrieking horns, just like the ones he heard for nights on end as a high school student in the KC bars. Charlie Parker and Bix Bierderbecke showed him how improvisation in prose poetry could be structured like a sax chorus—note clusters multiplying from one another in uncertain directions, the form and the form alone becoming the body, the vestment of composition.

This method stood Tate in good stead through the 70s and 80s in collections like *The Oblivion Ha-Ha* and *Riven Doggeries*. A narrator, often no more than a solipsistic, self-contained eye, would sit abashed as creatures, concepts, and flea market thing-a-ma-jigs floated like Thanksgiving parade balloons into his field of attention. They were burlesque comic "types;" compressions of high mimetic and low-brow phrases ("Frivolous Blind Death Child"); characters who were usually collectors of abuse and subsequent resentments; and pure ciphers—animal-vegetable-mineral mixtures who talked back, took a few steps, then turned into something else.

In subsequent collections (*Worshipful Collection of Fletchers*) these "small movies" (as one critic called them) became monochromatic and repetitive. Narrators and observations seemed much too interchangeable. If you'd read one poem you hadn't read them all, but you could skip the next three or four. This doesn't make for energized poetry, even cutting some slack to prose poetry.

And as with some Surrealism and all highly stylized, "clever" forms, these pieces drew far too much attention to their outward features, leading to suspicions there was little below the dazzling surface water. Like Borges' *Ficciones*, Tate's "dreams of a robot dancing bee," however lovely, however delicate, seemed highly cerebral and gamey, emotionally vacant, empty-hearted. The interplay between observer and observed was that of two constructs, reciprocal machines. It was hard for themes to develop in such poetry: yearning, searching and finding were substituted by laughter at such endeavors. This hyper-irony was summed up in one of his brilliant, heartless lines I used as an epigraph for a book of my own: "Of course it's a tragic story; that's why it's so funny."

Not so with *Ghost Soldiers*. And Simic, however observant, is wrong if using the foregoing "out of nothing/anti-poetry" quote to describe this new collection. For all the undirected meanderings, for all the chattering, squiggly spins of the radio dial, rich and topical themes emerge out of these hundred-plus pieces. Two arise in particular abundance. First, the relation of parents to children. Second is what could be seen as at least one of this bond's destroyers: wars and their aftermath. In 'Father's Day,' the narrator watches the ladder of bonding opportunities—hard work, but graspable with determination—slip finally out of his hands forever:

> My daughter has lived overseas for a number of years now. She married into royalty, and they won't let her communicate with any of her family or friends. She lives on birdseed and a few sips of water. She dreams of me constantly. Her husband, the Prince, whips her when he catches her dreaming. Fierce guard dogs won't let her out of their sight. I hired a detective, but he was killed while trying to rescue her. I have written hundreds of letters to the State Department. They have written back saying they are aware of the situation. I never saw her dance. I was always away at some convention. I never saw her sing. I was always working late. I called her my Princess, to make up for my shortcomings, but she never forgave me. Birdseed was her middle name.

The war poems are the masterpieces here. Too widely spaced to be a 'cycle,' they throb and beam their tropes of senseless loss off one another. Parades of the dead march by like figures in a Bosch canvas, leaving the speaker to pass through their chilly wakes and putrid, standing air. Dialogues are filled with ambiguities of security and protection, what counts as a "mission" and how it would be "accomplished":

> There were some bald men in a field pushing a huge ball, but the ball wasn't moving. . . . A woman walked by and stopped beside me. "What are those men doing down there?" she said. "It's a warrior thing," I said. "They're working out some technical problems. They're protecting us from evil, but the plan is still in the stages of development." "Does that big ball represent evil" she said. "It's either evil or good. They're still trying to work that one out," I said. "Some men live on such an exalted plane, it's a wonder anything ever gets done, " she said. "I meant that as a compliment of course."
>
> ('Special Operations')

It doesn't get any more Pure Tate than this. The herd ends up following whatever the half-assed philosopher kings *say* they are doing; if anything remains to be understood, it is all outside of the little peoples' ken, as only the wise men can judge their own actions. The freedom-fearing woman, like a serf out of Chekhov ("What is it about us that fears liberty?"), catches and checks her own incipient skepticism brilliantly, sadly: "I meant that as a compliment, of course." They are stick people but their language—fleetingly glimpsed—gives them the fullness of crushed spirits, Nietschean sheep, Republican wives. Samuel Johnson (or was it Eliot?) criticized Chaucer for lacking a "high seriousness," and Tate has been a magnet for similar charges. But while keeping all of his zaniness and verve, Tate has really written in *Ghost Soldiers* a book of subtle, softly echoing anti-war poetry. "Sure it's a tragic story; that's why it's so funny." But still it is tragic, first and foremost. The farces of the world don't make the world a farce; it still cries out to be made better.

'Stamps Are the Flags of My Small Country': Poets Writing Letters

The Letters of Ted Hughes
Ed. Christopher Reid
Faber and Faber, 756 pages

Words in Air: The Complete Correspondence between Elizbeth Bishop and Robert Lowell
Ed. Thomas Travisano with Saskia Hamilton
FSG Adult, 928 pages

Poets operate in the most elevated literary language, words that are, as Ezra Pound said, 'charged with meaning to the utmost possible degree.' At a slightly lower register are prose artists, less intense than versifiers but still seeking maximum valence from each phoneme, every unit of punctuation. At the lowest level, the deep sea divers of literature, are the letter-writers: self-conscious but more relaxed; studied yet supple and limber; espousing awareness but less harried by the punitive superego of style.

It so happens that poets are our best literary correspondents: better producers of missives than they are of memoirs or essays or criticism. The greatest example, of course, was John Keats, a man who not only produced a body of brilliant verse by the time of his death at twenty-four, but also letters that created canon-changing concepts like 'Negative Capability' and 'cold pastoral.' Like Chekhov's stories, these letters struck deep in the hearts of readers, and produced there a profound, ineffable alteration. People have been waiting for another Keats since his death in the early nineteenth century, and may well have to wait forever. There was Dr. Johnson, a splendid letter-writer but not really a poet. There was Coleridge, closer to Keats in genre but with a longer life span, and so slightly less deserving of our amazement.

"Letters," Janet Malcolm has written, "are the great fixative of experience. Time erodes feeling. Time creates indifference. Letters prove to us that we once cared." Letter writing is also, to state the obvious, becoming a lost art in the age of e-mail, of everything Electronic. Hemingway famously said it was gratifying to write letters because 'it is fun to get letters back.' (Brad Leithauser wrote a great poem out of this quote alone.) When I wished to write for a certain publication, I proposed it to the editor in an old-fashioned paper letter. Sure enough, she wrote back, a little bewildered but delightfully grateful at the anachronism. And we were off to the races, or at least to the inkwell.

2.

People my age began college in the Sylvia Plath Era (early 70s), and her widower Ted Hughes was almost daily burned at the stake by well-meaning but single minded feminist critics. What remained lost to so many was his being the closest thing to a contemporary English poetic genius, second only to the younger Seamus Heaney and the still-living Larkin and Auden. He was clearly the greatest nature poet in the language since Lawrence. His hawk series is the gold standard of bestiary verse cycles, and he unashamedly explored that richest and most mystical terrain of animal consciousness.

What is amazing in Hughes is how much of his primal, blood-moon, psychically violent poetic treatments receive their first blueprints in missives to fellow artists and friends. Christopher Reid has taken 2500 pages worth of letters, stretching through five of Hughes's seven lived decades, and pared them mercilessly down to about 750. *The Letters of Ted Hughes*. Like Robert Graves, to whom some of the originals may have been addressed, Hughes was drawn to highly complex symbolic structures. Where the gyre system of Yeats was crafted from unearthly, intersecting abstractions, Hughes got his pastiche of shamanism and the group unconscious from the foul rag and bone shop of the British countryside.

This comes across in the letters he wasn't forced to write, but felt obliged to, to the Queen Mother when he was serving as Poet Laureate. Hughes draws soaring, Blakean diagrams on the etymology of the Queen Mum's name, with foxes and owls and meandering limbs of diagrammed sentences one can only imagine her nodding over after her legendarily copious bedtime gin and tonics. And much like a shaman, Hughes saw the poet as a healer, a bearer of medicinal powers that found tap-roots in ancestral magic and undiluted beauty rather than must-infested deities.

The letters well chronicle the war of imaginative systems Hughes maintained with critics and fellow symbol hunters and gatherers. After his virtually unreadable book on Shakespeare's mimetic structures, Hughes answered pans of his tome with observations that 'King Lear was the Llud who was Bran,' and 'Apollo, Asclepius and Bran were Crow Gods.' Of course, he signed himself onto whatever lineage this was with declarations that 'My hawk is the sleeping, deathless spirit of Arthur/Edgar/Gwyn/Horus—the sacrificed a reborn self of the great god Ra.' Sensing our need for reassurance with these references and correspondences, he concludes 'I don't just jot these things down, you know.' Fine, but we still don't get most of the allusions without annotation, something we are not used to in his kind of especially accessible 'earth poetry.'

There is enough mention of Plath and his subsequent wife, Assia Wevill [her 'thickened mongol-tent of hair'] to keep the gossipers happy. (Upon learning that Wevill also put her head in an oven and brought their toddler with her, an undergraduate friend of mine titled a freshman composition 'Ted Hughes: Bad Luck With Girls.') Hughes states that Plath biographies are 'a perpetual smoldering in the cellar for us; there's always one or two smoking away.' But guarded as he was with his (their) children, shielding them from critical buzzards feasting on 'the cornucopia of her dead body,' his best treatment of their union is not found here but rather in the masterful, late-released poem cycle called, ironically, *Birthday Letters*.

The gems here are notes on poetic technique and academic stress relief dashed off to fellow artists: discussions of scansion with Robert Lowell, of the religious impulse with the diehard, crankily atheistic Larkin, and the simple peace of fishing and 'lake-wandering' with younger, later friends like the novelist Graham Swift. These letters, as much as his poems, are filled with what replenished his muse-well:

the stench and texture of animals and their unknowable, strangely imagined homes; the ululation of bird-crowded, piping orchestral forests; the sensation of teetering in a boat barely big enough to contain his giant frame, the line for his next idea laying slack on the lee water, waiting to stiffen with a strike.

3.

Sometimes the imagined, hypostasized recipient of a letter may bear little resemblance to the actual person who opens it. And sometimes correspondents have the power to change the exchangers of letters into something much closer to what their mutual readers wish them to be. *Words In Air: The Collected Letters of Elizabeth Bishop and Robert Lowell* (FSG, 2008, 875 pages), shows how much one can like the idea of someone better than the someone themselves, and how the fantasies built up by distance make for ravishing letters but greatly disappointing eventual meetings.

Each of these poets had numerous literary friends and spouses, but the closest to each were architects and novelists, leaving them with one another to bounce off ideas and supply suggested revisions. Accordingly, they were ferociously drawn to one another, and their exchange never faltered in three decades. All this survived mutual alcoholism, moral recriminations, and public scandals involving the major literary figures of our age. More than anything, each emerged from violently haphazard childhoods and needed, quite desperately, to be taken care of. They were one anothers' epistolary saviors, one thinks, largely because they never had to confront the glaring, painful mirror of frequent encounter. Yet their constant, mutual introduction was like a perpetual parting, and in that way a kind of unreal, infatuated affection. 'Love and death are made of the same stuff,' Jeanette Winterson has written: '[T]he moment of finding that you love someone is like the moment of knowing you will never see them again; its clarity is dazzling, and it alters everything—not just everything that will come after, but everything that has gone before.'

Again, letters gave each of these poets discursive freedom from poetry's formalism. Bishop lived in Brazil and could speak English with few others on a daily basis: 'Oh dear—now I don't want to stop talking,' she says at the beginning of one letter, 'so I'll write two—or 200—more sentences on this page.' Lowell was often recovering from a manic swing or depressive breakdown, unsteady on his poetic feet and needing unscrutinized prose to exercise himself back into rarefied language.

The exchanges are almost constantly humorous and entertaining. This is partly because their authors are conscious of the special role of letters in literary life. Bishop offered a course at Radcliffe in 1971 on 'Personal Correspondence, Famous and Infamous,' and wrote to Lowell the year before that '[A] very good course could be given on poets and their letters—starting away back. There are so many good ones—Pope, Byron, Keats of course, Hopkins, Crane, Stevens, Marianne [Moore].'

Many of Lowell's longer letters are hilarious comedy-of-manners send-ups of illustrious contemporaries and skewered, crank ancestors. There were Bishop's grim Nova Scotian parents, who gave her up, and their equally strange extended family and neighbors who took her in. Lowell was the quintessential American literary blueblood, unafraid of presenting his famous aunts and uncles as an abundant aviary, unfit not only for the practical world but also for their own self-created, eccentric atmospheres. He was a lost child among constantly aging yet seemingly pastless people. Living relics rolled their wheelchairs through the halls of Beacon Hill houses, weaving him into their underworld of shades, calling him by the names of the dead.

As one would expect, the finest portraits are of literary contemporaries, or—even better—revered demi-gods finally befriended and presented as emperors with no clothes. Lowell stays in the London flat of a former professor who he had deified, the magisterial William Empson of *Seven Types of Ambiguity*:

> Each room is as dirty and messy as Auden's New York apartment. Strange household: Etta Empson, six feet tall, still quite beautiful, five or six young men, all sort of failures at least financially, Hetta's lover, a horrible young man,

dark cloddish, thirty-ish, soon drunk, incoherent and offensive, William [Empson]. Frank Parker red-faced, drinking gallons, but somehow quite uncorrupted, always soaring off from the conversation with a chortle. And what else? A very sweet son of 18, another, Hetta's, not William's, Harriet's age. Chinese dinners, Mongol dinners. The house had a weird, sordid nobility that made other Englishmen seem like a veneer.

The ambiguities here are classist, generational, cultural, and above all genetic. Balzac couldn't have painted an odder or better detailed family of misfits.

Conversely, Bishop's letters have little sociological content, or even social observation. They are as vivid and colorful as her elaborately mannered but transparent lyrics. She escorts us over the Amazon's steaming tributaries and waterfalls, its mountains glistening with "little floating webs of mist, gold spider-webs, iridescent butterflies . . . . big pale blue-silver floppy ones." She has a toucan named Uncle Sam, wields her lover Lota's revolver, and acts as auntie to her neighbors' kids and cats and stone collections. She finds Lota walking in her nightgown out onto their veranda to see the stars "because they had never looked so close before—close and warm—apparently touching our hair." For all her painterly detachment, she honestly portrayed suffering, early on through her lost boy cousin ('First Death In Nova Scotia') and later in outraged letters about the Brazilian junta's murder of street children in Rio's hovel-hilled favelas. And she wanted to be able to better portray privation, concerned about the paucity of the human in her work and admiring Hardy's poems for their being 'about the real relations between men and women.'

Since both saw poetry as the deepest, most serene of moral enterprises, neither pulled punches in re-assessing old friends and castigating each other for violations of trust. When Lowell extracted portions of letters from his estranged wife [Elizabeth Hardwick] and spun them into the flawless poems of *The Dolphin*, Bishop was outraged. Dignity and confidentiality, central as they were to the human personality, were in that sense more important than poetry, indeed than any art. She quoted to Lowell Hopkins's notion of the necessity of the literary 'gentleman': 'It isn't being 'gentle' to use personal, tragic, anguished letters in that way—it's cruel.' When Lowell countered that '[N]othing is perversely torn and twisted, nothing's made dishonestly worse or better than it was [by what is written of it],' she stood her ground, saying '[W]e all have irreparable and awful actions on our consciences.' The trick was to keep from repeating them, especially in page after page sent out into the world.

After this, and with less than a decade for each to live, they flamed each others' kindling with Aeolian gusts blown over thousands of miles, all at the mercy of Brazil's mildewed, dilapidated airmail system. They traveled across dangerous continents, in dangerous times, to bask in the warmth of one another's insight. They finished one another's thoughts and first draft stanzas. For each of them, knowledge, wisdom and even hope were not given qualities of mind but rather fragile constructs, capable of disintegration at any time; for this reason alone they couldn't let the letters stop. Lowell loved her posting strings of words on bulletin boards for years until a line of poetry congealed—her essential method of composition. He saw each word as exalted, lucky to be so handled, thrown into the sky like confetti or graduation mortar boards, signifying revision but also completion:

> Have you seen an inchworm crawl on a leaf,
> Cling to the very end, revolve in air,
> feeling for something to reach to something? Do
> you still hang your words in air, ten years
> unfinished, glued to your notice board, with gaps
> or empties for the unimaginable phrase—
> unerring Muse who makes the casual perfect?

Raymond Carver: A Writer's Life

Raymond Carver: A Writer's Life
Carol Sklenicka
Scribner, 592 pages

For those who remember the publication of *What We Talk About When We Talk About Love* in 1981, its importance is nearly impossible to exaggerate. The end of the prior decade was scorched by academic scrivening formulas, or otherwise filled with the genuinely talented minimalism of Mary Robison and Ann Beattie. But Carver's lean phrases offered something more filling, and cast a light into a world the writing school algorithms could never get a bead on: alcoholics and deadbeats talking in their own scratched voices, adrift in a world of ostracizing, unfamiliar abundance. As Robert Pope said: "People imitated him and found the way back into high realism, which has little to do with Carver's stories ... [T]heir comedy is peculiar; He could have fit perfectly into the experimental period, but instead he became this salvation of American literature."

The facts of Carver's life are simple enough. While the blue collar atmosphere of his childhood friends' houses appeared stolid and predictable, the air in Carver's mill-town home quivered with menace. "Both parents' personalities were distorted by tension and anger, frozen by obstinacy," writes Carol Sklenicka in her new biography. According to Frank Sandemeyer, a co-worker of Carver's father in Yakima, Washington: "At the Carvers, [t]hings seemed as if the whole enterprise might fly apart at any minute." The atmosphere of his preteen years was captured in the germinal story "Nobody Said Anything," from his first collection *Will You Please Be Quiet, Please?* The story captures the theme that occupied Carver throughout his life: that of the divided self, which first manifests in the divided child. Like Pound's toddler of Dante standing rapturous before a fish's beauty in the Florence market, the young boy of "Nobody Said Anything" stands dumbfounded before a similar creature. But Carver's is a monstrosity, truncated and demeaned, the mythical symbol of the watcher's desire to be salvaged and redeemed: "He looked silver under the porchlight. He was whole again, and he filled the creel until I thought it would burst. I lifted him out. I held him."

After Carver met Maryann Burk in a Yakima donut shop in 1955, they began a family and a fierce itinerancy, Maryann finally settling them down to teach high school so Carver could write full time. Earning his degree at Chico State in California, Carver studied under John Gardner. The white-haired mentor, himself a mass of violent contradictions, inculcated in Carver both the desire to write serious literature and the warning that making a living that way was nearly impossible. Yet early publication successes coaxed him onward, kindling a bristly hope in his oversized athletic frame. On May 29, 1967, four days after his twenty-ninth birthday, Carver received news he called "the best thing that's happened, ever." "Will You Please Be Quiet, Please?" had been selected for *Best American Short Stories 1967*, and Carver returned to Iowa City, a young contender in the fabled Writer's Workshop's ring of champions.

Gordon Lish accepted his work for publication in *Esquire,* and Carver fell under the vain, manic spell of the man who was to tout himself as "Captain Fiction." Newly sober after years of binging, Carver entered that period of his life he called "gravy:" everything that happened to him after his last drink in 1977. While Maryann saw Lish as a Machiavel to watch closely, Carver was too weak and dazzled to question the editor's ruthless control, his merciless parings and reworkings. If, as Lionel Trilling would have it, authenticity and sincerity are the watermarks of valuable prose, the two questions that haunt Carver's output beginning in the mid-seventies can be called the questions of authentic content and authentic voice.

The slapdash merging of intended subject matter and actual subject matter jumped out at careful readers of *Will You Please Be Quiet, Please?* One got the feeling that the characters just might be fellow writing acolytes dressed up in the denim of steelworkers. Critics and writers like Dagoberto Gilb recognized that a genuine worker's flow of duties and obligations would prevent the ruminations seen on the page:

These stories didn't really seem to be about working people. Working people are energetic. They can be dangerous and energetic, but they are not sitting around. I could see where [Carver] came from the working class, but he wasn't it. His stories were about graduate students' lives, but he smartly made his stories about vacuum cleaner salesmen or whatever.

This problem began to be corrected as Carver's mastery of vernacular improved. The later stories of *What We Talk About When We Talk About Love* still foregrounded dialogue, but settings and behavior fleshed out a more believable proletarian world. Where before there were simply duos speaking in empty rooms, scenes now simmered with yard sales gone haywire, thefts and repossessions, wobbling men finding the keys to strangers' houses in their coats.

The issue of authenticity *of voice, of whose* writerly voice is really speaking, is the stuff of one of modern publishing's longest and most agonizing soap operas. The original versions of the *What We Talk About* stories, reprinted in a new Library of America collection of Carver, are dense with narration and have a more robust strain of dialogue. When these "A" versions were honed into the stories making up (what is now called) *Beginners* and sent to Lish, Carver had himself gotten them down to what he thought was "the bone." But the eventual "c" version brought into being by Lish shocked Carver, and left him vacillating between assertions that the editor was "a god" and a feeling that sounded like one of his inquisitive, mystified titles—this is not what I meant to say at all. As Sklenicka explains, Lish's perspective of the completed work-the almost skeletal sheen and polish of his version-took precedence over the original expressions, desires, and tastes of the artist. Lish offered no further proof for the necessity of his heavy hand than the fact that neither Carver nor his agents had been able to place the original copy with major magazines. Lish answered one of the author's letters with Socratic rapid-fire: "Which has the greater value? The document as it issues from the writer or the thing of beauty that was made? *What remains* is an artifact of power."

Though this writer certainly has his problems with Lish, I tend to agree with Captain Fiction here. The efforts of Tess Gallagher and others to reissue *Beginners* as the "real" *What We Talk About* was ill-advised. At its worst, it bordered on farce and was, albeit counterintuitively, an insult to the author. As Carver's good friend Richard Ford said (outraged at Gallagher's revisionism), a writer writes for readers, and the last step toward the reader is the granting of freedom to the editor with whom the manuscript is entrusted. Lish correctly persuaded Carver that earlier versions of the book were sentimental and structurally baggy, and he was right in saying that the final thing was the most beautiful.

Sklenicka's history of these struggles is compelling, though her prose can be clumsy and turgid. What she handles best is the dichotomies, the contradictions that lie behind the personalities of the greatest artists, what Updike said was "the good and bad in every man, that is more interesting than whether he is actually good or bad." This encompasses both craftsmanship and morality. Sklenicka shows how Carver could be like Faulkner. When writing badly, he wrote truly abysmally; when writing well, his words possessed the power of revelation. She recounts his undivided loyalty to friends and supporters and his late-life lover Gallagher, existing as it all did beside his grim view of his "baleful" children and his terrible mistreatment of Maryann. Carver's disparities were exemplified in his physical presentation. When I heard him read with Gallagher at the old Venice Jail (apropos) in 1988, scarcely a year before his death, he recited the late, majestic story "Elephant." An awe settled over the audience, after lavish, reverential introductions. But his high, tinny voice grated, seeming to so contradict the frame it came from.

All in all, Sklenicka has done Carver and literary biography a great service with this volume. The notes on sources and tables and grids of first publications form a beautiful history of 1980s magazine prose, and her treatment of Carver's late, supremely nourishing friendships (Ford, the brothers Tobias and Geoffrey Wolff, William Kittredge) are especially touching and subtly presented. Her chosen excerpts from the stories return you to the jolts those lightning-rod paragraphs had when you first read them, like my favorite, the opening sentences of " Mr Coffee and Mr Fixit":

> I've seen some things. I was going over to my mother's to stay a few nights. But just as I got to the top of the stairs I looked and she was on the sofa kissing a man. It was summer. The door was open. The TV was going. That's one of the things I've seen.

Thank you, Mr. Carver, for so sharply condensing tens of thousands of words of Freud. And thank you, Mr. Lish, for condensing this out of whatever was its original form.

Days Are to Be Happy In

Making Toast
Roger Rosenblatt
Ecco, 287 pages

The poignancy of this Larkin line is hammered home in this vivid new memoir just out from *Time* columnist Roger Rosenblatt. When Rosenblatt's adult daughter, Amy, died of an asymptomatic heart ailment in 2007 (and on her home treadmill, no less), he and his wife drove to Amy's home in Maryland. A prominent pediatrician, his daughter had three children under seven at the time of her death. One of them, granddaughter Jessie, asked Rosenblatt how long he and his wife were staying. "Forever" said the author.

This memoir captures the ensuing year with captivating, insightful vignettes of the three grandchildren living the lives of primary school waifs and masters. The grandson Sammy enters kindergarten, that forbidding portal to academia slathered over with all the innocent detritus of the nursery. Jessie loses at least one tooth. James, a.k.a Bubbles, learns to talk, speech descending upon him in the hypnogogic haze he inhabits between grief and non-comprehension of death.

Rosenblatt is not reluctant to reveal his own profound and terrible grief. But he and his wife—re-naming themselves Boppo and Mimi—resolve to channel this negative energy into structuring "the choreography of everyday life" so essential to young children, for whom routine is the referent for all other aspects of existence. Rosenblatt and wife continue their daughter's ornate breakfasts, the kid's piano lessons, even cross-country vacations with all their pet-congested, loss-plagued, vehicular foibles. Rosenblatt, himself a poet, uses as a framing device Yeats's great "Poem For My Daughter," and these lines reify the sanctity of sameness to very young minds: "How but in custom and in ceremony/Are innocence and beauty born?"

Indeed, Rosenblatt saw in his daughter all that Yeats's poem wishes for a female offspring. The author speaks of her as a living presence visiting him with all her tones and texture in the venues where she was most a mom and a daughter: "The distance of death reveals Amy's stature to me. My daughter mattered to the histories of others. Knowing that did not prevent my eyes from welling up with tears for no apparent reason in Ledo's Pizza the other day. But it is something."

The tightness of Rosenblatt's prose, its overall economy, is also fresh and revitalizing. Rosenblatt is a poet, essayist, playwright, and screenwriter, and he tackles the overused genre of memoir with appropriate openness, balanced at the same time with restraint and dignity. As one communicator opined: "What is the worst a parent can contemplate? The death of a child. And the next most awful thing? Her own death, before her children are ready to lose her" [Dinah Lenney].

Rosenblatt carries on in the only way he can: honoring his daughter by passing on the love he had for her directly to her issue without sentimentality, self-pity, or overstatement of her struggle. The book is wise and generous, and, again to quote Yeats, "inhabits that eerie realm of life-in-death and death-in-life." This is accomplished by Rosenblatt's fostering a respect and love for the quotidian, the "crap-work" of everyday life that creates patterns of safety and comfort not just for his charges, but for him, his wife and son-in-law. Sometimes it detracts from his writing, but life itself must come first:

> Late one morning I am alone in the house. I cannot remember another time when this was so. Harris is at work. .... Sammy and Jessie are in school. Bubbies is at his gym with Ligaya. I am supposed to be writing. Instead, I wander about the empty places—the playroom, the children's bedrooms, the halls. The only sound is the whir of the refrigerator.

In the morning of life, we rage to live without dead time. At its evening, and with responsibilities born abundantly from our dreams, we settle into routines that provide depths of understanding and a new alacrity of mind. Rosenblatt's becomes in the end the most sanguine sort of grief-memoir, a demonstration of the joy that is born hiding, then slowly comprehending, its contrary.

Racine on the Prairie: Richard Ford's Canada

Canada
Richard Ford
HarperCollins (Ecco), 446 Pages

Flying over the Great Plains to visit my sister in the Twin Cities, the far fields of both Dakotas stretch out in hundreds of miles of unruffled tableland, the gold and grey and russet of wheat stone-still from this altitude but undulating to their walkers and drivers in whatever breezes the passes allow. My perspective is a vista of breadth, a land unto itself that stands apart from what the ground observer sees: an ocean of crops unrivalled by any landscape save perhaps for the Asian steppes. You could say we inhabit different lands—the walker and the flyer—and that we could cross this border of altitude to see the diversity of the same terrain from the other's person's point of vision.

This is a land Richard Ford knows well (his third novel, *Wildlife*, was placed here), and serves as the setting of his newest novel, the first since his groundbreaking and highly acclaimed Bascombe trilogy. The year is 1960. America has a young, inspiring President, a robust economy, and the menace of Soviet missiles far away but never out of mind. (Notably, many of their U.S. Army counterparts lay in silos beneath this unassuming ground.)

A family of four lives a relatively uneventful life in the Montana railroad and farming city of Great Falls. The father is one of those handsome Centurions whose life reached its apogee during his recent military service. He wears his still name-tagged but bar-stripped jumpsuit as a reminder of days he bird-dogged girls, drank half-pints of Yellowstone bourbon, and—descending from year to feckless year in his early thirties—didn't have rent to pay and two children to raise. His wife is an Upper West Side intellectual, having married below her station but seeing something inspiring, apocryphal and opportunity-providing in this endless nothingness. She is also at once a doting and somewhat detached mother.

The narrator is their adolescent son, one of two twins, who sees a queasy chaos in this benighted grassland, and attempts to make it cohere with pattern-focused hobbies like chess and beekeeping. He craves a pattern for the wheat-sea's formlessness, beating back with games and strategies the lassitude that may doom him to being one of Cather's 'Obscure destinies.'

Their father sells cars but sweetens his income with gray market [read: stolen] sides of beef slaughtered and smuggled by local Indians. When he gets deep in hock with them and is warned to make good if he values the safety of his family, he hatches a plan to rob a bank just across the state line in even less hospitable North Dakota. He and the wife do just that, are trailed and reported and arrested; not to worry, this is all unspooled in the first pages of the book. Much of the novel then consists of the son Dell's ruminations of what happened, what could or should have happened, and on the terrifying force and effect of sudden, unforeseeable shifts in fortune—the razor's edge between psychic peace and the make-do backwash we flounder in just after catastrophe.

Before the parents are tried and sentenced to their North Dakota penitentiary bids, Dell's sister runs off to San Francisco and the boy is transported—before he can be adjudged a ward of the state—to live with his mother's relative's relative in far Northern Saskatchewan. Here, the metaphorical underpinnings of the book—crossing borders, leaping boundaries—comes to its acme, and the narrator wonders at his fate and its possible directions of resolve. He does all this thinking as a sort of child slave, having been apprenticed to a jack-of-all-trades named Remlinger, a cunning American exile whose shady past parallels those of Dell's parents, the figures who got caught, who couldn't get away.

Remlinger's own schemes, and what caused him to come to rest as a flim-flam man and Dell's rescuer, unfold in an ultimately cumbersome wrap-up that we need not go into here. What fascinates about the book is its unique style, and its skillful characterizations not only of people, but, much like in Hardy, the harsh landscape in which they find (or send) themselves.

Dell speaks with a single voice, but with two vocalizations, ranging, sometimes in the space of a single page, between the guileless view of an astonished 13-year-old and that of the more somber, philosophical register of the actual writer of the narrative, the much older Dell and Ford's diffidently exploring, morally Socratic stand-in. The effect is dazzling, with the man-child's unassuming, flatly descriptive major chords colored deftly by the minor notes of the summarizing elder. This is a prairie of the imagination, with bold columns of confident sun tempered by shadows of doubt, by the constant positing of counterfactuals and what might have been if just a different road—never mind the 'right' or 'wrong' one—had been taken through the mirage-making, dizzying grasses. Indeed, Dell is something like the boy narrator of Chekhov's great novella 'The Steppe'—young enough to still appreciate and invest in his will, old enough to know the terrible constraints of external circumstance.

The second stylistic device is Ford's ability to conjure life-changing, fate-sealing instants with the gentle voice of a master questioner, the constantly self-searching doubter and then just as effective re-affirmer of his conjectures. There is controversy with the self, but there are no gnarled, edgy sounds scraping up against the singing lines here. There is only the mellifluous, smooth, utterly diffident sub-speech of the inquisitor constantly interrogating himself. Dell old and young is a whispering, mellowed Hamlet. The debates with himself, their transcendental atmospherics, make Ford the heir to two other masters of this style—Peter Taylor and especially Robert Maxwell (whose influence he stresses in the acknowledgments.)

The Maxwell comparison is the highest compliment I can pay to a writer. And *Canada* may be Ford's best book yet, this coming from someone who regards his Bascombe Trilogy, along with Updike's Rabbit novels, as the chronicles that readers in one hundred, two hundred years will consult to see how we lived, to feel our texture as a society, and to understand what borders we were given to cross.

Eros, Builder of Cities

Sex & Punishment: Four Thousand Years of Judging Desire
Eric Berkowitz
Counterpoint, 443 pages

As my favorite social historian, Fred Schneider of the B-52s, likes to say, there are three basic urges: hunger, shelter, and 'getting some.' Take the last of this triad as your basic ingredient. Start with pre-Christian societies and civilization's strong discontent with the non-procreative erotic. Add layer after layer of aromatic, perfectly-spiced anecdotes about lust-driven schemers and their ultimate, illustrative and usually quite terrible fates. Baste slowly in a shimmering prose style that will be envied by the best essayists. Voilà. Bon Appetit. Serve hot. Large portions.

It is the mark of an excellent new writer to take a heavily treated subject and approach it with new energy and direction. Eric Berkowitz has done this with *Sex and Punishment: Four Thousand Years of Judging Desire.* He takes us through several millennia of sexual stasis and deviation with marvelous velocity, grace and precision. He instructs and delights, and within these Aristotelian parameters he harnesses (and preserves!) the lurid verve of the Hefners, the Jongs, and the lugubrious Frank Harris of *My Secret Life.* [Full disclosure: Eric was a law partner of mine some years back and while I would like to tell him to keep his day job and give up scrivening, I cannot, for reasons that follow.]

Where else to start but with the Greeks? In small, gossipy Athens, where a man's reputation was always up for review, adultery laws were face-savers far more than guides for behavior. No sex act was intrinsically prohibited for, as Plato said, the various acts follow any act's gradient of quality. "A love affair itself is neither right nor wrong," he said in the *Meno,* "but right when it is conducted rightly and wrong when it is conducted wrongly." Sex was often, for young men, exchanged for an elder's tutelage, and in Greece's homoerotic hothouse, a boy submitting too easily to his tutor was seen as female or bestial; if he resisted too much he stood to lose the older man's pedagogy and sponsorship. Laws fell into place around this social arrangement; to transgress was simply to throw off its equilibrium.

Discussions of Rome's imperial bedrooms follow, but Berkowitz is most interesting when exploring ages whose sexual history has been given short shrift, as in the Middle. In many ways the *moyen age* was utterly practical, with (especially) Mediterranean societies deeming prostitution "absolutely indispensable to the world" and taking the opportunity to tax it heavily. But money was never the key component of harlotry under the law. A strumpet could merely be a woman who had been available to "a number of men," the magic number of five somehow sufficing. In the monastic countryside, nun-prostitutes were required to remit fees to their convents, or keep their proceeds to give later to chosen pious causes. Clerics and not constables were the sexual police of the age. Laws prohibiting certain acts almost always had a racist or ethnic cleansing component: homosexuality and bestiality were invariably perceived as forces of either Islam or Judaism. Each were conduits to hell, their practicioners vividly pictured as agents of Satan, horned and bearded and chained and tailed.

The book moves through the early modern period, with Charles II not daring to institute a code that would curtail his debaucheries. The Protestant Reformation contained elements of rebellion against priestly lechery, institutionalized molestation, the tincture of the Papacy in the pure, clear vessel. By the time of de Sade and the Bastille, sexual freedom joined the battle against monarchy and theocratic nationalism, its leader a prophet of deviance who spent his prison hours carving wood phalluses and widening himself nightly by riding "the sweet Fafnir."

The Renaissance is treated mainly through a British prism, with its societal sanctions of sex ridiculed by geniuses like Shakespeare, Jonson, and others whose condemnation of society's retribution became accepted, if not revered. *Measure for Measure, The Winter's Tale* and other works served to highlight the hypocrisy of sexual bans more effectively than tracts of essayists or the proclamations of the Roundheads. Oddly, artists like Milton, whose 'Defense of Divorce' is an anti-Papist masterpiece and has been relied upon by modern feminist writers like Margaret Talbot, nonetheless succumbed to the sexual curdle of fellow Puritans, at least when called in to vote with them on policy positions.

The fine polish, that powdered wig perfection of the Augustans of course masked a lust that no law could get ahold of. Samuel Pepys's libido was especially powerful, and the legal apparatus of his time seemed more concentrated on sedition than prohibiting the upstairs-downstairs groping and buggery that can be read between the lines of his masterful *Diary*. The chambermaids who combed lice out of his hair and helped him dress could expect his hands to travel up their legs as they worked, and he had a penchant for being masturbated by a maid in stagecoaches on the way to Parlaimentary debates (no doubt on vice laws). Bestiality was especially rampant in the England of the time, and when a Scot, David Malcolm, was caught copulating with an animal, he fell to his knees and begged for mercy by explaining how many times he had theretofore tried it without success, and wished to be allowed his hard earned consummation. Bestiality was almost always associated with witchcraft, and while these practicioners were at it, they were most catholic in their taste: cows, goats and deer were favorites, but other unwilling sexual receptacles included boar, foxes, and "large hares." The punishment often involved burning at the stake rather than hanging, as the earth was deemed necessary of clearance of a pervert's flesh.

By the time of American slavery, of course, sexual crimes broke down rigidly along racial lines. The Southern states mandated castration for black men who even attempted to woo the kin of their white masters, though simple execution was the more common punishment. The hammer came down hard during Reconstruction. "After the Civil War," Berkowitz writes, ""[R]acial tensions . . . .reached their apex, and a man's dark skin was proof enough that he was a rapist; juries were instructed to infer that any sexual encounter between a black man and a white woman involved intent on his part to commit rape. Between 1700 and 1820, more than 80 per cent of the men executed in the U.S. for rape were of African descent, and 95 percent of females in these cases were white.

For a writer, including Berkowitz himself, the most fascinating chapters turn on sanctions of pornography, or literature than was mistakenly pushed under that rubric by particularly conservative British, French and American administrations. *Fanny Hill,* stories by de Maupassant and Zola and Flaubert, and of course D.H. Lawrence were the focus of authorities, driven by the belief that such writing should be more aggressively prosecuted than sex itself, as the former gave rise to the latter through "lustful incitement, deleterious and langorous preoccupation." Control what goes out in brown paper wrappers and you've won half the battle for the potential reader's heart. The postal systems were crawling with censors and seizers and name-takers. Law courts invoked a kind of strict liability that put in the dock writer, publisher, distributor, and the reader lucky enough for the prior three to have beaten the odds. The *Chatterly* ban was the broadest and most effective, some believe because the book involved heterosexual buggery, something the British bench found particularly unnerving.

Berkowitz's book is a wonderland of the forbidden, and of society's attempt to keep it so, despite all odds and its being predictably destined to ultimate failure. It is a mural sometimes done as miniature, sometimes as epic, but always with a craftsman's hand—a sprawling story told with uncommon precision and purity of expression. In past ages, the bluenoses would have Berkowitz himself belonging in prison. But his book belongs in your hands and on the shelf of any reader interested in, as Lord Rochester said, "[O]ur long and fruitless bridling of lust."

Under the Overpass

Lost Memory of Skin
Russell Banks
HarperCollins, 416 Pages

Russell Banks spelunks the caves of the taboo like no other master of American prose. In *Affliction*, it was fratricide and incest and propane-tank arson erupting amidst the gray brush of rural winter hollows. In *Cloudspitter,* his magisterial saga of John Brown, he showed how inspirational talent and homicidal mania could exist in the same brain, feeding and enriching one another. In *The Sweet Hereafter,* children, a whole school bus full of them, could pass from the earth in an instant, a supposedly benevolent god standing in the wings and, like Joyce's paradigmatic artificer, blithely paring his fingernails.

But no one until now has had the insight and courage to tackle the world of what has come to be called the "[registered] sex offender." How could sympathy be garnered for people *that* presumably low on the moral chain of being, people down on the level of those who kill their children or fly planeloads of people into buildings? They must, society seems to say, be deserving of all their universal, unquestionable negatives; any other weaker view leaves the assessor themselves upset.

"It's become a national preoccupation," Banks told Charles McGrath of *The New York Times,* "this fear of sex crimes." "It's almost like the Salem witch trials," he said, "[But] where is the fear coming from? I don't think it's about sex so much as some deep-seated sense that we've failed to protect our children."

In *Lost Memory of Skin,* Banks takes a group of homeless marginalists and adds that tincture of perversion ["the feely-thing"] that keeps society from allowing them a footing for possible recovery. The main character is the Kid, a teen on the cusp of adulthood—actually a virgin—where "sex offense" is by no means clear and thus even remotely irredeemable. The label itself is worse than any prison, and the Kid's very movements are a means of Foucaultian constriction—an electronic ankle bracelet keeps him defined and detached from schools and playgrounds, which amounts to almost anywhere, and requires unaffordable electricity to recharge. Living some of the year in Miami, Banks was taken with a group of real-life sex offenders living beneath the Tuttle Causeway in DM2 nestled against tony neighborhoods.

The irony, the circular dilemma, of course, is how society's "zero tolerance" has emptied its enforcement mechanisms of all subtlety, compassion, and tolerance. In a legal system where a nineteen-year-old has "normal" sexual contact with someone two years his junior or an investigative journalist mistakenly brushes over an FBI-monitored website, there simply are no second chances. The die is cast, their fate is sealed, and Foucault's "discipline and punish" becomes an especially insidious "classify and exclude." This rigidity surfaced in earlier recent history, with the application of aggravating circumstances in death penalty trials, and the Rockefeller drug law's removal of judicial discretion in sentencing. The post-McMartin molestation hysteria and the sheer existence of the Internet have turbocharged our longstanding sexual judgmentalism, creating a wasteland of souls barred from nearly everything at the advent of their lives.

The Kid begins to win the reader over not with his victim's status, but with his pluck and sparkling eccentricity, toting an Iguana around like a collared poodle. When the Professor, a surprised academic sociologist, shows us to study his young subject, the latter's openness makes us open up even more to him and wish for his redemption, whatever that might look like.

But the professor has demons of his own. He is arrogant, generous, brash, and endlessly inquisitive, but his obsession with homelessness may owe an explanation to his stint as a "slimy" government official informer in the 60s; it may also be a view he refuses to test by conjectures and refutation like any good social scientist. Where is the clinical data for his thesis that pedophilia is a response to powerlessness and disorder, and of modern media's sexualization of children in advertising? Is he really as detached as he claims to nubile sexual allure? Is he an actual example of what others are—under his hypothesis—falsely tagged with? Ambiguities like this keep followers of the Kid and the prof on their toes, watching Banks weave earnest personality development out of the thickest of society's sexual hypocrisy and queasy moral insecurity. We are willing to stick with them because they are battling a whirlwind, their two selves joining in a teleological puptent that shelters and values insight:

> The kid turns and peers up at the huge fat man blocking the late afternoon sun. The Professor chuckles. He's used to chuckling; it's his default form of laughter. If he must show pleasure or amusement or delight, he'd rather be seen as a chuckler, another stereotype, perhaps, but a slightly more serious one than that of the jolly fat man. He eases himself down to the ground and takes a position next to the Kid that effectively blocks the wind. The Kid tries again to light his stove and this time succeeds. The two sit there and watch the flame flare yellow and settle quickly back into a steadily purring blue blur.

The Duke of Self Regard

Selected Letters of Norman Mailer
edited by J. Michael Lennon
Random House, 2014, 867 pages

Those of us who grew up in the 60s and 70s were exposed not so much to the writer as to his public personae. We saw the head butts with Gore Vidal on Dick Cavett and otter talk shows, coupled incongruously with Mailer's amazing erudition on almost any subject thrown his way. We saw the parody (and nearly self-parody) of the New York mayor's race with his ticket-mate Jimmy Breslin. We endured *Maidstone* and other film forays. We more than endured the feminism debates with Germaine Greer at Town Hall during the release of *The Prisoner of Sex*.

Though Mailer never got to the point—as he said of Truman Capote—of replacing his writing with a social life that became his "real work," it was damn close for a while. He had the non-fiction masterpieces of *The Armies of the Night* and *Miami and the Siege of Chicago* behind him, but would have to wait a decade until his fiction would crest, through a long-awaited self-effacement of the narrator, in *The Executioner's Song*, the Gary Gilmore novel told in a majestic duet of "Eastern" and "Western" voices. It was the home run of a novel he had not enjoyed since *The Naked and the Dead*.

Now we have the letters, and, as Hemingway said, 'It is fun to write letters because it is fun to get letters back.' Many of the missives herein were one-offs to other celebrities (often non-literary) that he hardly knew; many are long essay-disquisitions to pet-project recipients of the time, especially the prison bird Jack Abbott, whose writing Mailer justly praised but who failed to respond to Mailer's half-baked program of rehabilitation.

There are some letters that illuminate his (and many working novelists') mundane and tormenting labours. To Gordon Lish, as *Executioner's Song* was germinating, he wrote "The Gilmore book has me working like a lawyer preparing briefs; I think I have two thousand pages of notes already, and not a line of manuscript." Mailer had not yet broken through and abandoned the 'Aquarius' personae that animated *Armies* and other successful novel-as-history experiments, so his flailing left him with little but compliments for other writers, which are generous, encouraging, and abundant. This to Abbott: "You have one talent that very few writers have, even good professional writers, and that is a personal tone . . . . .[There's a psychology to convicts and murderers which has never been touched by anyone, except for that author sitting next to God himself, Old Dostoevsky.]" Tone and style, especially when coming with the effortless virtuosity with which they visited Mailer, would be the key out of his own true prison of self-doubt, a place never inhabited by certain "naturals" (Bellow, Malamud) he did not count himself among. The many letters to Lillian Hellman show his admiration for the "natural voice" of her then husband Dashiell Hammett: "I had considerable respect for Dash, and not because he would refuse to face into knotty problems, but would . . . dismiss them by an exercise of his personal style."

What one marvels at here, of course, is the range of Mailer's interests. He jots off praises to the old Beat buddy Michael McClure for his *Meat Science Essays;* hobknobs with Bellow and the Kennedys ("Jack didn't look like a president, too pretty; he looked like your ski instructor") in gathering notes for *The Presidential Papers,* and tells Graham Greene he will simply have to wait his turn for a more substantive letter. Bad manners though it traditionally is, he actually answers his critics. My favourite was a letter to William Buckley castigating him for letting (the great critic) Hugh Kenner, then a *National Review* staffer, trash Mailer's *Deaths for the Ladies:* "Bill, one wonders whether you are not managing a farm team for the Book Review at *Time.*"

For every wonderfully funny, juvenile fight over sports statistics with Red Smith or Sonny Liston, there are earlier, searingly astute snippets on the big (besides his own) books of the day: Heller's *Catch-22;* Updike's *Rabbit, Run* ("its great, bending arcs of despair"); Baldwin's *Another Country,* and Roth's *Letting Go.* He could see the genius behind Sartre's novels, but deftly warned away readers from the great man's "ultimates and principles." He gave unlikely praise to Isherwood's Weimar stories as the inspiration for *Barbary Shore,* and displayed increasing obsession with (to quote Vidal) the National Security State, and his ambitions of writing its ultimate history in his CIA opuses *Harlot's Ghost* and (the much better) *Oswald's Tale.*

Of all possible things, theology surfaces in late letters as a constant preoccupation. He fashions his own doctrine and then bobs and dances around it like one of his beloved prizefighters. His fluency is staggering but beguiling. He explains to some recipients his notion that God puts at work certain forces of good and evil in the world, and lets them war with one another. Accordingly, "[H]e is not all-powerful; he exists as a warring element in a divided universe, and we [humankind] are part of—perhaps the most important part of—His great expression, His enormous destiny." He also believed that certain evils of the human heart could "invariably be saved by art."

This certainly was not the case with the aforementioned Abbott. As soon as Abbott was released from prison (with Mailer's help, just as Sartre had helped free Genet), he stabbed to death a waiter in a Greenwich Village restaurant in some dispute over use of the restroom. As J. Robert Lennon says in his admirable preface, Mailer finally recognized the "folly that sinners and criminals could *invariably* be saved by art."

The best letters here have Mailer writing admirably about the process of composition, and of course, with characteristic pugnacity, lighting into his critics. Especially after he learned to box, his desire for physical confrontation became puerile. He describes vanquishment "eating at my heart like a cancer." But the same correspondent could brim with charm and almost unqualified offers of assistance and encouragement. He was enormously generous with money, scowling at critics of the first mega-advances he got from Little, Brown with the exclamation "I have *nine* children." He was a beacon to grieving friends, writers on a bad publishing streak or suffering from block, and spent his "public" time finally in a prolonged presidency of PEN [during the critical Rushdie *fatwa*], steering clear of the former mayoral politics and rescue of felons. Though his writer's crow's nest in Brooklyn Heights was off limits to everyone, his home in Provincetown was virtually a commune. It drove crazy all of his wives save for the last and longest, the very public Norris Church of Little Rock, Arkansas.

Lennon's selection of a thousand letters, from fifty times that number, is nicely balanced between the peaceful and the provocative. He displays, as the critic John Aldridge once described of his work, "the various ways a man may sin in order to be saved." Sticking one's finger into any section of this book yields rich, plentiful passages. A few float on the waters of the drowned. But most fly up, over every dark thing, to join the company of the saved. I last saw him a year before his death, squired along a Beverly Hills street with two canes and his powerful son John Buffalo [full disclosure—John Buffalo was my editor at *High Times*], and he looked happy—writing-happy, fighting-happy. Not ready to give up anything.

Modernist, Downhill Racer

Litterchoor Is My Beat: A Life of James Laughlin
Ian S. MacNiven
New Directions

If you could do anything in life, what would it be? A serious literary novelist? A hockey forward or a tech lord? Maybe you could try to live sideways as one of Jonathan Lethem's flawed superheros, like Vestman or False Dave? Let's put the question differently. If you came into a fortune as a Harvard sophomore and one of the world's greatest poets looked you in the eye and said "Do something *useful*," what would it be?

James Laughlin, heir to the Jones and Laughlin steel fortune, was in Rapallo in the late thirties, having attained an audience with Pound, who called his tutoring of the young poet the "Ezruniversity." The bearded one's "usefulness" advice was taken with the knowledge that virtually none of Pound's friends, save for Hemingway, had steady publishers. James Laughlin came back and, armed with a Buick full of manuscripts and access to a friend's Heidelberg offset press, began the great and famous publishing house of New Directions. William MacNiven's *Litterchoor Is My Beat* follows Laughlin from the silver spoon manor to the garrets of writers the world was ignoring, but in whom he believed with prescient, unerring conviction. What we need now is more Laughlins, with the tiny handful of publishers in the U.S. having fulfilled our worst expectations, owned by less than a handful of conglomerates and basically making major publishing decisions in their marketing departments. 'JL,' as he was known to friends, saved from oblivion those who would never have found a place in that juggernaut—the Oppens and Levertovs and Duncans, the ones whose pavannes and divigations were, again in Pound's words, making it new.

The history of New Directions became the history of Modernism's visibility and influence, its march out of the shadows of

American cultural and public life. Laughlin did not just bring into print Kenneth Patchen, Djuna Barnes, and a whole lot of Lorca. He didn't just take chances on outsiders, but salvaged untouchable works from established figures. Of course he re-issued *The Great Gatsby* when it went out of print. But he also published *The Crack-Up*, mental illness being a subject Scribner felt should remain hidden in the happy family of established authors. It was a move that dazzled even the officious Edmund Wilson, Fitzgerald's old Princeton roommate and a standard bearer of the official canon. The book is small, as thin as the unravelling tapestry it accounts. But its phrases have become indispensable on our tongues, like there being no second acts in American life, or that in the dark night of the soul it is always three o'clock in the morning.

For a number of decades, New Directions had to simply absorb the losses of masterworks guaranteed not to sell: Pound's *Cantos*, the spidery, filamental notebooks of Robert Walser. But by the sixties, a new openness boosted the popularity of poetry to where Levertov and Patchen, as well as Gary Snyder, could have best sellers. The house's first million-copy sale was appropriately that of a similar publisher poet, Lawrence Ferlinghetti's *A Coney Island of the Mind*.

Laughlin's own verse ranged from slim haiku to the mock epic. He seemed to follow the influence of whatever (not always first class) talent he was publishing at the time. If he could be compared to anyone it would be Dr. Williams—a rough-hewn, straight-backed stare at the structure and scales of the everyday marvelous: a bicycle or a pitching wedge, what clotheslines could tell us about perseverance, and chimney smoke about hope, and hope's evanescence. Dr. Williams had told him that "Anything is good material for poetry," and Laughlin agreed.

Pound slashed at the verse Laughlin handed him, so that other editors like Williams and Louis Zukovsky did not have to. MacNiven notes that Laughlin found in Pound not so much his real father who had abandoned him in corporate oblivion, but an "intellectual father, a soul's father." Laughlin didn't swallow, as did many acolytes, everything Pound dished out. To his credit, he vigorously confronted Pound on his anti-semitism and his pathetic fascist sympathies.

In writing his verse, Laughlin would make sure that the length of a following line was within two typewriter spaces of the line preceding it, which he called "typewriter metric," the mechanical space count having an equivalent value as the letters of words. His subjects varied from the Great Depression to magical realism where 19th Century poets showed up on the subway, to the acceptance of the suicide of his son, who stabbed himself numerous times in a bathtub, "Four hours," Laughlin wrote, "just to wipe the blood away."

Other tragedies and shortcomings plagued him: thrice-divorced and with scores of mistresses, his erotic poetry was abundant but received no publishers and little attention when brought out by smaller houses. His family ostracized him—abandoning the family business, a stalwart, shining star in America's manufacturing economy, was unforgivable. He was blind in one eye, but used it effectively in Cyclopian motifs and allegories.

This writer would regard Laughlin's enviable life as a sort of vacation, but the question arises of what *he* regarded as fun, as the experience of "getting away." The answer was skiing. He'd gone to Harvard rather than the other elites who beckoned him, given Cambridge's proximity to New Hampshire's White Mountains. In Europe, slaloming the Alps and Dolomites hooked him completely. His other "doing something *useful*" became ski resorts—not just visiting, but starting new ones. After World War II, he founded with several fellow literary ski bums the Alta Basin resorts in Utah, which made him a fortune New Directions could never provide. It was the source of consternation to his writers, never being able to find him as he disappeared onto the world's most enviable slopes. Williams became furious when his novel, *White Mule,* showed signs of best-sellerdom, and Laughlin, with little office staff to speak of, was in the New Zealand Remarkables and unavailable to order a second printing. Rexroth and Delmore Schwartz had similar experiences, writing letters to the trades and never forgiving him.

He was a poet's poet and a publisher's publisher, and he wrote to his last breath at 83, turning out over 1200 fine poems in the more sedentary (he finally broke his back on an icy slope) last two decades of his life. He approached death with the joyful misanthropy, zaniness and self-deprivation that proves endearing and effective, and is often the closest we can come to wisdom. He embodied Lionel Trilling's notion of the supreme author being first and foremost a vessel of authenticity and sincerity. One of his last poems was "The Junk Collector": discursive, light yet mordant, anticipating the self-consuming, tossed-off conversational strolls of Frank O'Hara and James Schuyler. And it is "typewriter metric" at its brief best, muscular and slim as a whippet:

> what bothers me most about
> the idea of having to die
>
> (sooner or later) is that
> the collection of junk I
>
> have made in my head will
> presumably be dissipated
>
> not that there isn't more
> and better junk in other
>
> heads and always will be but
> I have become so fond of
>
> my own head's collection.

Thank God he didn't go into the steel business, that his head's collection was reflected in the actual cold type of shelves upon shelves of bookstores and libraries. And that his list, without peer, may well be with us, in the words of his first cantankerous teacher, "[T]ill time hath broken/ down all things/ save beauty alone."

A Manual for Cleaning Women

A Manual for Cleaning Women
Lucia Berlin
Farrar, Straus & Giroux, 446 Pages

The stories of Lucia Berlin (how's *that* for a Cold War mother's name?) are utterly raw in their emotion, smarting like scuffed knuckles or strings of firecrackers, each new one snapping with pain in the echo of the one preceding it. The tales are narrated by a seemingly straight, middle-aged mother of four (which L.B. was) who sinks into addiction, petty crime, and unexplainable flight from unseen tormentors in the American Sunbelt of the fifties, sixties and seventies. Their miseries lie open like the viscera first apparent to the surgeon as he opens the wound along his marker. That bright, that perfectly horrific. These are worlds of pain from a narrator slipping into poverty alone in spite of what Phillip Dick called the "Perky-Pat Layouts" of the post-war economic boom, those natural communities of mid-20th-century abundance.

But even as they display true misery, their stylistic delivery is laconic, spare, diffuse. The lines along the page look not so much like locutions as much as mere revenants of sentences. Punctuation is unorthodox and sometimes inconsistent. If Celine were wandering across Tucson's trailer parks instead of war-torn Germany, the layout of the pages would be very similar. As her executor Steve Emerson has written, Berlin avoids the comma that results from a pause that would not be heard in actual speech, or that results in an undesired slowing of any kind. At the same time, the cadences can feel rushed and hectic. She has drawn comparisons with the first-person stories of Denis Johnson's *Jesus's Son*, but the narrator bears the responsibility of her four children seriously, so the vision is not drug-addled or hallucinogenic.

But what amazing stories these are, and how deprived the modern short tale has been by her itinerant, hard-to-find appearances in journals edited by Saul Bellow or the Black Sparrow Press anthologies where they were eventually gathered in the nineties. She has an almost supernatural ability to tell a story from the perspective of the non-literary storytellers she grew up with, filtered through a smugless knowingness and affection for those she describes. Her stories have the illusion of a loose naturalness, but at the same time a solid beginning, middle and end. They open and shut like a music box. Their music is dusty, deludedly hopeful, salving and bandaging the wound like a palimpsest letting the blue smudge of blood show through.

The sixties come more alive here than in anyone's fiction or non-fiction, and that includes Carver, Didion, those who have etched out a branded grit and desperation for what their narrators deliver. There are lots of laundromats and lost TV game shows. In 'Carpe Diem,' the mother telling the story puts us exactly where we need to be, looking through exactly the lens that does it justice:

> So many laundromat attendants I have known, the hovering Charons, making change or who never have change. Now it is fat Ophelia who pronounces No Sweat as No Thwet. Her top plate broke on beef jerky. . . .When she comes down the aisle with a mop everybody moves and moves the baskets too. She is a channel hopper. Just when we've settled in to watch *The Newlywed Game* she'll flick it to *Ryan's Hope*.

The rightness, the click of completeness and the ending *lift* of the trash TV reference are seamless, the sacred stuffed screamingly down into the profane by someone who has come to know too much to be happy. An Elmore Leonard narrator would have no familiarity with Charon, and a Bellow or Martin Amis character wouldn't even know what a laundromat was. This is the kind of incipient enlightenment someone like my own mother underwent when returning to college in the mid-sixties, raising three of us, my sisters and me wondering what she was doing with those SBX-bought Norton Critical Editions.

The sheer messiness of life brims over for narrators who had the glamorous, Jackiesque sheen of the author herself (look at the jacket photo!). She meets other mothers who have descended into parental abnegation and misanthropy, waiting for their issue to become tweens and run away: "The mother. She hated children. I met her once at an airport when all four of my kids were little. She yelled 'Call them off', as if they were a pack of Dobermans." It gets even better when the narrators are kids themselves: "All the clean restrooms were on the other side of the road, on the left side. But Mrs. Snowdon couldn't make left turns . . . It took us about ten blocks of right turns and one-way streets before we got to a restroom . . . I'd already wet my pants by then but didn't tell them, drank from the cool, cool Texaco faucet."

The stories I feel closest to are set in the Oakland-Berkeley flatlands of the seventies. I was an undergraduate then and Berlin, somehow, kept gravitating back to that sun-blasted hodgepodge of students, welfare moms, immigrants and would-be artists of every stripe. (Of course, she was a cocktail waitress somewhere along San Pablo Ave.) She took up nursing ("It's good, you can meet doctors that way. Dying rich men who are patients.") "Emergency Room Notebook, 1977" packs a wallop and draws the Denis Johnson comparisons. Of course, this narrator knows every conceivable variety of overdose: phony, incompetent, sure-to-succeed: "Exam week at Cal. Many suicides, some succeeding, mostly Oriental. Dumbest suicide of the week was Otis. Otis's wife, Lou-Bertha, left him for another man. Otis took two bottles of Sominex, but was wide awake. Peppy, even." Who would call peripheral Asian characters Orientals but someone of that time and place? And not lost on us who watched TV the decade before—Otis was the town drunk in *Mayberry RFD*, who locked *himself* into a jail cell every night for safekeeping.

I have locked myself into this collection, turned the key, and fallen asleep with it every night since the book came out in early August. Scenes will drift into your dreams whether you recognize a reference or not: "It's Marlene the Migraine, an ER habitue. She is so beautiful, young. She stops talking with two Laney College basketball players and stumbles to my desk to go into her act. Her howls are like Ornette Coleman in early 'Lonely Woman' days . . . all I can see is her elegantly manicured hand, extending her Medi-Cal card above the desk."

Berlin finally found a place in Boulder, where the poet Ed Dorn ran creative writing and brought her onto the Colorado faculty and where she still wore her hair—on into the nineties—like Barbara Eden in *I Dream of Jeannie* (did I tell you to look at the jacket photo?). She was the most popular teacher in the English Department's history, though old habits die hard. She complained of the impersonal atmospherics of Colorado liquor stores, "Gigantic, Target-sized nightmares, where you could die from DTs just trying to find the Jim Beam aisle."

She wrote to Emerson from there, dying in the University Hospital, disappearing into the shady pantheon of her characters:

> Bay Area, New York and Mexico City [were the] only places I didn't feel I was an other. I just got back from shopping and everybody kept on saying have a great day now and smiling at my oxygen tank, as if it were a poodle or a child.

She wrote till the end (2004), with even her titles starting to swell and boost with beautiful, colloquial helium: "Let Me See You Smile," "How'd You Get It So Hot?" and my favourite, "So Here It Is Saturday." Her last letter was to August Kleinzahler, the San Francisco poet and discoverer of great, neglected talents like hers: "Augie, so what is marriage anyway? I never figured it out. And now it is death I don't understand."

The Captive Sylph

Shirley Jackson: A Rather Haunted Life
Ruth Franklin
Liveright, 656 pages

Ruth Franklin's masterful, deeply insightful biography lays bare Jackson's buried, tormented life, a mass of often toxic contradictions that make the 'The Lottery's' townspeople both understated and wholly explanatory. The Library of America has re-issued her stories under the sure hand of Joyce Carol Oates, but Jackson needed a Boswell for her odd New England peregrinations, and she has found it in Ruth Franklin.

Franklin has an uncanny ability to put the zoom lens on Jackson's use of place—both terrain and dwellings—as a metaphor for human arrogance and fear (two sides of the same coin). This, for example, from *The Haunting of Hill House*, illustrating as well her complete control of the rhythm and timbre of her sentences and paragraph structures:

> [The house] reared its great head back against the sky without concession to humanity. No live organism can continue for long to exist under conditions of absolute reality; even larks and katydids are supposed, by some, to dream. Hill House, not sane, stood by itself against its hills, holding darkness within; it had stood so for eighty years and might stand for some eighty more. Within, walls continued upright, bricks met neatly, floors were firm, and doors were sensibly shut; silence lay steadily against the wood and stone of Hill House, and whatever walked there, walked alone.

The book posits Jackson as a major artist who arrived at the perfect time to write "the secret history of American women of her era," and most certainly women writers of that time. Her role as an artist more successful than and financially supporting her fellow writer-academic husband adds the toughest of ironies in the mid-Twentieth Century sociology of letters. The better her books sold, the more jealous he became, a jealousy revenging itself in affairs, indifference, and anger at his marginalism and derivativeness.

Jackson wrote in distinct but (again, because of the time) interlocking genres. In her mass-market fiction for mainstream women's publications, the atmospherics were comic and never rose above keeping boisterous kids in the corral. But in her novels and stories, the mood could only be described as American Gothic, where the homemaker was trapped in a claustrophobic prison of maternity and dependency. Soon to follow was Wordsworth's twin cliffs of his own young contemporaries—"despondency and madness."

Jackson had escaped her mother in an early marriage to Stanley Edgar Hyman, a brilliant and contentious Jewish intellectual she met at Syracuse University. But Hyman turned out to be exploitive, bullying, controlling and selfish. He recognized her talent and encouraged her writing—as well he should, since her income kept them going for years—but he also kept her insecure and subordinate by flaunting his affairs with thinner women, pressuring her to write commercially geared stories, saddling her with the sole care of the house and the children (he helpfully bought her a dishwasher to increase her productivity). Jackson accepted his infidelities and his sense of entitlement, and blamed herself for being fat and lazy.

When he got a job as a professor at Bennington, she became a supportive faculty wife and a tireless, inspired hostess for his friends and colleagues. But she felt like an outsider and freak in the small Vermont village where they bought an enormous, ramshackle old house. The racism and anti-Semitism of the conservative community showed up in many of her stories, along with cold mothers, matricidal daughters and vain, cruel husbands.

Behind her cheery masks, Jackson was hiding an angry vengeful self, dreaming of divorce and flight to a place where she could be alone and write. As the pressures of her domestic role and her own work multiplied, as the marriage became unbearable, she became morbidly obese. She was also a heavy smoker, an alcoholic and an addict of amphetamines, tranquilizers and other prescription drugs. In her last months, her agoraphobia became so severe that she was unable to leave her room.

But on and on she wrote, constantly sharpening her hatchet's blade. Drawing on journals, diaries and unpublished fiction, Franklin builds up to an explosive ending, as Jackson recorded lurid nightmares, plotted murderous fantasies and planned her escape to "that great golden world outside" in which she would be independent and free. "Writing is the way out," she told herself in those psychologically tumultuous years. Writing with growing power, discipline and control, she produced her two greatest novels, "The Haunting of Hill House" (1959) and "We Have Always Lived in the Castle." (The former was made into a supremely horrific film.) Franklin shows Jackson as a deeply gifted master of tone and setting, and a prism of the socio-economic trap into which a female author—especially a writing mother—could not help but be snared.

Barque of Hobbes

The North Water
Ian McGuire
Henry Holt, 257 pages

I am not greatly familiar with the literature of the sea. I know my *Moby Dick* and *Billy Budd,* but I have yet to open Patrick O'Brien, Herman Wouk, or those many who ply what—describing this book—Hilary Mantel calls the "[M]asterful reconstruction of a lost aquatic world." Melville's lesser known *Beneto Cereno,* about a slave ship mutiny, and Poe's *Narrative of A. Gordon Pym,* are my strong favorites from a limited diet. As for now, I do not expect to find anything better of this "lost world," and the human heart's darkness that fogs it like a Norse mist, than Ian McGuire's just-released *The North Water.*

Told from the perspective of an Irish surgeon in need of work, it is a tale of a whaling crew in the mid-Nineteenth Century hunting waters off Greenland and its Northwest Baffin Lands. The captain, Brownlee, is an able mariner, but with nefarious insurance schemes up his sleeve. Cavendish is a navigator who is a little more honest, and serves, along with Dr. Sumner, as a mediator between the brutal, enthralling savageries of the heartless seamen. The German Henry Drax, a principal (and quite skilled) harpooner, is something God seems to have forgotten to finish—perhaps out of shame or distaste—when fashioning the most vicious human receptacles of evil. All are British save for Drax and Dr. Sumner, who they at once condescend to and admire for his nationality and his indispensable healing talents.

As in *Billy Budd,* there are mysterious fatalities and misapprehended suspects. A cabin boy examined by Sumner is suspiciously tight-lipped about his savage rape, and when he is later cut to pieces and curled in a pickling barrel, a "nancy boy"—seen often with effeminate shore mates and an imbecilic loner—is interrogated and chained in the hold as the whaler plies north, racing against the dying hunting season that settles into Lancaster Straight.

The style is ravishingly direct, an echo chamber of the world of men confined to a single purpose but in a place that spawns and incubates their incipient brutality. This description of Drax, as he is examined by the doctor for signs of being the rapist:

> His chest is dark-pelted, broad, and stoutly muscular; his belly is proudly bulbous, both his ankles are covered in a checker-work swirl of blue tattoos . . . He is standing fully naked now—thick-limbed, fistic, unashamed. His face is burned brown and his hands are black from toil, but the rest of his skin—where it is visible beneath the mats of dark hair and panoply of tattooing—is a pure pinkish white like the skin of a babe.

McGuire deftly lets the bestial grow and occlude the angelic in the description, passing like a black cloud over the last smooth sands of innocence. McGuire's genius is similar to poets such as Heaney: strange substantives abound, dazzlingly designed for poetic diction, but just inaccessible enough to transcend the imagination's feeble dictionary. The floating world is a linguistic stew of bucket-rinds, hatchway casks, flensings and mottles and cleats and swills. It is the brute music of men, only men, and it has the somnolent drone and clang of the bells of walking oxen.

Once a shootout darkens morale, McGuire has a tendency to tell too much and show too little about the dolorous new atmosphere of the below decks. This is especially unsettling in that the directness of his realism leaves no doubt of implications. It's as if a fat, spidery Henry James walked across the clear, declarative sunlight of a page of Hemingway.

The wheels of justice, the sails of destiny move the cursed crew forward with startling, always plausible narrative mechanics. Civilization, i.e. the port of Hull and its waiting gallows, is like a magnet that pulls, certain and unseen, this band of souls to the sorting-out that awaits them.

There is little wasted here, nearly every page knocking you like the icy plaster of a frozen wave. The inner and outer are melded by narrative tension—its tightening and loosening tracing the interior storms of desperate men, thrown toward doom with something like a blasting, propulsive lightning. It is as if Hardy, with his "personality of landscape," had written a sea novel. The passive surgeon is the perfect all-seeing, self-doubting eye that keeps the drifting vessel barely keeled. Until it's not. The question here is never whether one will survive, but only for how long. It won't make you want to be a whaler, or even to ever go to sea. But you will wait on the foredeck like a spotter for this writer's next burst of soaring, sky-splitting craftsmanship.

Blood Soaked Plain

Killers of the Flower Moon
David Grann
Doubleday, 336 pages

David Grann has a way with creating razor-keen suspense out of already tension-filled historical narratives. *Killers of the Flower Moon* brings salient illustration to a centuries-old story that resonates even now. Just as he took us through struggles to find a lost city on the Amazon—the abject misery and hopelessness of the journey—he channels his outrage into an insistence that the oppressed Native Americans here have a voice, albeit, for some of them, from beyond the grave. In this new powerhouse, he brings us back to our own country, the southern Great Plains, where a series of calculated, shocking murders were disguised behind an altruistic movement of assistance, truly a wolf in sheep's clothing.

The "benevolent plan" of the Interior Department and the cavalry was to relocate the Osage Indian tribes from their ancillary lands in Kansas, which they in turn had been pushed to only a few decades earlier. The new location in Oklahoma was arid and rocky, and had little planting soil and zero ground cover. Bison had populated the crossings, but other Plains Indian tribes had depleted the herds, and the new transplants—robbed of their all-purpose sustenance—began suffering from malnutrition and diet depletion illnesses.

But there were riches under the land. Prospectors hand dropped wells and found supplies of oil that were rivalling those that had caused the Texas boom. At first the prospectors treated the tribe honorably, cutting them into leases and royalties. It enabled the tribal leaders to build spacious cabins in an otherwise hostile dust bowl. They lived well, hiring other rival tribes as house servants and rig and deerick workers. These new-found Oklahoma Osage suddenly became one of the wealthiest group of fin-de-siècle Americans.

But when the oil money truly became an investment worthy staple, the government's paternalism devolved into vicious ripostes to anyone who resisted them. They decided the Indians simply could not manage their own wealth or oversee the lease areas and equipment. What the ground had given them, quite by happenstance, the white man was determined to fleece them of. White guardians were assigned, "authorizing and overseeing all of their spending, down to the toothpaste they purchased at the corner store, Grann writes. "The guardians were usually drawn from the ranks of the most prominent citizens in [Osage] County."

The guardians skimmed millions of dollars from the tribe. The Gray Horse, a company town with merchants of the same name, increased prices for the Indians, but not their overseers. As the new century progressed, in a series of slow-moving, terribly efficient massacres, the tribe began dying in just such a manner that observers called it a Siege of Terror. Everything began happening all at once, and every episode was got more and more horrific.

Grann's laboratory specimen of white oppression is Mollie Burkhart, an Osage squaw who had become the wife of a white man. Several of Mollie's siblings suddenly died of a mysterious "wasting illness." Another sister, Anna, was dispatched, execution style by a white merchant with a pearl handled revolver. Then the mother came down with the same wasting illness. Finally, Mollie herself became deathly ill. Grann writes: "She barricaded herself in dread, knowing that she was the likely next target in the apparent plot to eliminate the entire family."

Though no one was able to solve the murders—evidence was spoliated and witnesses vanished—the case was assigned to the young J. Edgar Hoover, looking to build the profile of his young Federal Bureau of Investigation in Washington. It was one of Hoover's best early pieces of work, rivalling that of the Dillinger assassination and the infiltration of the Chicago, Detroit and Cleveland mafias.

But the Texas Ranger that Hoover deputized as an FBI regular,

Tom White, had to work through a labyrinth of double and triple agents, and sheer decoy witnesses set up in a puzzle palace managed by a single, crafty mastermind. This Great Oz of Duplicity was discovered only after near-genius detective work, and only after White had become an arranger—indeed a connoisseur—of plots and false trails and investigatory legerdemain himself.

Grann has built a book (it is truly a narrative edifice) that will stand beside classics of Indian oppression like *Bury My Heart At Wounded Knee*, Peter Mathiessen's *In The Spirit of Crazy Horse*, and Peter Cozzens's *The Earth Is Weeping*.

Killers of the Flower Moon belongs on the shelf of anyone interested in America's long war against the people who first inhabited its land, gave it a fabric of glorious and mystical traditions, and eventually were killed off or at best disenfranchised in slow deracination. It reads like a thriller, its pages flying away like Osage ponies running over the doomed hills.

Spies and Prophets

The Road Not Taken:
Edward Lansdale and the American Tragedy in Vietnam
Max Boot
Liveright, 338 Pages

We are used to the political configuration of a country starting from the bottom up. This is what the Framers saw as the task of representative democracy. Obviously, Americans like to see a similar pattern in other countries. Call it nation-building or spheres of influence, we measure the legitimacy of a government by how the least among them, the people, are treated.

But what if we wish to influence another country's political direction, especially if war has appeared there as an unavoidable stepping stone? Should it be the "top down" approach of rarefied diplomacy, neutrality, something in between? Edward Lansdale had a unique, well-advised answer. He called it "civic action," denoting the practice of giving a rural population a stake in an insurgency so that we—the influencers—appear to be something other than the enemy.

As Max Boot demonstrates in his *The Road Not Taken,* Lansdale was a brilliant, innovative stealth aviator in the OSS, the precursor to the modern CIA. After rising to major general in his WW II exploits, Lansdale first tried civic action while advising the Philippine government during a Marxist rebellion in the early fifties. The Filipino commanders were "shooting through two peasants" to hit the communist guerilla standing behind them. Moving in (literally, roommates) with the defense minister, Roman Magsaysay, Lansdale taught him that Mao Zedong gave the best advice on winning over an oppressed population—"keep the closest possible relations with the common people." Mostly this meant avoiding ambushes and indiscriminate airstrikes, which multiply civilian casualties and frighten an already benighted people. Lansdale gave primitive cameras to Filipino soldiers, so they kept accurate casualty figures and avoided civilian victims. This grass roots approach to body counts was successful, and avoided the top down misrepresentations later given for that phenomena, which came to be known as the order of battle. (Vietnam Commanding General William Westmoreland notoriously thought higher North Vietnamese casualties were the only requirement for winning the "war of attrition" in that country. In fact, the opposite was taking place—less North Vietnamese were dying, American casualties were muted and then falsified, and by the time of Hue in 1968 the attrition myth had been flipped on its head as the U.S. began, by any intelligent estimation, to lose the war.)

Rewind to Lansdale's arrival in Vietnam, circa 1954. He told American Ambassador Lawton Collins to seize control of rural areas of the south being abandoned by the communist Vietminh, who had defeated the French at Dien Bien Phu. Collins and his generals would not listen to their old OSS maverick, whose approach focused on protecting and educating—via a non-communist Maoism—the local village leaders and militia commanders. He not only befriended them, but also cozied up to Prime Minister Ngo Dinh Diem, who he would try to educate in the constantly shifting vicissitudes of guerilla warfare. Diem had too much baggage and too strange a family for Lansdale's former employer, the CIA, to abide, and was viewed as weak against the rising popular front of the Vietcong. Lansdale's influence hit low tide in the 1963 coup of Diem and his relatives, its blood-spatter rife with CIA fingerprints. (This writer once listened to a rare White House tape of JFK expressing into a dictaphone his "condolences to the Diem family," an odd sentiment in light of their slaughter on his indirect orders.)

Ironically, Lansdale's civic action approach showed signs of success in a strategic-hamlet program, winning over rural peasants by reducing communist infiltration through pacified or "protected" communities. But it was too little, too late. Lansdale came back to Washington, confronting Robert MacNamara, whose notion of the order of battle, wooden and outdated and as mathematical as Westmoreland's, showed Lansdale that the "best and the brightest" were in fact working in paradigms of dangerous ignorance.

Lansdale ended his Vietnam involvement in 1968, just as black pajama-clad Viet Cong rang in the lunar new year with the Tet offensive, blasting their way over the walls of the Hue Citadel and, for good measure, the U.S. Embassy. In hindsight, LBJ's national security advisor Walt Rostow commented that Lansdale's belated, ignored approach of "civic action" exhibited a "kind of last chance" to avoid the fragmentation and collapse of American military efforts.

Boot's book is ripe with the panache and swagger that made Lansdale so engaging. Dashing as a movie star, he cultivated, right down to the moustache, his resemblance to Clark Gable. He loved fast cars, planes, speedboats and women, and may have been the closest thing we ever had to a real-life James Bond. The longstanding rumor that Graham Greene used him as the template for his Indochina masterpiece, *The Quiet American*, is probably false. Greene was in Vietnam in 1952, with Lansdale not "officially" arriving until 1954; Lansdale claims he met the British novelist, who denied ever running across the colonel. Lansdale is probably the prototype for Burdick and Lederer's *The Ugly American*, a book far inferior to Greene's and often confused with it. This is especially so given its portrayal of the Lansdale figure, Col. Edwin Barnum, as boorish, egotistical and cruel. Lansdale was, in fact, and as Frances Fitzgerald wrote in *Fire in The Lake*, a man "of artless sincerity, who never thought in terms of systems or larger social forces." He believed in insurgents as people and as embodying the peoples' will, which had to be maneuvered constantly upward and often (Mao again) through the barrel of a gun.

The Mind Makes Up the World

From Bacteria to Bach & Back:
The Evolution of Minds
Daniel C. Dennett
Norton, 476 Pages

In his mid-career books like *Brainchildren* and *Consciousness Explained,* the philosopher and neuroscientist Daniel Dennett seemed hell bent on showing how a comprehending mind could be built from a mindless process of natural selection. How this happens has perplexed philosophers since Aristotle, who blew Aeolian wind into the skull, and Descartes, who proved the irreducibility of consciousness but fobbed the leap from matter to thought back to his Catholic God. And not a lot of progress has been made since then—the same problem of what a mind *in fact is* has perplexed the heaviest hitters like Kant, Hume and Wittgenstein, and even though our understanding of the inner workings of proteins, neurons and DNA is more profoundly realized than ever before, the matter of how our minds came to be by arising out of them has largely remained a mystery.

In examining the building blocks of consciousness, Dennett starts with billions of years of what he calls "irreplaceable design work," performed not by God but by natural selection. Natural selection takes the crude functions that exist in sentient but non self-conscious animals and builds on them. The functional components from which selfhood develops appear to slowly grow through evolution in what he calls a "sort of" form. An example is free will, at least as it is currently understood. The amygdala, the part of the brain that registers fear, may not have true autonomy. In fact, it is something of an industrial robot of the mind, a little like the spleen is to the dead blood cells of the body. But as eons went on, its power augmented to where it enabled the mind to sense and then avoid danger. In this manner, the path of automatic, instinctual fear that we see in almost any animal led, according to Dennett, from determinism to free will: "A whole can be freer," he writes, "than the sum of its parts." What began as a reflexive protection impulse evolved into a process of assessing, gauging, choosing the path of least danger to the knowing subject.

The approach has been, of all the schools of the philosophy of mind, given the rough label of "functionalism." The workings of neurons and cognitive systems simply turn richer and more deft in their functioning. Suddenly impulse and instinct give way to the enormous qualitative leap into consciousness. The physical remains a physical process—there is none of Ryle's 'ghost in the machine'—but something rises up in the cranial vault that is ghostly, spectral, seemingly untraceable to anything as crude as a physical process. The narrative arc of functionalism is easy to follow, well argued, but at least for *this* philosopher of mind, has always seemed to leave something out. In the formulation of one of Dennett's critics, physicalist hypotheses skip over the process by which "the water of the brain becomes the wine of consciousness."

Accordingly, one of the obsessive, briny focuses of this book is Dennett's war with David Chalmers, another big-brained, furious debater on the origins and ontology of consciousness, whose basic approach to things is called "instrumentalism." (Their debates were profiled brilliantly in a New Yorker article by Joshua Rothman.) He is one of the critics who see Dennett by-passing the challenging issue of getting from brain data to the trick of the brain that seems too dazzling to be of common, merely human origin. Dennett feels that all one has to do is to explain the functions, and that there does not have to be a hard boundary between first-person experience and third-person explanations. They would simply be two different perspectives on the same phenomena. Take the two perspectives on a sugar cube—the description of a sugar molecule and the taste of sweetness: "From the outside, it looks like neurons; from the inside it feels like consciousness."

This will not do for Chalmers, who feels that cataloguing the third person data could not explain the existence of a first person point of view. Dennett demands that Chalmers formulate an experiment that would at least make the notion of "first-person data" or "experiences" provable or non-provable. Chalmers so far hasn't come up with same. Chalmers is more open to odd epistemologies in his search for what it means to think. He has lately explored arguments in favor of "panpsychism," the idea that consciousness might be "a fundamental property of the universe," upon which the brain somehow draws." This is similar to William James's neutral monism, which has a tidy explanatory power. Cut one way, the history of the world is simply the history of objective physical objects; cut another way, it is the psychological history of human beings.

All of this and more in the ever-shifting world of logico-analytic philosophy is on display here by one of our liveliest and most readable philosophers. Dennett's appreciation of the artistic consciousness is unique, attractive, and shows that he looks as much for sparkle and verve in the world than the question of what about it makes philosophical sense.

A Pugilist at the Riots: Mailer's Sixties

Four Books of the Sixties
Norman Mailer
Library of America, 879 Pages

Mailer was a better journalist than fiction writer. Between *The Naked and the Dead* (1946) and his brilliant *The Executioner's Song* (1979), few of his novels matched his long essays on contemporary culture, social affairs, film, and other writers. This new volume from the LOA shows Mailer as really one of the inventors—along with Tom Wolfe, John Sack, Gay Talese and a few others—of what came to be called the New Journalism. It was a genre in which the old self-effacement of the journalist was largely scuttled, and the narrator's personality entered with a vengeance and vigor that made him a character as worthy (usually) of our concern as any of his subjects. With two books, the case can be made that the Sixties really wouldn't have been the Sixties, as we know it, without Mailer's reportage.

The first book was *The Armies of the Night*, his account of the 1967 anti-war march on the Pentagon, which he attended along with fellow literary figures like Robert Lowell and Allen Ginsberg. Sub-titled 'History as a Novel; the Novel as History,' Mailer himself appears as the narrator Aquarius, fitting the age and painting street scenes with an unforgiving, dazzling pen. He follows the marchers until he, along with Lowell, Ginsberg, Dave Dellinger and others, are forced by organizers to essentially lead the charge, linking arms in the style of the civil rights marches.

Mailer's descriptive powers are unmatchable when applied to the canvas of real life, in a way he was never able to equal in the largely voice-driven novels. Mailer was arrested at the Pentagon event, consistent with his long fascination with incarceration as a subject and metaphor. Scenes of blocked bridges, tear gas clouds wafting over the Potomac and into monuments, and his sketches of oddball officials like Sen. Fulbright and the D.C. police chief all contain Chekhovian touches of the slightest minutiae—the way hair and fingernails were trimmed, the tone of sloganning voices and echoing police orders, the sleeping tent-armies of demonstrators lining the river like the pre-dawn Shakespeare's Agincourt Battle in Henry V. Willie Morris set aside an entire issue of *Harpers* to contain all 50,000 words, and it was an overnight, justified literary sensation that garnered him the 1969 National Book Award.

The Democratic National Convention in August 1968 was hot on the heels of the Pentagon book, and Morris again signed up Mailer to cover what would become *Miami and the Siege of Chicago*. *Esquire's* Harold Hayes had commissioned Mailer to cover both the 1960 and 1964 Democratic Conventions, and with Mailer's dance card taken, Hayes assigned Terry Southern, Jean Genet, and William S. Burroughs to cover the Chicago juggernaut. These three musketeers—a shy, drunk pornographer, a convict, and a junkie—all had prodigious, hallucinatory perspectives on the coming event, but they weren't the most reliable of narrators. (Hayes thus sent a young editor, John Berendt [the later author of *Midnight In The Garden of Good and Evil*] to herd these cats and translate Genet's French.) Burroughs provided appropriately dystopic coverage, and probably the best writer among them—Genet—had such a sadomasochistic twist to his homosexuality that he began professing desire for many of the Chicago police who famously bludgeoned demonstrators. ("Their blue helmets make me think they are angels descended from heaven").

Much of Mailer's *Siege of Chicago,* for my money one of the greatest pieces of post-War 20th century journalism, is nothing more than a domestic version of his war reportage. There were ghastly casualties in Chicago, but no one was killed. Mailer observes, from a penthouse in the Conrad Hilton on Grant Park, the CPD's truly savage charges against the marchers. Helmeted officers pushed scores of demonstrators through the first floor's plate glass window, prompting outcries from McCarthy and Senator Abe Ribicoff on the convention floor. Mailer frets about going down to the street, fearing that another jail stint would keep him from wiring his copy to Morris at *Harper's*. As an alternative, he headed back toward the hall and tried to organize two hundred delegates to march alongside the demonstrators. This was not successful, and soon delegates were nursing broken noses and head gashes. Sneaking away, Mailer meets the *Post's* Pete Hamill for drinks, getting so plastered that the two of them, goading national guardsmen in a razor-wired jeep, almost get arrested after all. Mailer is still Aquarius, the peace-loving autodidact who also aches for the *mano a mano*—this time with law enforcement—that landed him in the D.C. tank for a night.

Mailer weaves in the powerful and contemporary televised debates that enveloped these demonstrations, fueling their descent into violence. The most famously visible was Mayor Daley answering Ribicoff's criticisms of the cops, calling the senator a "Jew bastard" and inviting him to have carnal relations with himself. On ABC, two of Mailer's sparring partners, William Buckley and Gore Vidal, insulted one another to the point of fisticuffs, which Mailer the boxer would have welcomed. But there were Yippies to interview, armored jeeps to chase down, tear gas to wash out of his hair.

Mailer's most powerful portraits are of the candidates themselves, Nixon and the Minneapolis "drugstore liberal" Humphrey, champion of Daley and the older unions and ward bosses, but carrying the inherited Vietnam War on his back like a poor, plodding plough horse. In this passage from the Nixon/Miami segment, how deftly the author vivisects the psyches of the candidate's "great, Silent Majority of Americans," without condescension or stereotyping:

> There was no line like the wealthy Republicans at the Gala, this was more a pilgrimage of minor delegates, sometimes not even known in their own small city, a parade of wives and children and men who owned hardware stores or were druggists . . . a widow on a tidy income, her minister and fellow-delegate, minor executives from minor corporations . . . editor of a small town newspaper, professors from Baptist teachers' colleges, a high school librarian, a young political aspirant and young salesman—the stable and the established, the middle-aged and the old, a sprinkling of the young, the small towns and the quiet respectable cities

of the Midwest and the far West and the border states were out to pay homage to . . . the representative of their conservative orderly heart, and it was obvious they admired him in a way too deep for applause . . . moving forward in circumscribed steps.

And there is poetry and rhapsody in Mailer's descriptions, linking the countries' metropolises like bangles on a long-worn, grubby bracelet that he shakes, bauble by bauble, metaphor by metaphor, until he comes down to the anthemic embrace of the City that Works:

> Chicago is the great American city. New York is one of the capitals of the world and Los Angeles is a constellation of plastic, San Francisco is a lady, Boston has become Urban Renewal. Philadelphia and Baltimore and Washington wink like dull diamonds in the smog of Eastern Megalopolis, and New Orleans is unremarkable past the French Quarter. Detroit is a one-trade town and Pittsburgh has lost its golden triangle. St Louis has become the golden arch of the corporation, and nights in Kansas City close early. The oil depletion allowance makes Houston and Dallas naught but checkerboards for this sort of game. But Chicago is a great American city. Perhaps it is the last of the great American cities.

Mailer took the "tough, spare, particularly American" form of writing Hemingway had handed him, applying that palette to an incredibly divided, uncharacteristically politicized population (sound familiar?). His jabs and left hooks fly like lightning as he punches every other working reporter out of the ring.

Where the Days Go

The Order of Time
Carlo Rovelli
Riverhead, 239 pages

What is time? Is it something real, or is it simply part of our human perceptual framework, one of the categories of pure understanding Kant posited in the Eighteenth Century? Those categories, he believed, require that episodic actions be sequenced out and not experienced in a simultaneous mush. Is time something that actually exists "out there" or is it a useful measurement of change, with no actuality in and of itself? Carlo Rovelli is one of those scientists and scientific writers (he is a quantum physicist) who can take the most abstruse concepts and add to them the spark and music of poetry, all of it somehow comprehensible and delightful.

Newton thought time an absolute concept, that there was an "absolute time" ticking relentlessly across the universe. It kept ticking even if there were no objects in space, no human subjects to experience it—as Heidegger famously did—as "the essence of boredom." This is, indeed, how most of us give time its "felt life." It is its main feature as a phenomenon if we stop to think about it.

Rovelli also considers Aristotle's belief that "time" is something utilized by the brain for different purposes. It doesn't exist "out there" like air or the oceans. It is simply a "measurement of change." If nothing continued to change, the Athenian would have it, time would for all practical purposes be non-existent. Again, Newton would disagree—if the universe was somehow frozen, like in the famous Ed Wynn 'Twilight Zone' episode, time would tick on at different speeds depending upon the influences of light and gravitation, and what then were perceived of yet not named as the "weak' and "strong" forces.

Einstein, the third of Rovelli's "Great Three Dancers" (like something out of Hindu myth) said both Aristotle *and* Newton were correct. Aristotle correctly noted that time had a "flow," what the logician (and metaphysician) Quine called "a river process," that made sense only in relation to a before and after. And Einstein also saw Newton's "absolute time" as having a plausible existence—but only as a special case of Einstein's relativity-based "spacetime" theory of gravity, in which space and time were simply two sides of the same barely comprehensible coin.

Einstein thought of gravitation as the universe's most important force, as a field, a sort of sheet upon which spheres like the sun and earth moved, staying out of one anothers' way by bending time down to a slower process than if it had never been gravitated. Rovelli feels that reality is really just a complex series of events on which we cast, like shadows, our experiential episodes—past, present, and future. The universe obeys the laws of quantum mechanics and Newton's thermodynamics, out of which time emerges from the gravitational field. Its different "speeds," to risk making the argument circular, accelerate or affect "drag" depending upon its gravitational position and purposes at any one time, and for many different observers and sets of instrumentation.

The way this works is that events (the given time and location at which something might happen), rather than particles or waves, are the basic constituents of the world. Physics's job is to describe the inter-event relationships as though describing a weather storm—"[A] storm is not a thing, but a collection of occurrences." From our perspective, each of those event/occurrences looks like the interaction of particles at a particular position and time; this is fine so long as we realize time and space are not some framework containing the events, but really just a "web" of their interactions and the force of causality between them. Rovelli concludes:

> There is no single time: there is a different duration for every trajectory, and time passes at different rhythms according to space and speed . . . . the substratum that determines the duration of time is not an independent entity different from others that make up the world. It is an aspect

of a dynamic field. It jumps, fluctuates, materializes only by interacting, and is not to be found a minimum scale...

The third segment of the book delves into the theory of knowledge and focuses on how certain illusions arise from the universe's scaffolding of quantum mechanics, thermodynamics, electromagnetism, and other "fields" similar to that of the "sheet" of gravitation. Our perception of time's flow (he quotes Rilke's greatest verses on this) depends on our inability as knowing subjects to comprehend the world in all its detail. Quantum uncertainty means we cannot know the positions and speeds of all the universe's particles in one conceptual glance. If we could, there would be no entropy, no "unravelling" of time, no step into the waterflow of the "river process." His explanation of this occurrence cluster and how we cannot step back from it enabled him to originate this 'thermal time hypothesis' and quantum gravity looping with the French mathematician Alain Coines.

The book is elegantly translated from the Italian by Erica Segre and Simon Carnell. It is colored by not only Rilke snippets but by an ode (starting each chapter) from the last great Latin poet Horace, ever transfixed by the faster passage of time he experienced on his estate after contemptuously leaving Roman politics. The book explores questions very much alive and very much contested in quantum physics. The other, less testable and more bizarre comprehensive picture of physics is that of string theory, which gets more press than Rovelli's loop quantum gravity simply by virtue of its oddness and sci-fi features like parallel universes.

This writer, trained in philosophy, is astonished at how well Rovelli grasps many concepts in the philosophy of mind and language, disciplines so essential for the conceptualization of physics. He marvelously picks apart Hilary Putnam's view that Einstein's simultaneity allows for future events to exist presently in Putnam's "Twin Earth" epistemological games. Putnam has it that if the earth and (what he calls in his papers) Twin Earth are approaching each other, an event A is simultaneous with an event B on Twin Earth, which in turn is simultaneous (for those of us on Twin Earth) to an event C back on earth, that *is in the future of A*. Putnam mistakenly views "being simultaneous" as "being real now" and deduces that this has to mean the future event C is presently real. The error is to see Einstein's simultaneity as having an ontological value, whereas it is only a definitional convenience that reduces a relativistic notion to a non-relativistic notion through an approximation process. (Non-relativistic, or purely philosophical simultaneity, is a reflexive and transitive process, where Einstein's is purely mathematical and explanatory—the two have no ontological relation.) As Wittgenstein would say, with his customary, guileless beauty, "The only correct answer is that the question makes no sense."

Once in a great while a science book comes along that is so much more. Lewis Thomas's *Lives of a Cell* and Greene's *The Elegant Universe* are examples, as well as the works of the late Steven Hawking. Rovelli's book is one of those. They occupy a very narrow shelf on which this one belongs.

The Shadow in the Garden

The Shadow in the Garden: A Biographer's Tale
James Atlas
Pantheon, 400 pages

In this guidebook for the derivative artist known as the biographer, the esteemed polymath James Atlas does not brook idols easily. He is fair, but is severe about social critic Dwight Macdonald, who spent many hours editing Atlas' fine life of Delmore Schwartz. Atlas gives many examples and creates little bubbles of mini-bios as he goes. An envious blowhard, Macdonald exclaimed that "Hemingway couldn't write" and that the learned man-of-letters Edmund Wilson was interested only in "showing off how much he's read." Atlas later notes that Wilson "never showed off his vast erudition." Finally, Atlas found the "fierce, irascible, antagonistic" Macdonald intolerably oppressive.

Atlas' portraits of Alfred Kazin and Richard Ellmann are accurate. Kazin, whom Schwartz called "a serious menace to criticism," was venomous, retributive and bitter. Ellmann, whose life of James Joyce is the greatest modern biography, was brilliant and kind. But in a fit of pique Atlas misjudges John Bayley, who refused to tutor him at Oxford. Bayley was an exceptionally stimulating lecturer and teacher. His memoir of his wife Iris Murdoch descending into the darkness of Alzheimer's, "Elegy for Iris" is not "pitiless," as Atlas asserts, but self-sacrificial and sympathetic.

The Shadow in the Garden contains beautiful, forceful writing but does not adhere to a traditional narrative structure. Atlas follows chronology, even if he returns to the same subjects in different chapters and drops derivative sketches of Greek and Roman historians where appropriate. The book is abundant with needed footnotes, and in these Atlas is also generous. But sometimes it seems as if the reader must jump between parallel texts. It's a good thing Atlas didn't touch upon the philosopher Karl Popper, whose footnotes often swallow the text like Ouroboros devouring its tail.

Atlas describes following the author's trajectory from birthplace through foreign travels to the grave ("Death," Atlas sadly observes, "is the biographer's worst enemy"), studying unpublished letters and manuscripts in widely scattered archives, searching for school records, finding family and friends to interview, and discovering that famous older people are often quite lonely.

During interviews with Bellow, Atlas did not use a tape recorder. Bellow learned to draw people out and remain silent, to take notes while eating and (sometimes) getting drunk, adding to his notes immediately after leaving. He refereed fights, often about money, between the children of different wives. Responses from valuable sources ranged from "I curse the day you ever heard my name," to when Bellow tried to extract a privately owned manuscript by Somerset Maugham to "I've been waiting all my life for you to come" from the daughter of Robert Frost's lover.

But there's no need, as Atlas suggests, to "get it all in." Not everything matters, and you don't have to scrutinize "every electric bill, every grocery list, every torn envelope." Biographers should remain an unobtrusive presence, concentrate on the reader's interest rather than their own obsessions, and focus not on the facts of the live but on what these facts *mean*.

Atlas, who can't quite break free from his subject, ends his book with a description of his own life that inadvertently recalls the sad end of Schwartz. The writer took out his garbage, suffered a heart attack and died in the elevator of a seedy Times Square hotel. Atlas, in a burst of welcome empathy with his subject, races his trash out to the hall drop shaft and then races back before anything terrible can happen.

Audacity and Distraction: Two Very Young Critics

American Audacities
William Giraldi
Liveright, 462 pages

Attention
Joshua Cohen
Random House, 560 pages

Though there is abundant talent floating about in fiction, poetry, and memoir, few realize how true this also is of literary criticism. It may be that the latter is a form merely brushed past in most serious readers' reading, giving rise to the notion that the literary critic slogs on at the peripheries of literature, shouting comments in from time to time, but not building any kind of ouvre of her own as an independent practitioner of craft. Even those who see book essays as a genre unto itself, building, through consolidating progress, into a body of work either within or outside a tradition, few seem to pick up collections of criticism as did the literati of past decades. There were days when a volume of critical essays by T.S. Eliot, F.O. Mathiessen or Edmund Wilson would be anticipated like a new novel. Before we say "no more," consider what follows.

Two young critics have arrived who recognize and remind us that the critical perspective is also an invaluable second set of tracks in the literary train yard, a *ferrocarril*, that performs the mirror-work of flashing back the narrative dialogue of literature, in turn a mirror—in Stendahl's phrase—of nature and of the figures of life. William Giraldi's *American Audacities* is a rich mine of splendid essays, its sections broken down into literature's two great forces of anxieties (rebellions) and influence. Joshua Cohen's critical pieces in the longer, baggier *Attention,* have less of an organizing principle than *Audacities*, though his doorstop of a tome is not without its gleaming interstitching of insights and vibrant asides.

First to Giraldi [full disclosure: Billy Giraldi and I have been acquaintances and fellow editors for about twenty years; I have published his stories in a quarterly I edit]. Giraldi correctly sees himself as part of a tradition. In this way he resembles Harold Bloom, Edmund Wilson and his beloved Lionel Trilling, critics who straddled the mid 20th century like colossi, and who Giraldi invites us to delight in and learn from. Giraldi—also a fine novelist/story writer and spot-on memoirist of his family's Italian macho culture in *The Hero's Body*—quotes Stanley Hyman on Trilling in a way that is equally applicable to himself. "A critic is someone practicing something 'primary and autonomous, something that is 'literature itself.'" "Our world," Hyman wrote, "is a multiverse and complex one, and our criticism reflects that; unless the critic's equipment is similarly multiverse and complex, he will be turned away at the door of literature."

Giraldi is at his best when examining intra-traditions of prose authors like the 'Catholic Writers' who emerged in the middle of the last century. Of Flannery O'Connor, he marvelously examines her puzzling characters as dispensing with "the dubiety of faith," a literary population very old-fashioned in having "things figured out for themselves and [not much bothering with] the nuisance of self-doubt." The short story master O'Connor, he rightly notes, sees that kind of diffidence as leading to the greatest Catholic sin of despair, a condition more novelistic and perilous, and explored by the (Catholic) long-formists like Graham Greene and Walker Percy. In her short, eccentric, hugely influential tales, O'Connor's freakish characters try to attain the two incompatibles of "Christian judgment and grace from God." Giraldi is astute on how O'Connor could be a practicing Thomist and yet realize "all is chaos in search of grace, all is enigma unveiled but unresolved, and no credo is the clear victor." She steers clear of past Catholic novelists closing their artisans' eyes and adopting a doctrinal vision, resulting in "[A]nother addition to that large body of pious trash for which we have long been famous."

Giraldi compares O'Connor with a modern master of spiritually lost characters, the Denis Johnson of *Jesus' Son*. Based on my earlier reading of reviews of Giraldi's book, I was ready for a point-counterpoint send-up of the more modern author, whose influence can sometimes seem outsized. But Giraldi provides probably the best assessment ever written of Johnson's precarious collection, and its magnetizing influence on younger writers. He contrasts Johnson with his flabby, morally vacuous predecessors like the Bret Easton Ellis of *Less Than Zero*, and we get passages as graceful and adept as Giraldi's prose fiction:

> Johnson's narrator is part messiah because he's been charged with salvaging himself from devils most of us will never be sunk enough to know. We go to *Jesus' Son* precisely because in its most sublime moments it reveals to us a condition both lesser and greater than human. We go to it for its flawlessness of aesthetic form, its transformative spiritual vision, the lovely stab of its humanity, and the beauty, the deathless beauty, of sentences that sing of possible bliss.

I'll take riffs like that over the paragraphs of almost any novel one picks up these days. Going back to the Catholic writers, Giraldi spots the intrinsic embodiment of doctrine within human behavior that has been the success ingredient of most "religious" writing since Dante, where "[T]he religious elements aren't obnoxiously grafted onto the narrative but emerge intrinsically from the circumstances of the characters." Well said. Like the Dr. Williams of "No ideas but in things," Giraldi, adroitly and with much-needed topicality, notes that no faith goes any further than any one believer's actions here on the postlapsarian earth. Giraldi, obviously raised as a Catholic, echoes Walker Percy in that faith's particularly felicitous use by the novelist, giving any prose writer "that dramatic itch for sin, for judgment and damnation, for the rottenness of the world and the holy in us all."

Joshua Cohen has dazzled American readers with post-modern fiction opuses like *The Book of Numbers* and the more accessible *Witz*. His essays, as opposed to Giraldi's, are more wide-ranging than just literature, and have their particular obsessions, most of them perfectly timely and almost irritably recognizable. How deeply examined and yet how purely odd is his 'On Distraction,' which starts with the sentence (he was born in 1980) "[I]f anything distinguishes my generation of American writers, it's that everyone in my generation became a writer simply through the act of going online." He observes that the sheer quantity of information bestowed by living within a digital universe (he brilliantly chooses major evening news items of Sept. 10, 2001) renders us "incapable of absorbing [everything that] was happening; we are only capable of reacting to it." And given the near impossibility of absorbing that the next day's explosions of jet fuel across two buildings could melt that grade and tonnage of steel, 9/11 had to be "an inside job" (by Israelis? By Saudis in collusion with the Bush administration?), which in turn ushered in the new, frightening violence being done to facticity.

The new war on news and facts finds fertile ground in Cohen's dizzying abundance of digital information, which leads its subscribers to a "constant state of distraction." Distraction relieves the mind of the hard work of putting facts together into a meaningful pattern. So vast segments of the population accede to not only "news" commentators doing the meaning extrication, but, more dangerously, their deciding what did and did not take place—what is there in the first place to apply meaning to. (Cohen's subtitle to the collection is 'Dispatches from a Land of Distraction.') The digital age's mass mental confusion can result in comic superficialities, like Trump's lies about, *inter alia,* the size of his inaugural crowd and his intention to say "wouldn't" rather than "would" at the Helsinki debasement summit. But taken to its extreme it can numb us to events to which outrage and dismay are the only human, only responsible reactions (the primary school shootings at Sandy Hook in 2012), leading to the appropriately responsible societal improvements.

Cohen is better at these essays on social affairs, since his literary stabbings seem very much axe-grindings. In examining current events, Cohen becomes an admirably Tom Paine type polemicist. "When our media fill the air with trashy breaking updates, when our elected officials lie, what they're doing is creating a *distraction* so as to command our attention for their profit, or steer our scrutiny away from the more dire of their crimes," he writes.

> And in turn, when we feel overcome by this assault, when the sheer variety of its indecency has worn us into boredom, we withdraw and *distract ourselves*. And so what had been a technique for subduing the vulnerable is still with us, but now it's also become the technique by which we subdue our intelligence . . .stuck between the external forces that disempower and control us, and our own internal drives to preserve, protect and defend our hearts and minds. In my opinion, there has never been a better time to recall this: the democracy of our *distraction*.
> "I'm writing it down here," he finishes, "before I forget."

The Master's Farewell Gift

Last Stories
William Trevor
Viking, 223 pages

William Trevor was, by all critical accounts that matter, one of the two greatest writers of short stories, in English, of our age. He died two years ago well into his eighties, at his home in rural, Protestant Ireland. His female equal, the only slightly-younger Canadian Alice Munro, was honored the year before that by the Nobel Committee with its literature prize. It was a great vindication of the short story for those of us who write and publish them. ("Novels are a marriage," Norman Mailer once snarled, "Stories are a one-night stand.") At the New Yorker, which grabs at everything their respective agents ever submitted, the two of them were known by the editorial staff as the King and Queen of Hearts.

The hearts Trevor deals with are by turns exalted, frustrated, thwarted and redeemed. Or not. Many belong to couples who have spent their lives together, either openly or (often) in secret. Some beat in the chests of the rebellious young who raise their love up against Catholic strictures like candles in Babylon. Many of the examined loves here are stymied by poverty, misunderstanding, the demands of religious orders and religious wars, or the simple shunning of benighted, backwater Irish villages.

Trevor, like the Chekhov he most resembles, works largely by indirection. He avoids judgment and yet his detachment still vivisects the most intricate workings of romantic narratives. He examines unfulfilled lives and desires by leaving them free to wander through the pages untrammeled by authorial intervention. His characters, sometimes damaged beyond repair, lack the passion in characters of many tale-tellers. But it comes off as the price one pays for reticence, solemnity, and wisdom.

Penelope Fitzgerald, herself a master and acolyte of Trevor's, admired Trevor's combination of compassion and authorial effacement. She loved the value he placed on innocence, the way he created "a magical sense of time passing," his interest in "the dispossessed, the defiantly eccentric, the non-communicators . . . all who despair but do not care to admit it." She called him (so justly) "the most crystal clear of writers," but one "who maintained, as he often wrote, that 'black and white are densities of more complicated grays.'" His characters' unforgettable, astringent mixtures of personality are the battleground of both bewilderment and enlightenment. "Every good story has a mystery," Eudora Welty wrote, "—not the puzzle kind, but the mystery of allurement; as we understand the story better, it is likely that the mystery does not decrease—rather it simply grows more beautiful." There is no better description of the joyful misanthropy of a Trevor story.

In his early collections like *The Day We Got Drunk on Cake* and *Lovers of Their Time*, one marvels at classic after classic of the canon. In "Mrs. Silly," a boarding school boy is embarrassed by his eccentric rube of a country mother. She comes to Dublin for a Parents' Day. After ignoring her in front of his dandyish urban friends, walking always a full room's length in front of her, he is later overpowered by guilt, driven and derided by his selfish vanity. In the title story of *Lovers of Their Time*, a pair of adulterers find their trysting place in a cramped rooming house near Victoria Station. Peopled by similar sinners, the Sixties aerie eggs them on with the merry, cleansing textures of Beatles music. The arc of their union is traced from 'A Hard Day's Night' to somewhere around the White Album. These stories can contain a stitch of cruelty, especially those dealing with the Protestant-Catholic "Troubles" that have plagued his homeland for centuries. This writer's favorite is the ice-cold "A Bit of Business," the title referring to how utterly normal, unassuming tradesmen, IRA provos, are dispatched to carry out the execution of a (very) young political enemy.

There is no falling off in this final collection of *Last Stories*. Trevor unwittingly left it to us as a funereal consolation. In "The Piano Teacher's Pupil," found on his desk when he died and published in a June 2017 New Yorker, a spinster pianist is so enamored of one of her prodigies, and possibly in love with him, that she forgives his kleptomanic lightening down of the home where she gives him his lessons. In "The Crippled Man," external deformity conveys a full spectrum of various lives of pain, all concentrated within one landlord. Two East Europeans come to paint a house where he lives with a female relative in "miserable tedium and animosity." When the immigrants come back for their pay, he has utterly vanished. They assume the woman has killed him, thrown his body in the bogs, and gone in to the annuity office to cash in his pension. They are only abashed, neither horrified nor angry, because this, too, was often "the way things were done" in their own backward and terrible country.

However atrophied one's existence, one wants a death that is dignified, that self-validates and gives meaning to the suffered life. Yet this is precisely what is snatched from the main character in "Mrs. Crasthorpe." An alcoholic ex-prostitute, she lives in a side street hovel with a son who gets arrested for exposing himself to her as a joke. Brandts and Canadian geese circle and bob around their mishaps in huge lake-like puddles, like vivid, jittery, waiting demons. The hand of fate fumbles with her to the very last. His son is unable to afford an ambulance when she dies. Her corpse is transported to hospital in a garbage truck, "in the refuse men's enormous vehicle, a reek of whiskey emanating from her sodden clothes." The shades that misled a life accompany Trevor's characters into the afterlife. They continue stumbling. They are dismantled by the smallest shocks, like brushing against mildly electrified wires. They continue the difficult work of being confused.

Chekhov, his literary progenitor, once said that the task of a story is to pierce deeply into the soul, remain inside for the shortest while, succeeding only if it produces "a great alteration there." Trevor's effortless virtuosity—more black magic than prose style—does exactly that, and in spades. *If* there is an afterlife, he might very well be there, sitting in the half-light going over proofs, turning and turning his dark pages.

Writers and Horseraces:
The Reticent Genius of Gerald Murnane

Stream System: The Collected Short Fiction of Gerald Murnane
Farrar, Straus & Giroux, 681 pages

If Proust lived in Western Victoria, Australia, rather than in the Place Vendome, and if he'd had the same trouble sleeping—the downstairs party sounds of his mother and guests—he would be and write something very much like Gerald Murnane. Murnane's world is one entirely of memory, of sensations that comprise and preserve the earth for a knowing subject who happens to be trying to write his life. All of it happens in the grassy wastes of Down Under, a merciless and testing scrim of terrain, terrain, terrain. There is absolutely no one writing now like him, no writing like his remotely produced by anyone else. His relaunch into the forefront of world literature began largely with Mark Binelli's April portrait of the writer in *The New York Times Magazine*. Binelli has performed an enormous service to fiction writing, radically extending the body of 20th and 21st Century Antipodal letters.

Murnane's characters can be said—at least in the novels—to follow normal narrative structures and progressions, but stay fixed on obsessions of departure, directions, orientation, unnatural concerns about returning to uncertain tertiary domains. Like Murnane himself, his population of characters, usually nameless, have never departed their countries, never ridden in an airplane, never worn sunglasses or used a cellphone.

Like Beckett, their foibles, like losing hats or pendants or keys, hint at the flimsiness of human continuity and dependability. Losing their movie ticket might send them out of the assurances of personalty, and will make them wonder whether the film they planned to see exists, or ever existed. All things in Murnane, as Yeats said, hang like a drop of dew upon a blade of grass.

He has perfected the vehicles of modernism with none of the

stunts and gimmicks that so often make a text seem like a directionless roundabout. A character derivates from another, passes beautifully back into himself, and then finds that the Other's retained memory contains a lot of the original narrator's concerns—thoughts both erratic and meticulously organized. There is wild abundance in these progressions, but all tightly confined, like a primordial jungle stuffed into a clear glass terrarium.

He eschews metaphor, but the finally chosen ones are immaculate. An uncle's girlfriends are presented as a "lost country." Obsessed with the clamor of the racetrack, his infield spectators watch the flow of hides like dust blown through an empty riverbed. The narrator pursues some kind of stasis, but is slapped with wave after wave of Heraclitian chimera.

The landscape of Australia is a brambly, unwelcoming Eden, yet one whose loss (on a trip, say, or an imagined trip to Hobart) is mourned with great self-reflective grace and solemnity. The pages are filled with taps coming out of walls, the precise configurations of stones, moraine maps, buttes and plateaus, and sheep grazing ponds that rise from the ground into Dali-like aerial smiles, living paintings for the sheltered and thwarted. Words hypnotize and enchant; others curse and bewilder and blind the more scrofulous characters: *quinsy, impetigo, seizure perspective.* Scrofula itself.

As in Calvino, the narrator is often writing about a writer who may be writing about the narrator. The sharpness of natural imagery buffs up against the Protean incoherence of identity. Identity is then restored by action, however inconsequential or profound:

> During the year mentioned in the first sentence of this story, whenever the man mentioned in that sentence foresaw as appearing in his mind the images of some of the details explained in the previous paragraph, he observed that the sequence of images he foresaw as appearing in the mind of the man (or rather the image of the man) while he knelt on the bed and performed the acts reported in the previous sentence . . .

'Velvet Waters,' from his first story collection.

The loops complete themselves once an action or series of inactions restore personality to the subject. His ruminations dissolve him, like ashes blown off of a log. But the fire abides, and the core of bewitching descriptions, events piled upon memories of events, bring the speaker back to himself as assuredly as any Beckett clown.

A sort of cult has assembled itself around Murnane, fictional variations of which give him startling, delightfully comic material. Though short-listed for the Nobel as frequently as the late Phillip Roth, Murnane has gone to great lengths to ensure a veneer of obscurity. He tends bar in a West Victoria golf club. As Will Heywood observed after a Paris review interview, "[M]urnane has never been in an airplane, never worn sunglasses, hasn't watched a current movie in decades; can recall by memory the names of thousands of individual racehorses, along with their individual colors; keeps meticulous files detailing every aspect of his life . . . His readers talk about his books in reverent tones, carrying his work along by word of mouth." Like Homer or primitive, third-world oralists, his work and life weave into one anothers' assemblages; he and his characters are kept from vanishing by sheer, compendious cataloguing—by taxonomies of their "keeping going."

By way of impossible summary, after he abandoned traditional plot and character following 1982's *Border Districts,* Murnane's work became highly essayistic and exhaustively explanatory. As Binelli observes, the typical Murnane story unfolds like a procedural, unravelling out from a half-remembered glimpse of something—a simple well handle or some florid speck in the brown like a jockey's racing silks (his true, admitted obsession in life is the infield and the betting window). Other memories will follow, be they anecdotes, ruminations, mental footnotes, and mini stories within the story. It can all "seem digressive, until the methodical obsessiveness of [his] self-interrogation becomes clear. He's searching the furthest reaches of his memory for clues, hidden meanings, details that may have slipped away." Then, as Binelli observes, "The digressions turn out to be leads, and in the end, there's no writing shop epiphany, but rather that thrilling moment when the circles and arrows linking up the photographs thumbtacked to the squad room wall form a previously unseen web of connection."

Sticking with connective webs, one might start this collection within the gossamer threads of the aptly named "Control Web," where misogynistic impulses seem to be the natural legacy of war. In "The Interior of Galaande," the main character circumnavigates, digresses around himself as he seems—yes, Beckett-like—to be vanishing both from real and imagined worlds, hovering at the very edge of a desperate fictional lifeline. Wherever one starts in this feast of a book, they confront a mastery and uniqueness that results in a little self-cursing for having found the treasure too late. *Where has this guy been all these decades?* This reviewer—who endeavors to keep abreast of Australian writing—has seldom entered an undiscovered country so immediately magnetic and thrilling, all in a prose whose effortless, subtle music rumbles like a far off, forward-marching storm.

Wake of the Flood

You Think It, I'll Say It
Curtis Sittenfeld
Random House, 226 pages

Curtis Sittenfeld, whose novels like *Prep* and *American Wife*, showed an early and easy fluency, has shown herself to be an equally adept master of the short form. Each of the ten stories in *You Think It, I'll Say It* (marvelous title) shows the sharp contrasts between classes, genders and locales in a nation she herself—especially post-Trump—as adrift and viscerally divided.

Gender fluency presents itself in "The Prairie Wife," where a woman fantasizes into *schaudenfreude* an old friend's crashing, disintegrating healthy-living empire. The narrator finds it hard to believe that her old summer camp friend can be as guileless as she once was, and not the kind of "greedy, phony hypocrite" one assumes as essential for empire making in the 21st century. The narrator is startled to see a jealousy in herself, apologizing to a mate that—with "full-time jobs and young kids"—entertainment and excitement is not the coin of the upper middle class realm. The brass ring of true success keeps racing away just ahead of everyone.

In "Plausible Deniability" (for you Reagan veterans), a woman explores her erotic feelings for her brother's wife. They disguise the erotic, transgressive charge of their e-mails under discussions of classical music. The narrator has been accused in past relationships of being heartless, unreachable, and she surmises that bisexuality—albeit with a risky prospect—is her ticket out of her emotionally stony history of personality. But she runs up against a surprise.

In "A Regular Couple," a high powered female lawyer finds herself stalked, to a mild extent, by a fellow mean-girl high school bully, while both are on their honeymoons. Lingering suspicions of her old rival cause the narrator to question her own appeal to her new mate, with events spiraling downward from there. Strange prejudices and idée fixes shock the speaker as much as us, her observers. Sittenfeld is a master of peoples' attempts to judge, to interpret others, and have that attempt thwarted and often revealed to result in the opposite of what was expected. One never ceases to be surprised at her turns of character, and to sense—unlike Nabokov's chess pieces—that they sometimes surprise her too.

Sittenfeld has cornered the market on a class of characters seldom focused on in contemporary fiction—middle aged women of middle America. She empathizes as well as she describes, and her imagination, though not fantastical, works well with both an inner life, a given external veneer, and a backstory that is never less than perfectly placed and perfectly believable.

Here is a novelist who is every bit as good in the short form as in the genre in which she made her name. And that's saying a lot.

Love Is the Crooked Thing

The Only Story
Julian Barnes
Knopf, 247 pages

How deep does love's sense of duty go? How long do we stay with someone who our heart lays claim to, but who is bent on a path of self-destruction and non-existence? Lionel Shriver has explored this dark landscape within the terrain of parent and child. Leave it to the ever fresh, ever abundant Julian Barnes to explore it as the blasted earth laying between a romantic couple, as he does in his new novel, *The Only Story*.

In an upper middle class Surrey village, Paul meets the older Susan at a tennis club. She is married, a sort of Northern Mrs. Robinson, with two children, and a loathsome cruel husband, who enables Paul to see his intercession as a kind of fable of rescue. The cuckold is brutish and short, and slams his wife's face against the doorjamb.

Barnes modulates between first, second and third person voices with great deftness. The first person serves their early erotic explorations: "It wasn't until we were in bed that I was rummaging and rooting around her body, into every nook and cranny, every over-examined and under-examined part of her, that, crouched above, I swept back her hair and discovered her ears."

This is a woman nearing her fifties, and for the just post-teenage Paul, she is truly an undiscovered country. As he settles down and they continue their liaison, the dark acres of her thirst for alcohol widen, and Paul, maddened with love for her, nonetheless begins questioning how far his assistance will drag them both.

It becomes an anchor, a deep and growing weight on their souls. Here, the little-used second person serves the narrator well. Is she a binge-drinker, or an occasional lush who only goes off the rails on weekends? Barnes's command of tone allows the story-teller to question his own motives, as well as his subject's. Is he bent on going off into death with her, or dragging her back into the cognitively lubricated place they shift between.

As she descends into blackouts and hospitalizations, Barnes shifts the engine down to the third person, so necessary for the detachment the narrator needs for the high, open ground of judgement and consequence.

In the popular mythology of tabloids, someone like Paul ends up being the leader of a small country (or a minor figure in a large one), elopes with his mistress and then lives happily ever after. As drink consumes Susan's body here, we see all the opposites coming true. One goes back to her ears, those bright flowers first discussed within the forest of her hair.

> Things, once gone, can't be put back; he knew that now.
> A punch once delivered, can't be withdrawn.
> Words, once spoken, cannot be unsaid.
> We may go in as if nothing has been lost, nothing done, nothing said; we claim to forget all; but our innermost core doesn't forget, because we have changed forever.

Paul goes on to say that the strength of the heart never fits its wanting, that accuracy and completeness are not, as they are in logical systems, anywhere near its purpose: *"In love, everything is both true and false; it's the one subject on which it is impossible to say anything absurd."* Romance has all the topsy-turvy breathtaking direction of the old philosophical paradoxes.

But unlike them, it causes pain, constant and relentless questioning. Barnes's essays on death and bodily deterioration dazzled us when he wrote of his mother's demise in *Nothing to Be Frightened Of*. Here, in the freer, open landscape of fiction, we watch the narrator waste away with his wasting love-object. If first love fixes a life forever, young Paul here fastens on the magnetic, true north of the first love being an addict. It is a line of magnetism that will, like gravity, bend all his future relationships. It destroys and instructs at the same time. Its narrative fixes and pulls you as powerfully as it does the narrator.

Men Without Women

Good Trouble
Joseph O'Neill
Pantheon, 247 pages

Joseph O'Neill composes so completely from the man's perspective that one expects the #MeToo era out of him. It would miss the point, however, as the depth and textures of his female characters are amazing to behold. Simply because the genders bounce off one another like magnets doesn't make the depth of their struggle dolorous; in fact, it makes them highly illuminating.

Though gender relations are the drawing mechanism for many of these stories, life phases and stages of aging are equally foregrounded here. Another fascination of O'Neill's is the ethicist Parfitt's notion of what we owe to one another—how far out people whose lives we've merely passed through might stay tethered to us. Nowhere is this better explored in "The Trusted Traveler." There, a couple skirmish over how welcome they should make an old writing student in their sequestered "retirement cabin." The wife is most forgiving at accommodating the stranger, even though he is a mooching lout, who offers all manner of unwelcome and unsolicited advice. O'Neill describes the "strangely fictional few hours" that transpire in this encounter. His passage through the house lets the couple assess their current hacking of the thickets of age, contemplating how they will move down, eventually to the level grey of death.

An awkward visit to a fertility clinic in "Ponchos" illustrates the male agony mirroring the woman's sub-conscious rage to conceive. The semen-gathering scene alone is worth the price of the book. Later, the narrator/seminator is ribbed and in turn repartees with his Irish pub mate. Few subjects are more permitted and more subject to good comic relief than Irish persecution.

In "Snowden" a poet-titian is asked to sign a petition for the release of Edward Snowden, and his side rumination on the Nobel justification for Dylan's prize, magically sends him out of his writer's block.

There is much, much comedy in the domestic gender wars. In "The World of Cheese," which starts as a debate over their son's circumcision, evolves into the husband's hilarious side-trip into cheese snobbery, and eventually into reveries on such vacuous rabbit hole openings as "the state of the upper middle-class adventure."

Through the prison of he said, she said; she did, he didn't, and other lines and orders of battle, O'Neill brings us bracingly through the world of Londoners and Dubliners with too much money. And not because of what they have done, but because—like John Lancaster's characters, they have long ago bought a house.

How much does money change us? How much spousal tension is based on money and how does it become so comical? The stages of life resist being staged here, or at least too studied. O'Neill's great prose keeps the reader, just like his characters, just off-balance on the careening log that chutes us down to Lethe's water.

River of Dreams

The Man Who Made the Movies
Vanda Kreftt
Harper, 412 pages

When one looks at cinema's founding fathers like Jack Warner, Louie Mayer and Daryl Zanuck, there is always the missing but indispensable figure of William Fox. If Zanuck and crew were celluloid software designers, as it were, Fox was both the hardware engineer and product (franchise) visionary—really the Steve Jobs—of cinema's turbulent infancy.

Though his name lives on in the great studio he founded, everything seemed to go right for Fox, until it didn't. He began with a small theater in Brooklyn. He had the prescience to expand that into a chain, then leveraged it into even larger revenue outlets, including foreign venues. Early careers fell deftly into his hands, principally that of Theda Bara and Tom Mix. In the late 20s, he occupied a position much like that of Saul Zaentz, an artist with impeccable taste and money to boot. The first among his 1927-29 successes was Murnau's 'Sunrise,' a film whose critical street cred cannot be overemphasized. He was foregrounded among silent film-era producers, and stayed that way until the den of lions began to circle him.

In 1929, along with so many others, he was sideswiped by the Wall Street crash. Shortly before that, an auto accident had laid him up for most of that ominous summer. He had wanted to merge Fox Theaters with Loews releasing company, a vanguard distributor that kept relatively free of equity security entanglements. The crash obliterated his ability to merge the two companies. He essentially lost control of the Fox Film Corporation, at one time a $300 million empire of deluxe studios and theaters that easily rivalled Adolf Zukor's. The increased speed of his downward spiral is heartbreaking. He was the victim of multiple double crosses and all manner of financial legerdemain. He had enemies among the U.S. attorneys spearheading antitrust statutes like the Sherman and Clayton Acts. Merger of his company with the more flush Loews empire was seen as horizontal integration, leading to at least the "monopoly power" requirement of the new acts, even if not actually forming a monopoly.

When Fox approached trial, he was alleged to have attempted to bribe a federal judge. This led to another litany of charges and prosecutorial scrutiny. Attorney defense costs caused him to file for bankruptcy. When his defense failed and he was convicted, he appealed. The conviction was upheld in a published opinion. His nadir came when he began to serve jail time for the bribery. His health deteriorated during his imprisonment, and he spent much of his incarceration in infirmaries.

What Fox embodied, and what Krefft's attention to detail brings out so well, is the Horatio Alger journey of the East European immigrant. His parents brought him over from Hungary, already reeling under the post WW I apocalypse. He began by selling candy on the streets of Brooklyn and Manhattan. By his early twenties he was financing talkies and launching the careers of obscure stage actresses and Vaudevillians. He was a man of principle, staying above board in the days when the "casting couch" determined who did and did not get into the studio *du jour*. Notwithstanding the bribery allegations, his discipline and personal integrity were models for those who quickly followed him.

Krefft's knowledge of the industry and her feel for the essence and character of Fox is uncanny. The book rises from the genre of biography and becomes a vital history of early American moviemaking. She is especially deft at showing how a financial adept can also be hoodwinked by slightly more sophisticated charlatans, especially when masses of money are moving quickly and the laws of business expansion are embryonic. The details of his financial dealings may seem excessive, but they flesh out this portrait of a dreamer whose dedication to his discipline overshadowed that of nearly all his contemporaries.

Norman Mailer said that while the published word embodied America's waking existence, it was movies "that formed the dream life of the race." Krefft has given us a vital picture of the incipience of that dream life. Without Fox nothing would have developed the way it did. He had Mailer's intuition of a national subconsciousness, what could be called a collective memory and what Yeats called the *spiritus mundi*. He knew that there were certain subject matters—among them the conquest of the American West—that needed solidification in an art form that mere books could not sufficiently capture. He got the material made, got it running in the projectors, and founded gilded strings of palaces for them to run in. He lived and died the American Dream, and this account of his destiny is also the account of the formation of our ongoing, indispensable dream life.

Righting the Brain

The Mind Fixers:
Psychiatry's Troubled Search for the Biology of Mental Illness
Anne Harrington
Norton, 369 pages

Anne Harrington is a historian of science at Harvard, one of the best chroniclers of the history of psychology and psychiatry, especially the latter's move from nurture to nature in the post-War decades. The latter necessarily entails a revisionist thesis, an analysis of the movement away from Freudian-dominant paradigms to a biological basis for much of what we have come to call "mental illness."

Like philosophy, the psychiatric disciplines tend to proceed as reactions to preceding systems. Freud's theories of childhood traumas, archetypes and wish fulfillments arose in response to 19th century biological theories of mind, many of them detritus from the eerie dark ages of that period's "science" of human behavior. Fleiss and others who influenced Freud also repelled him with their primitive theories of organic causation in brain processes and disease. But the swing to organic causation of "disorders" was a kind of excess stroke of the pendulum. The "bio-thesis" coincided with deinstitutionalization of mental hospitals, with counter-cultural (R.D.Laing, Adam Phillips, Alan Watts) attacks on "establishment psychiatric power," and with the American Psychological Association's takeover by clinicians re-arguing mental illness's probable tissue, chemical, and electrical basis.

The postwar return to biology, Harrington argues, has been pretty much an academic and clinical success, but not without a lot of resistance and theoretical bumps in the road. There is a settled framework now for the two main types of illnesses as biological and pharmacologically co-constructed phenomena, and not psycho-dynamic, socially created processes or entities. A lot of this arose from changes in the leadership and direction of the National Institute of Mental Health, and some of the work of Thomas Insel. The Diagnostic Handbook of Mental Disorders or DSM—one psychiatrist dubbed it his "favorite work of fiction"—also had a lot of pages to fill and a lot of chemistry and molecular structure to explain.

One of the problematic side effects of the foregoing was an obsession with managing dopamine and serotonin levels, which in turn transformed the pharmaceutical industry into the bête noir of "big pharma" and its notorious direct marketing of psychotropic drugs to consumers first in print, then in broadcast media. Although tens of millions of people began prescriptions of drugs to control behavioral hormones and molecules, the question remains whether we truly, epistemologically learned anything new about types of consciousness emanating from negative changes in physical brain states.

*   *   *

Harrington is not seeking to lessen the dispensation of "mind drugs," which can actually involve a dizzying number even for a single patient. One psychiatrist of my acquaintance notes how a scrip is often given for each (sometimes overlapping) symptom: 1-2 antidepressants; one benzodiazepine (tranquilizer); one mood stabilizer; one anti-psychotic or "boost" agent like Abilify; one stimulant; and one or two sleeping aids. Especially with respect to the anti-depressant SSRIs (serotonin re-uptake inhibitors), some astute writer patients have come to wonder whether their personalities come from a nature/nurture mix or, rather, the shelves of their crowded medicine cabinets. There has to be, Harrington agrees, an end to the complete medicalization of human suffering. But drug companies, in their assistance in taking the patient constituency from neurosis to "regular unhappiness," have no interest in their doctor-clients underprescribing, and shareholder value is shareholder value. (Note the recent scandals with the Sackler family's Purdue Pharma, sued in over thirty states for overprescribing opiates.)

Harrington answers her own question by proposing a de-centralization of psychiatry from biology, and a positioning of medication as one path among options, as well as alternative modalities such as talk therapy that preceded most modern psychopharmacology. She calls for what could be labelled a psychiatric pluralism, the blending of alternatives into a single, focused, and—most importantly—patient-friendly set of realistic goals. The book remains, however, a fix on a historical context, a readable and free-flowing synthesis of mind/brain medicine and an admission that for all its progress it is still largely a process of trial and error, of what Karl Popper called conjectures and refutations. Her history nicely deconstructs what scholars like Nikolaus Rose and Joelle Abi-Rached have denoted the emergence of "the neuromolecular conception of the self." These notions dovetail interestingly with recent work in the philosophy of mind and the philosophy of language. It partakes equally with concepts of personhood and their commencement in time, as well as the problem of other minds. She does this all with a sensitivity to understanding "the actual diversity of the suffering they [drugs and therapies] seek to alleviate. In this sense she appreciates humans not just as neurological beings, but also as metaphysical ones, and knowing subjects aware of their ontology and seeing their existence not just as a unity of physical effects but as a unity of their concerns.

Above all, Harrington is a master narrator. She combines anecdotal episodes—often from high levels of organizations like the NIMH and APA—with everyday case histories of suffering, "ordinary and not-so-ordinary" unhappy consumers of medical services. The book moves, as any good history should, from the individual to the universal, weaving complex science and personal history together with a readable, engaging fluency. Of particular note is Harrington's ability to take the ideological Freud-biology skirmishes and set them squarely in the context of several specific forms of disorder, namely schizophrenia, depression and bipolar disorder. This book will serve as a useful historical reference for mental health practitioners, a guide to current therapies for the most prominent disorders, and an invaluable contribution to the history of ideas.

Who Was the Shining Path?

The Shining Path:
Love, Madness & Revolution in the Andes
Starn and La Sterna
Norton, 384 pages

In the torpor of South American politics in the 1970s and 80s, a movement surfaced in Peru, where income inequality is well-nigh medieval and government suppression of any kind of dissent was savage and rapid. Out of the jungles of the western part of the country a shadowy movement formed. At first they simply held testimonials and workshops on how to organize. Then they moved on to arming willing recruits and building an intimidating cadre of effective guerillas that began to gain traction in farming villages and even toward the suburbs of Lima, where literally hundreds of thousands of residents look up at you from trenches along the airport tarmac when you arrive. Like the runway squatters in Mumbai, they are so poor they pass their estates to progeny in fee simple, building houses of tin, cardboard and wire out of the materials thrown away in nearby industrial districts.

As it came to fruition, the movement came to be known as the Shining Path. At first described only as a communist insurgency, they soon crafted a multi-point socialist program modelled on Mao's red book and later writings of Lenin. So they were essentially Maoist, kind of like the governments of China and Albania. Anthropologist Orin Starn and historian La Sterna (*The Corner of the Living*) detail how the organization—motivated by that great Communist longing to redeem humanity from misery and injustice"—ignited a vast rebellion, spottily successful, to destroy the capitalist government. Though they preceded and followed his administration, their attacks were largely focused against President Fujimoro, one of more than a few Japanese leaders of the country, whose daughter also ran it for a time and was deposed herself and later indicted, still living in Lima under house arrest. The phalanx of Shining Path's leadership was pretty straightforward and careful about collateral damage in the early and formative years. However, once Fujimori's army closed in on them, there was a brutal counterinsurgency involving torture, killings, and truly indiscriminate massacres, growing in size as the skirmishes magnified and brought in more recruits. Each act of suppression, including mass burials of guerillas, brought more and more young men (and women—it was radically feminist) to the quartermaster's huts for rifles, machine guns, grenades and light tank weapons.

Basically, because of the velocity of the movement's growth, the population got into the crosshairs fairly early. Each step forward among the village people seemed to result in pauses and hesitations, not just because of Shining Path's own reprisals (they were nothing if not vengeful) but also the indiscriminate nature of the government's crackdowns. The conflict spread to the massively populated, congested and inefficient capital. Photos were circulated in the press of mass killings by both SP guerillas and the government. Bodies were stacked like cordwood—the primitive, black-and-white photographs looked like photographs of the liberation of Dachau or Sobibor. Still, the movement kept its basic attractions. Poverty was so systemic and markets so rigged to corrupt oligarchs (including Fujimori himself), that everyone seemed to support the guerillas, though no one would cop to doing so. All signs of support had to be hidden; all expressions of affinity remained mental constructs, never reduced to writings or plans of any sort.

The movement had an extremely charismatic and literate leader, Abimel Guzman. He had a gentility and polish that was sometimes hard to sell to an indigenous, bitter, illiterate peasantry. (This model was repeated and preceded by many Central American movements.) In his Maoism he resembled Pol Pot, but he had no agenda for the liquidation of whole classes as Lenin did for Kulaks and Pot for "intellectuals," apperently anyone wearing spectacles. Guzman was characterized by his equally bright senior staff as the "Communist warrior and philosopher king," who spearheaded the movement and fed into its missives and programs an indiluted, unrepentant Maoism. The

Maoist features were attractive to the agrarian population much like Mao's ideas resonated with peasants and farmers during his Long March through the 1940s. (Peru has a very limited industrial base; proletarians and lumpen proletariat were thus scarce; it had to be a "revolution of the farmers and villagers".) Other primary figures included Augusta La Torre, Guzman's wife and the "bull woman" (playing on her Spanish surname), who was herself killed in combat during the long insurrection.

Elena Iparaguirre was another high level commander who Guzman fell in love with. An additional figure was Gustavo Goritti, a journalist who chronicled the war like Herodotus did with the Greeks, fighting along side, weaving in and out of the trenches and moving the machine gun forward. This book amounts to a more gritty, detailed and personal account and this moves the ball forward from David Scott Palmer's collection 'The Shining Path of Peru,' which is excellent but never gives you the journalist's take because of its being a collection of essays. La Sterna is particularly good in showing—from the perspective of a professional historian—the fanatical and somewhat outmoded devotion to a galvanized terrorist philosophy, and the military's bloody response, which led to the death of at least 70,000 Peruvians. What is most fascinating about this book is how it is panoramic, almost cinematic, during Peru's rocky transition from military dictatorship to elected but extremely unstable democracy. The authors take readers to the very center of the rebellion's leadership, and the pinpointed areas of population it terrorized and reduced. There were neutral parties and mediators, people like the black activist Maria Elena Moyano, and the great novelist Mario Vargas Llosa, who many Shining Path did not trust and who had to, especially after his run for the presidency (chronicled in *A Fish Out Of Water*), still keep his Flores neighborhood townhouse under guard because his neighbors numbered among Fujumoro's leadership.

The book is a meticulously researched and harrowing account of how a dweeby professor and his seriatum of fiercely revolutionary wives conceived and orchestrated what, at its acme, was the most feared communist insurgency on the continent. Guzman took as scripture the edict of his idol that "Revolution grows out of the barrel of a gun." He also subscribed to the Little Red Book aphorism of "Correct ideas come from the people," though it was a harshly top-down, pyramidal and stratified leadership structure, one that brooked no second-guessing the Big Man. There is a famous photo of Guzman behind bars, wearing a horizontal striped beach shirt and looking like the parody of a late 50s beatnik. He stares through the bars to the distant horizon of freedom, and in that way looks lofty and erudite and principled. But his hands and fingernails and dark with soil and blood, the symbols, to him, of any agrarian struggle worth that holy name.

This will be the definitive Shining Path book. Its research and high quality of writing leaves others in the dust. In the history of South America's western countries' revolutionary movements, this is the book historians, journalists and lay readers have been looking for. There is little in it to fault and much there that will make it impossible to best.

The Supreme Court and the Illusion of 'Voter Fraud'

One Person, No Vote
Carol Anderson
Bloomsbury, 271 pages

Why did Trump win the election in 2016? Flyover state resentment of liberal, coastal elites? The specter of globalism, with a nativist, protectionist response by Trump voters? Other forms of nationalism, like the belief other countries don't pay their share of alliances like NATO? *Extreme* forms of nationalism with nativist, racist threads, like the first views of undocumented aliens Trump stumped on? Or was it just the recurrent belief that nobody in Washington pays attention to the little man, and the view that the Democrats—though that is their mantra—have forgotten Joe Sixpack and thrown in with Wall Street and the financial services sector of voters?

The answer is a little bit of each of the above. But let's focus on one that partakes of each but is really none of them. It begins with a still-shocking fact: black voter turnout fell by *seven percent* in the '16 election, a staggering proportional number given the fact that less than half of our eligible voters goes to the polls anyway. Was that because, as Fox News suggests, blacks did not repay the favor of eight years of one of their own by also boldly putting in a female president who, after all, clarified that she had their interests at heart? There is another answer to the "7% Question," one argued effectively by Emory University sociologist Carol Anderson in this book.

The 2016 election was the first in fifty years to be held after recent erosions in the Voters Rights Act of 1965 ("VRA"). Three years before, in *Shelby County v. Holder,* 570 U.S. 2 (2013), a five-to-four majority of the Court, led by Justice Alito, ruled that red state voter "rolls adjustments" were constitutional because requiring those states to submit to federal vetting was "based on data over 40 years old," making evidence of minority voter suppression "no longer responsive to current needs." The Court concluded that such federal scrutiny of state voting rules amounted to an impermissible burden on federalism and its respect for equal sovereignty of the states. Sections 4(b) and 5 of the VRA required the federal preclearance of state methods of prohibiting voting. The Court did not strike down Section 5, but without Section 4(b), no state jurisdiction would be subject to Section 5 preclearance unless "Congress enacts a new coverage formula." *Id.* 17. Five years after the ruling, nearly a thousand polling places had been closed, with many of them in predominantly African-American counties, in regions as diverse as Mississippi and my native often outcome-determinative Ohio.

The ruling, argues Anderson, essentially left minorities, especially transient ones, completely at the mercy of state legislatures. Her writing has the cool detachment of peer review prose, but often breaks out into bracing polemic, obviously timed to this coming November's midterms. Anderson is following up on her superb 2016 book *White Rage,* which deftly examined resentment voters mention in the first paragraph of this review. Her basic theory there was that periods of black progress (read: much of the Seventies after the Civil Rights Act, and eight years of a black president) "wreaks havocs subtly, almost imperceptibly, in the legislatures and the courts."

Anderson has it that the *Holder* ruling is one of the "last gasp attacks" on minority voters' access to the polls. Earlier methods were dressed up in the genteel garb of bringing post-Reconstruction and post 1964 'integrity' to the polling process. But these were quickly seen for the ruses they amounted to, the main ones being 'literacy tests' and poll taxes. Besides rulings such as *Holder,* Anderson sees the second barrel of the shotgun as gerrymandering and rank fabrications of "epidemics of voter fraud." She makes an excellent case for both the evils of redistricting and the ludicrous Breitbart nightmares of illegal aliens and ex-felons bussed into polling places by Blue State agendists.

Anderson adroitly explains many of the disqualification methods, and shows why they are empirical and statistical travesties. Anderson describes Georgia's Exact Match system (don't ask) and the Interstate Crosscheck system, all cloaked in antiseptic phrases like "voter roll maintenance" as having a disastrous effect on the minority vote. The tiniest of bookkeeping errors can lead, under these "failsafes," to purging entire households and neighborhoods of eligible minority voters. Anderson's examples will make the hair on the back of your neck stand up. I was listening to it on a CD and nearly drove my car into oncoming traffic—always the sign of a good read. Anderson gasps at the sheer wonder that 1964 and 1965 were nearly fifty-three years ago, and that evolving standards of fairness should, by 2018, have hardened into federal statutes and decisions that still, more than ever, protect the vulnerable from being turned away from the curtain and stylus.

But do you have to even guess at the current administration's view of the "menace" of voter fraud? Trump posited that swaths of Clinton popular votes were 'fake', were bussed in, duplicate counted, or something of the sort. Though Attorney General Jeff Sessions has garnered my sympathy over his recent treatment, this is a man who, as an Alabama federal prosecutor, (unsuccessfully) prosecuted three black activists for attacking that state's "voter maintenance" subterfuge. And Sessions said, quite recently, that the VRA was "an intrusive piece of federal legislation." The result? He is requiring *forty-four states* to detail their plans for voter maintenance, with the deadline thankfully falling after this November. Anderson also points out that the current presidential Advisory Commission is led by Kris Kobach, a Trump enthusiast running for governor of Kansas and who has been a sort of Moses of poll list stripping. Er, I mean voter maintenance. The co-chair of the Commission is none other than Vice-President Pence, hardly a guardian of the minority voter.

Anderson sees silver linings in the voter-manipulation thundercloud, principally Doug Jones's Alabama upset over the ensconced Republican incumbent Roy Moore. But at the same time she wonders why allegations of child sexual assault must be what brings a titan down. Why can't it be efforts like the NAACP providing transportation to areas decimated by poll closings? Anderson's bottom line is that a strong democracy encourages voter inclusion. Of course, if there is evidence of voting integrity problems, and not just speculation, then the state should take necessary steps to correct them. But the alleged anomalies and unfairness must be proven, and not mere fantasies leading clumsily to administrative disenfranchisement. Fifteen states including DC use same day voter registration, and North Dakota doesn't have any pre-voting registration requirements at all. These states have not reported one instance of voter abuse.

In this fantasy, "fake news"-suspected time, Anderson points out that conservatives often have an almost instinctual view that minorities and left-liberals will cheat like poker shills when left to their own devices. One of her favorite voter fraud stories is also mine, from Robert Caro's ongoing LBJ biography. Johnson and his cronies were ballot-stuffing, chalking names off Texas hill-country gravestones back in the 40s, during Johnson's first run for Congress. A (short) assistant came timidly up to the candidate and reported that one gravestone was so old he couldn't trace the worn-away letters with paper and chalk. The 6'5" Lyndon grabbed him by his collar, lifted him up, and said. "Son, you get that name—that man has as much right to vote as anyone else in this cemetery."

Apocryphal material like this (I actually tend to believe the LBJ story) cannot animate the formulation and enforcement of our voting laws. But listening to certain TV networks and candidates, and even parsing the evidence-bereft, sweeping and sloppy logic of *Holder*, can sometimes make you wonder.

From Langley to Lahore: America & Pakistan

Directorate S: The Cia and America's Secret Wars in Afghanistan and Pakistan
Steve Coll
Penguin Press, 757 pages

There is no more dicey, dangerous geopolitical dance between two significant powers than that between the U.S. and Pakistan. The two countries are often on the right side of history, sometimes together on the wrong side, but much of the time it is mixed—all of it depending on the enigma of *which* Pakistan one is talking to. In 1971-72, when Kissinger saw an entrée to China that could only be brokered by West Pakistan, we (at best) stood aside and (at worst) assisted in that (largely Punjabi) regime's suppression of the East Pakistani Bengal muslims creating the independent nation of Bangladesh, far over in the delta lands northeast of India. Gary J. Bass revealed much of the back story on this in his *'The Blood Telegram: Nixon, Kissinger, and a Forgotten Genocide'* (2013). "Blood" here denotes not only the sordid, disgraceful spectacle of what was spilled in Dhaka, but also the actual surname of the Nixonian diplomat who back-channeled what turned into an endless three years of exile, slaughter and famine.

Steve Coll's *Directorate S* concentrates on Pakistan's pivotal, indeed indispensable roles in our battles with Mideast terrorism, particularly against Al Qaeda and the Taliban. Reviving the epic of his Pulitzer-winning *Ghost Wars* (2012), Coll, the dean of the Columbia Journalism School, tells the story of Pakistan's assistance in our "forever war" (Dexter Filkins's phrase), as well as when it stood aside and dithered, and concludes with the treachery it deemed necessary to keep its own leaders from the lead rain of Afghanistan's gathering political thunderclouds.

Coll starts with Bush II's Operation Enduring Freedom, when our outrage at 9/11 sent us blundering into attempts to forge common ground with Afghan and Pakistani counterparts, entities with all the substance and consistency of a Waziri desert mirage. In nearly 600 interviews, particularly with intelligence operatives, Coll shows how endless negotiations, visions and revisions, led us into one disastrous strategy after another. Coll keeps a suspenseful pace by zooming between the highest executive and military policymakers (Cheney, Tenant, Hayden, Panetta) down to the CIA field operators, station chiefs and deputies trying to stay alive in order to do their work "inside the wire."

Coll sees two sources of our intelligence agencies' failures in the region, particularly their failures with Pakistan. The first is the legendary enmity between Washington and Kabul. This has, of course, its historical roots in the 'Great Game' for Afghan influence between Russia and the West, going back to at least the mid-nineteenth century. But more recently, Coll sees the Afghans as similar to the Vietnamese, a people so long conquered and exploited by outsiders that they deem everyone an enemy, and all of existence, both in this world and the next, as a perpetual battlefield. After Russia's debacle with Kabul ended, the war-weary people suddenly had U.S. and U.N. soldiers on their doorstep. The longer the Americans remained there, bribing warlords for terrorist leaders' whereabouts, the more difficult it became to convince the Afghans that we were there with a purpose, or at least a willingness to assist in building a country out of fractured tribes. Eventually their suspicions were confirmed by our treatment of Hamid Karzai, the West's chosen "leader of a free Afghanistan." Karzai, deep in a fog of insecurity and paranoia, came to see us as an occupying power, particularly when we (correctly) accused his family of corruption and when he began brokering deadly deals behind our back.

Coll's second *bête noir* is, again, our historical tension with Pakistan, exacerbated by our friendship with India even when the latter drew perilously into the Soviet orbit. One key to this dysfunction is the Pakistan Army, a necessary institution which, like Turkey's, is a deep state phenomena that usefully stabilizes the shifting panoply of quasi-civilian leaders. The army calls the shots in all internal and external security, particularly through its intelligence apparatus, the fabled I.S.I. and its sub-agency Directorate S. (Carey Schofield's *Inside the Pakistan Army* (2011) is excellent on this.) The I.S.I., best known for perfecting the roving truck arsenal of nuclear warheads, appears at times to play everyone, and could easily spark the fuse for World War III.

The problem with I.S.I. and the Directorate is their breadth and surreptitious, shifting loyalties. Many in the state security apparatus seek the best geopolitical choices, and have loyalty only to the civilian regime and its attempts to keep stable with a menacing, neighboring India. But for every straight-laced, transparent officeholder, there are others, often semi-retired, who tumble forward into jihadist Islam and cover for Al Qaeda, the Taliban, ISIS, and more heads of the Hydra who have not yet surfaced and been identified.

The things we need from Pakistan are both concrete and ephemeral. First, they have to allow supplies bound for coalition forces to cross their airspace (we mostly have that). Second is the real Sisyphean number: we need their assistance, particularly their intelligence, in getting militant operating bases out of their country and away from the porous border with Afghanistan. Confidence is not inspired on the latter, given the fact that Osama bin Laden lived with his inner circle just miles from Pakistan's military academy in Abbotabad. Even after we gave Islamabad hundreds of millions in aid, even after elevating them to the status of a "major non-NATO ally" (come again?), segments of the I.S.I. were tipping off the terror camps to keep one step ahead of American drones. I.S.I.'s justification for all this was that it was defensive covert diplomacy, an "effort to push the violence 'caused by America' back across the border, into Afghanistan" and away from Pakistan population centers and tribal enclaves.

This argument has its complexities and nuances. President Musharraf's most trusted lieutenant, Ashfaq Kayani, argued vehemently that most of the I.S.I. was loyal and only some "wafflers" like Faisal Shahzad showed sympathies to the Taliban. But Shahzad was draped in the cloak of the senior army officer corps, and enjoyed access to government intelligence and weapons caches. Shahzad himself entered the U.S., packed an SUV with white plastic bags of explosive fertilizer, fusing the vehicle to alarm clocks as he left it in Times Square on Mayday 2010.

The bomb fizzled and the "Second 9/11" was not successful. But had it gone off, the fact the attack was prepared in Waziristan by the son of an air force marshal would have forced the Obama administration into an escalating military confrontation with Pakistan. As had been the case so many times with our putative "ally," swallowing the I.S.I. "us-too" arguments and trusting Pakistan had amounted to one step forward, two steps back. The "forever war" continues, across three presidential administrations, with the dead and bandaged still coming back to the homeland. The proverb that one must keep one's friends close and one's enemies closer presents particular irony with Pakistan. Is the dagger your cohort carries there for you to use, or is it meant for a mark on your back?

A Trial Lawyer's Book of Days

Beautiful Country, Burn Again
Ben Fountain
Ecco/Harper-Collins, 385 pages

Many attorneys ruminate in trial, and not always on the matters before them. One hopes that the lawyer Ben Fountain has someone else first chairing the critical portions of his proceedings. He joins predecessors like Scott Turow, Lou Begley and, most prominently, Louis Auchincloss in turning to essay outlines rather than doodlings at counsel table. After graduating Duke Law and teaching at some Texas law schools, Fountain slipped over into fiction, and won a few National Book Critics Circle Awards. (Disclosure: as a member of that body, I voted for his fabulous send-up of the Dallas Cowboys executive management, *Billy Lynn's Long Halftime Walk*; Fountain won.)

Now he is back writing about law and social affairs, much of it cast as a "Day Book" chronicling the 2016 election. His observations are tight and pithy, casting just the right grammatical net to catch slippery politicians on stage left and right in our current Theater of Polarity.

In March, 2016, in Iowa, he follows his fellow member of the bar, Ted Cruz, through his invocation of returning to "the Judeo-Christian values that built this country." Cruz is, to Fountain's jaundiced and disagreeing eye, an extremely intelligent and effective speaker—the "scary smart" that Cruz's Harvard Law professor Arthur Miller commended. Cruz takes a crowd down through his assessment of the Supreme Court after Scalia's death, when Kennedy still deftly hovered as the swing vote modulating the center. Describing an "activist, out-of-control court," the cadences are spectral, ominous; everything is so stressed that the truly stressed is left unitalicized:

> We are *one, justice, away,* from a leftist Supreme Court. We

are *one, justice, away*, from the Supreme Court concluding that nobody in this room and no American has the right to keep and bear arms. We are *one, justice, away* from the Supreme Court striking down every restriction on abortion, and mandating unlimited abortion on demand . . . . We are *one, justice, away* from the Court ordering veterans memorials torn down all over the country if they contain any acknowledgments of God Almighty.

"The chisels are ready," Cruz intones, "to hack off the crosses and stars of David from the headstones of dead veterans." As much "bad beef in this kielbasa" that Fountain sees, he marvels at Cruz's approximation of a litigators closing statement, the compression contained in combining terminated births with desecrated deaths, all at the hands of an out-of-touch, agendized and elitist Left.

Fountain is his most incisive in showing how Clinton lost in 2016, caught up in a thicket of Catch-22s and paradoxes from a Democratic Party leadership marketing itself as the blue collar champion, but nestling up to the top one percent financial sector moguls. He shows how Hillary led the terrible razor walk of appealing to rarefied, post Glass-Stiegel trading and securities interests while still cleaving to New Deal protections—the safety net—that animated her party for six or seven decades. But it was too late. Her message was contradictory. It presented itself as a con job that Trump successfully exploited, without much intelligence or historical perspective; the arguments against her she created herself:

> The holders of what might be called 'minoritorian' economic interests would, [under the Democrats] grow stupendously rich. Surely for them the New Democrats' "Third Way" was both coherent and compelling. A swing back toward New Deal populism—to "majoritarian economic interests"—would have served this new Democratic constituency about as well as a pitchfork to the head.

Fountain writes that for Hilary to show fealty to Democratic

Party values, she would have had "to claim, forcefully and without apology," the New Deal and Great Society legacies that had radically transformed American life for the better. He goes on: "The last thing [Clinton] wanted to do was declare there was a possibility for class struggle. But the Republicans...were happy to declare class struggle all the time; they are always waging a one-sided class war against the constituency the Democrats nominally represent."

Clinton was essentially trapped between the traditions of her party and what Republicans cast as Democrats' recently-shifted "super-wealth accomodation strategy." She stretched and straddled; she wrapped her arms around both sides, and people rejected that as phony waffling, deceitful legerdemain. Then she made a few appearances that Fountain literally could not believe, not so much the fact of them as much as their tepid justification. "That's what they offered" she told Anderson Cooper when he asked why she accepted a $225,000 fee for speaking to Goldman Sachs traders. Her brutal, simplistically direct adversary won; life, as Eliot said, cannot bear too much reality, i.e. too much compromise and embrace of opposing positions. It cannot, especially in these political times, lean in to compromise and credence for the views of the Other.

Fountain keeps the lid on, but only barely. He is clearly hopping mad at both political parties. He sat down with the writer Malcolm Gladwell who, in his book *Outliers,* saw Fountain as the only 'writer genius' to feature in his mini-essays on late bloomers. Circling back to the hypnotic Ted Cruz speech described above, Fountain described the eerie attraction of politicians. Substantively, he feels both parties have sold the country down the river, their front men and women so wedded to the "ambition trope" that they do not realize "We are not just units of production for some higher power to get the maximum economic benefit they can out of us." Yet in terms of style, "I feel a strange tenderness for politicians," he says, "because in some ways they seemed very vulnerable; and they are flesh and blood and they're putting themselves out there to do this thing that might destroy them." Not unlike writers, Gladwell added. Overall, Fountain describes how writing the book made him more radical. "I feel like the working and middle classes of this country have gotten the shaft over the last 35 or 40 years, and part and parcel of that has been a very effective sales job on the mind of America, this hard sell of free-market fundamentalism—it has benefitted a few people at the top and there's been scant trickle-down, and it made me angrier."

This book has an arguably unfortunate title for our incendiary times, recalling nods and winks at political violence like James Baldwin's *Fire Next Time*. The title actually comes from a Robinson Jeffers poem celebrating vitality in diversity, a theme Jeffers mined as California's poet laureate and environmental champion. The poem, dealing with earth and water spirits in his native Monterey, is called "Apology For Bad Dreams":

> Beautiful Country, burn again, Point Pinos down to the Sur Rivers
> Burn as before with bitter wonders, land and ocean and the Carmel water.

One can only dream of sitting next to Fountain at counsel table, peeking over at these jottings. The next best thing is reading this book, or any of Fountain's works. Lie back, pick any day of the day book, and live it with him. From law to fiction and back again can be an exhilarating journey.

Being Geniuses Together

Black Mountain College:
Experiment in Art
Vincent Katz (ed.)
MIT Press, 320 pages

Black Mountain College was an experimental institution founded near Asheville, North Carolina in 1933 by John Andrew Rice, Theodore Dreiser, and several others. It was founded on the principles of John Dewey's concept of education, with emphasis on the practicum, holistic learning, and a fluidity and continuity between the plastic, written and performing arts. Many of its students and faculty would go on to become enormous influences in various disciplines. Its earlier architectural and design faculty were exiles from the Bauhaus, and moved out of Germany and Austria just when the Werhmacht was locking up "decadent" artists. Its early members included Joseph and Anni Albers, Ruth Asawa, Charles Olson, Robert Motherwell, Cy Twombly and Robert Rauschenberg, Buckminister Fuller, John Cage and Merce Cunningham, Franz Kline and Elaine de Kooning. It its latest years, when literature came more to the forefront, it was the home of the Black Mountain poets whose sort of Socrates was Olson, soon exceeded by Ed Dorn, and the astonishing Robert Duncan and Robert Creeley. MIT Press has given us the most beautiful and definitive account of the place. Indeed, Yale's recent 'Leap Before You Look' pales in comparison, though it contains photos unavailable at the time of the MIT treasure trove.

The college had added complexities in addition to its role as an American home for Bauhaus exiles. It was operating in the South, albeit the gentile 'Upper South,' during a period of legal racial segregation at other colleges in the region, most notably Duke, the University of North Carolina (the oldest public university in the country), and smaller institutions like Appalachia State and Douglas College. The college existed in its own small town of Black Mountain, which had benighted racist enclaves even though nearby Asheville was a well-established, tolerant art colony city. One of the first dance students at black mountain was Alma Stone. She is long considered to be the first black student to enroll in an all-white institution of higher learning in the Jim Crow era.

Founders of the college believed that the study and practice of art were essential aspects of a student's general liberal arts education, and they hired Josef Albers as the first "arts" teacher. Speaking only halting English with a thick Bavarian accent, he and his wife Anni left Hitler's Germany as Freud left Vienna for London, and both Yeats and Joyce died on operating tables, in 1939, as the Anschluss rolled across the Polish frontier. Because of the shadow of totalitarianism that spurred its founders to leave their homeland, its faculty was committed to democratic governance and roles for women and minorities in its faculty, the choice of curriculum, and the institution's overall vision.

It was remarkable that Albers would invite artists and critics not necessarily in his camp. German educators were notoriously cliquish and haughty, and tended to keep their students as successors, if any were allowed. Certainly, all the people Albers brought were modernists, but they came from all cultures and all sides of each cultural divides. So many schools converged here that no one was foregrounded in any of the various disciplines: there was Neoplasticism in sculpture, Abstract Expressionism and New Impressionism in painting, Surrealism and Social Humanism in everything. Even after Albers left the inclusionism he fathered, it flourished. The musician John Cage became involved in Chance Operations and radical "accidental" harmonics, and modernism moved beyond abstraction into concept and concrete ontologies. Albers brought Walter Gropius over from the Bauhaus. Everyone there believed that art need not, and should not, be subjected to any other societal aim or preoccupation. As Albers wrote in the issue of the magazine *design* that contained many of the school's "manifestos" before the birth of *The Black Mountain Review*, "Art, then, can be considered an end rather than merely a means. So "l'art pour l'art" can be justified. To restrict art to a means of propaganda, for example, proves only a psychological, and thus a fundamental error." Not only did he believe art should never function as propaganda—an invaluable insight in the time of the Cold War—he believed other arts should not be subordinated to architecture, his own specialty that had been elevated and nearly pedestalized at the Bauhaus and in many other European institutions.

Twombly became interested in Dada and Surrealism during the years 1947-1949, and left Black Mountain to move to New York and join the Art Students League. When he returned, Twombly came into his most productive period, causing Robert Motherwell to write "I believe Cy Twombly is the most accomplished young painter whose work I happen to have encountered: he is a 'natural' in regard to what is going on in art right now . . . .his painting process is orgiastic: the sexual character of the fetishes half-buried in his violent surface is sufficiently evident (and is not allowed to emerge any more. Yet the art in his painting is rational, often surprisingly simply symmetrical and invariably harmonious."

For this reader, the literary figures were the most fascinating. When I was a freshman at Berkeley, Ron Loewinsohn taught a course on Olson, Duncan and Creeley called simply 'The Black Mountain Poets.' It was truly a life-altering class. Olson's concept of 'projective verse' and composition 'by field' seemed the next steps in poetic modernism after the colloquial permission given verse by Wallace Stevens and, most importantly, William Carlos Williams, the inheritor—at least in a purely American idiom—of the experiments of Eliot and Pound. In the early 1950s at Black Mountain, Olson and Creeley decided to mount an attack on academic poetry. They would not do it by infiltration or infusion, but by a flank attack in which the repositories of academic comfort would be scaled like the walls of Troy. Paul Blackburn and Larry Eigner and Joel Oppenheimer were brought in, whether as faculty or students was not clear—it never was. In one of the first publications of Divers Press, an offshoot of the college, Robert Duncan's influential poem 'Song of the Border-Guard' was printed with a cover by Twombly.

MIT has done publishing and modernism a great favor with this lavish book, shimmering with rare photographs and artist proofs even in its paperback format, though I prefer the hardback laying solitary on the coffee table of my writing shed. Katz's editorship is the book's true strength, gathering under single covers essays by Olson, Creeley, Blackburn, and even the dancers and choreographers. The design is immaculate, and the production quality absolutely first rate. When American cultural history is shelved along a single wall, this book quite simply cannot be absent. It is the definitive history of a group of artists and artisans whose influence radiated outward from the spoke of Asheville, its spindles flowing from that piney center into several generations of emulators.

Meltdown: What Was 'Chernobyl'?

Midnight in Chernobyl
Adam Higginbotham
Simon and Schuster, 538 pages

There is an old Soviet saying touted often by the late poet Joseph Brodsky, but not, of course, until he had defected to the West. "In the Soviet Union," it goes, "we pretend to work, and the government pretends to pay us." The charade suffices if the tasks involved are postal duties or the bagging of groceries. But when it involves a relatively new (three years old) nuclear reactor hidden in the Ukrainian forests, it is a recipe for a conflagration that poisoned hundreds of square miles, scores of miles up into the atmosphere, and hundreds of meters downward into the earth, imperiling a water table including the Knieper River, supplying drinking water for the metropolis of Kiev. On April 25, 1986, a safety test was scheduled for the Chernobyl reactor. The principal technician was on vacation ("We pretend to work...."), so a younger operator was put at the controls. To complete the test, the reactor had to be powered down. The supervisor of the inexperienced operator had only military training with atomic fission, knowing nothing about non-weapon civilian uses of the process. (Before taking his new post, he remedied his ignorance with a correspondence course in nuclear physics.) When the young man—knowing a power-down could compromise electrically calibrated safety coolers (rods)—questioned his boss's orders, the latter did what *Homo Sovieticus* did best. He blindly obeyed regional nuclear authorities and gave the green light, which quickly became a red one.

The decision to power down, ironically, led to a series of events in which all safeguards were weaned away, and the world could witness a disaster unfold so vividly it was registered in the orbits of space satellites. When control rods could not stop the wildly heating uranium neutrons that were the workhorses, the "fireplace logs" of the reactor, the spring midnight announced itself with a blast of unprecedented forest thunder:

> The entire building shuddered as Reactor Number Four was torn apart by a catastrophic explosion, equivalent to as much as sixty tons of TNT. The blast caromed off the walls of the reactor vessel . . . and smashed open the concrete roof, revealing the night sky beyond.

The reactor operated by controlled fission, in which energy bursts (fissions) of one atom's nucleus produce fissions in other nuclei. This came to be called a "chain reaction" in early atomic history, and to control fission speeds and their degrees of heat, the thermostats of various "moderators" were brought into play. Water is the most common moderator, but when the presence of a certain uranium isotope is highest, the water must be supplemented by other compounds such as graphite. Because of its precise configuration of fuels, the Chernobyl reactor was water-graphite monitored.

What was worse was the absence of containment mechanisms and protocols. Soviet atomic scientists were so convinced of the invincibility of the reactor (cue the 'Titanic' theme music) that they felt it could do without the customary containment domes—the giant concrete casings one sees, for example, at San Onofre when driving south to San Diego. If graphite is not mixed with water, it *hastens* fission, so after the blast the graphite became additional tinder, burning by itself for days and spewing radioactive particles into the air. Higginbotham called the money-saving decision to tip control rods with graphite an "absurd, chilling inversion of a safety device, like wiring a car so that slamming the brakes would make the vehicle accelerate." Accordingly, once the fission process was uncontrollable, safety workers could not seal off the reactor without fanning still-radioactive material into another sudden blast. There were also hundreds of tons of uranium down in the core, which heat levels could push toward additional explosions.

Rescuers had to move forward behind lead "pioneer walls," giant shields that enabled them to build a containment structure, akin to erecting a guardrail after a 25-car collision. Weeks later the famous Sarcophagus was ready to be paraded before the press, but not after thousands had been evacuated from close-in (to Kiev) cities like Pripyat, which had largely been built to house the influx of atomic workers moving west from Siberia. In the first few days of cleaning space for scaffolds to build the Sarcophagus, men were sent to the roof and sides of Reactor Four to scoop up uranium waste with shovels and small tractors. The life-span of these people ended up being 24 to 72 hours, a week if they were lucky. Anyone else involved in the clearing and building would be dead within years. Even early robots could not assist in the waste movement, their circuitry scrambled by rising waves of radiation.

Higginbotham brilliantly explains the utter uniqueness of nuclear energy, a one-of-a-kind unwieldy power anticipated by playwrights of antiquity in the Prometheus myth, and which calls into question whether atom-splitting should have ever been attempted by humankind. "Radionuclides," Higginbotham writes, "could be neither broken down nor destroyed—only relocated, entombed or interred." The process of *hiding* what was really transpiring led to almost immediate political fallout. Western newspaper accounts were accepting reports of 15,000 dead a week, while *Pravda* and nuclear commission press releases fabricated a death toll of 31. Chernobyl thus illustrated the perils of blind acquiescence to authority, the very building blocks of Soviet society and both political and military command structures. The new president, Mikhail Gorbachev, was spurred to push Soviet intransigence toward the makings of an "open society." But this resulted only in something akin to show trials. The collectivist spirit essentially evaporated, and there were both military and civilian kangaroo courts. Many of those scapegoated were already dead, and their convictions resembled the verdicts (and sometimes rehabilitations) of the more political show trials of the early Stalin era of the 1930s.

What happened to the reactor area itself? It is now situated in a vast "exclusion zone" of about 1100 square miles. A Ukrainian visa like mine (a journalist's) contains, under the national logo of a silvery trident, an "NZ" or "Nyet Zona" acronym, meaning you cannot get into the still populated pasture and timber country that spacecraft once saw as an eerie nightlight illuminating the darkness of southwest Russia. At the same time, and with a special visa and if one is *really* bored with Paris Disneyland, the zone can be accessed to reveal high-yield farms amidst a new "Radioactive Eden." The correspondence course-educated director of the plant served only half of his ten-year prison sentence. The chief engineer was diagnosed with "reactive psychosis" and confined in a psychiatric hospital. Nobel Laureate Svetlana Alexievich [*Voices of Chernobyl*] describes victims she met right after the incident, their flesh melting and sliding off of their facial bones onto hospital pillows. For all the human cost, Higginbotham has a talent for humor and mischief among the somber ruins, as when he interviews the female architect of the town of Pripyat. Still mourning the death of her husband and son from nuclear cancers, she shows up dutifully uniformed even while keeping mute about a lot of what she saw in clearing the "town inside the cloud." She brings him a packet of neutered, harmless radiation dust, after she had described it as smelling like rain, something that didn't quite register with the author. She opens the tiny garden seed packet that contains it, and, bending over the table, blows a slight amount into Higginbotham's nostrils. *"Tcha!"* ("There") she says, "If you needed to be afraid, I wouldn't have brought it."

West with the Sun

El Norte
Carrie Gibson
Grove/Atlantic, 437 pages

This amazing book begins not with an epigraph but with a quote from Walt Whitman. The prescient poet wrote that Americans had long ago swallowed "the notion that our United States have been fashioned from the British Islands," which he deemed a great mistake. Then comes the quote that forms Gibson's thesis: "To that composite American identity of the future, Spanish character will supply some of the most needed parts." Gibson develops this into the notion that Hispanic peoples do not constitute a separate history of outsiders and interlopers, but one that is central to how the United States developed." Would it that leaders like Modi of India had the same appreciation of infused populations—the Mughals or Muslims that he sees as 'interlopers'—as the good grey poet did. The same can be said for many leaders of the Middle East, and Russia with respect to the Chechens and peninsular Tatars. Gibson, from this starting point, backs up her themes with solid history, science, and cultural anthropology.

Gibson's history begins, as it must, not in pre-Columbian times but what must be called the Columbian or Spanish forays. The New World lay waiting with all its riches, a place the Iberian Peninsula, with its own sense of manifest destiny, saw plunging slowly but inexorably into the high, cold Atlantic. New places had to be explored and new peoples dealt with. After the North American continent was ruled out as India, all of Spanish and Portuguese civilization shared an obsession with a land mass then did not know the end of, but which had signaled abundance in what is now Florida and Central Mexico. Their search for exoticism was not disappointed, as Tenochtitlan (now the Mexico City basin) presented itself to Cortez (1519) as a wonderland in which he could not "describe one-hundredth of all the things which could be mentioned." An illustration he gave King Ferdinand began with a market in which more than 60,000 people came to buy foodstuffs and garments, "ornaments of gold and silver, lead, brass, copper, tin stones, shells, bones and feathers." Cortes was escorted by Moctezuma into what was described, in European tropes and archetypes, as a vast compound of palaces, apartments, libraries and warehouses, and even a zoo. As most people know, Cortes kidnapped the Aztec king but was later rebuffed, only after his soldiers infected the Indian warriors with a plague that would cause the capital to fall in the years after 1520.

Gibson's sweep is enormous, eight centuries starting with the Florida Spanish colonies and ending with US-Mexican skirmishes over California Hispanic settlements. She starts with the novel and largely unknown fact that there was an enormous diversity of people within Latin America even before the Spaniards blundered in. Over ninety languages were dispersed over a population of nearly 300,000 in Alta California alone. Christianity is often intertwined with conquest, and Meso-America was no exception. Priestly order started missions everywhere. But for all the benign aspects of conversion, Spanish soldiers guarding the clerics were bent on mayhem, rape, self-enrichment. The entire Mexican series of settlement—missions or no—were plundered and savaged by European soldiers and their hangers-on. And the Church's ambitions were not just to save souls. By 1823, even after numerous Mexican burnings and rebuilding of missions, there were 21 Christian sites spread along the California coast, dedicated to enslaving Indians after converting them.

Gibson debunks the "whites only" etiology of the U.S land mass extolled by historians like Samuel Huntington, who wrote that "America was created by... settlers who were overwhelmingly white, British and Protestant. Accordingly, swarthy indigenous peoples, however advanced and however much the subject of wonder, were seen as having the divided loyalties that came with a Papist fealty and a Spanish tongue. Spain kept hold of its grip on the New World by depending on the good will of local elites to enforce its laws and customs. As usual, it was the lower classes that suffered. Stylistically, Gibson's approach is unique. Rather than a traditional historical narrative, she writes as if in a long dialogue or exchanges of anecdotes on a pilgrimage, almost as if history were being signaled along the human circuits of something like the Canterbury pilgrims. Though filled with facts, dates, painstaking reportage and truly beautiful illustrations, the brilliance of the book comes through best in this endless dialogue of suffering and majesty.

Gibson nowhere leaves off her scrutiny of white privilege as a guiding force of conquest. She exposes the appalling hustle of divinely ordained "American exceptionalism" that has put a racist tincture into our personal and institutional relations with Hispanics. And these notions continued long after actual territorial growth ceased and its effects somewhat dissipated. Building engineer Montgomery Meigs talks about the planned frieze that would ring the U.S. Capitol. Meigs enthusiastically said the mural would picture "the gradual progress of the continent from the depths of barbarism to the heights of civilization . . . . the gradual advance of the white, the retreat of the red races." A later appointed governor of Puerto Rico stated that the native Hispanic population could not "supply the brains, character and other equipment necessary for carrying on the government of the territory."

All this was taking place while literature, music, and other cultural phenomena—all of it entirely original and entirely Hispanic—was flooding into the Anglo-American world, enriching it, infusing it with new concepts, colors and ideas. Gibson follows all the paths of bloodshed and conquest, and ends up leading us to the forest spring of the human imagination, which no oppressor can silence. The voices of the book take on new gusto. As the story progresses into the last two centuries, it veers deftly from macro to micro, taking in a more ground level perspective on the American-Mexican divide. She shows how directors both American and European could make films in Mexico with less financial and censorship restraints. She traces the emergence of Hispanic-rooted music from the 20s to the present. The film industry made domestic products tinged not just with Dolores del Rio but Lucy and Desi, Zorro, and Jose Jimenez. (The latter indulged Hispanic stereotypes, a subject the author's intrinsic morality condemns and does not spend a lot of time on.)

Gibson's book could not come at a more propitious moment. With a head of state denouncing a whole country and its people in unprintable expletives, characterizing its immigrants as rapists and "bad hombres," this book shows how much of what we are came from the vast, rich lands below us. And she celebrates the fact that that influence is growing. This book will make you join her.

In'Shallah

Arabs: A 3,000 Year History
Tim Macintosh-Smith
Yale University Press

Tim Macintosh-Smith is of Yemeni ancestry, raised in England and educated at Oxford. He has returned to live at least part of the year in S'aana, Yemen's dusty, turbulent capital. In this breathtaking book, he takes us through 3,000 years of Arab history. The unifier is not, as one might guess, Islam. Much of the volume deals with Arab life and customs as much as 1400 years before the birth of the young Mohammed in the Seventh Century. The far more sinuous and problematic chain that runs through the narrative is the Arabic language, with its near-infinity of dialects. The first known inscriptions mentioning Arabic date from 853 B.C. For hundreds of years, from Indonesia in the east to Mauritania, the westernmost reach of what could be called the Arab Empire, the script that worked its way into the Qu'ran was "the founding text of Arabism . . . with all the weight of a Pentateuch, a Magna Carta and the Declaration of independence. All of it emerged from the "golden swirl" that finally culminates with "La ilaha illa Allah," "There is no god but Allah." The first victory this ethnic group secured was the tongue that bears their name.

Though Macintosh-Smith goes on to say that "The grammar of the Arabs' history would be unstoppably active, and they would earn not just a capital letter but a definite article," there are two other forces of unification at work as well. One was Islam, the other the tide of warfare that swept these desert people from the moment of their inception in history. He starts when jewels and spices from oasis cities were the pre-Christian equivalent of oil. Caravans moved west laden with dates and incense, and returned with garments and stonewear incumbent upon a nomadic or itinerant life. There were the Sabaeans and Himyaris, the Abbasids who settled Baghdad and the unconquerable Umayyads who dominated the valleys beneath Asia Minor, in the kingdoms that came to be called Trans-Jordan and Jordan. The development of empires eventually brought the family of Saud, and the reciprocity of desert and village life, and the animated drama of the caravan, all of which are a constant theme in this rich, almost cinematically delivered narrative. It has the marvelous, brisk velocity of a good novel, and will be the gold standard of this fabulous peoples' histories.

After taking us through the pre-Islamic world, we land at the transformation that took place with Mohammed's prophecy in 622 A.D. Surrounding wars and clashes of cultures in zero-sum lands show that a key to Arab culture was their capture "on a rock between predatory powers." There were invaders long before Napoleon, but his arrival in Egypt in 1798 brought fashions and technologies that culminated with a Christian convert, the Lebanese Ibrahim al-Yaziji. Fighting over desert lands was given its film baptism by David Lean, who has Omar Sharif shoot Peter O'Toole's guide boy to death for drinking from his tribes' well. "You do not understand, English," said Sharif, demonstrating that the concept of sharing with outsiders was dangerous and perplexing, and could amount to disloyalty to one's own family. Of particular interest, and interloping, was of course the British Empire. During and after World War One, the creation of nation-states "on the back of a lunch napkin" (Churchill's words) left a line of disquiet from the Sykes-Picot pact to the much ballyhooed Balfour Declaration in Parlaiment, which delivered on the long promised wish for a Jewish homeland in the middle of historic Palestine. Of the British and Balfour, Macintosh-Smith proclaims that the English diplomats were, "more often than not, driving wedges into old splits."

The battles between Arab empires and Christian or Jewish neighbors persists into the 21st Century. In Northern Syria, particularly the "ISIS capital" of Raqqa, there was a tax on Christians levied in 640 A.D. It was reinstated by the "Islamic state" in 2014. Hopes for democracy and representative government across such a wide swath of territory have met with some success, but clouds block the sun at opportune moments. Much of it came down to Cairo's Tahrir Square in 2011, the birthplace of the first wave of "the Arab Spring." Would it lead to something like English colonists achieved in 1776, or would it sputter and invite bloodshed, like Tien An Men Square in 1989? Macintosh-Smith would have it that the only success has been the Western-oriented Tunisia, which made much of what happened in Cairo and moved it forward with geopolitical baby steps. The new kingdoms are ruled by autocrats the author dubs as rulers of conspicuous skyscrapers and shopping malls. The police-repressive apparatus of Egypt is probably worse now than it was in 2011 when Mubarak was deposed.

Gamal Abdel Nasser, the potentate of Egypt in the 50s and 60s, followed the rotund and autocratic King Farouk. Nasser was a dazzler, a handsome drake not seen in Islamic politics since the (ironically secular) Kemal Atatürk "Father of the Turks" earlier in the same century. First, Nasser humiliated the British over the Suez Canal. And it was this same blunderer who goaded Israel into the Six-Day War, and set sympathies for surrounding Arab states back at least a hundred years. Little was helped by his embrace of Russia, though as a nation Egypt was propelled forward by Soviet inspiration, education, technology, and a shared sense of marginalization from the Western world. One recalls the great news photograph of Nasser and Krushchev raising their joined fists together in a Bedouin tent, surrounded by exotic weavings and hopeful acolytes. It all crumbled after 1967, when a rollback of granted land stranded West Bank and Gaza residents under the thumb of the "Zionist infidels."

The great debate about "modernization" of the Arab world is deftly analyzed by the author. We are told that Arab and Islam are not synonymous, and yet Islamic culture, often very advanced for its time, provided a sort of "Arab information technology." This was cnveryed in the form of writing and painting, and when Arabic script, famously difficult for the printing press, began to be printed on cheap paper rather than the parchment made from Nile weeds. The class divisions within the identifying language also lead to dissidence, confusion and neglect. While printed Arabic lead to "new ways to use and control language and thus form identity," the Koran—as in the Hindi-Urdu distinction—insists on a "high" Arabic, a near Biblical tongue more proper even than the "Standard Egyptian." Proselytizers of the Qu'ran admit that an essentially nomadic people may have trouble finding madrasas, or schools, to teach it to peripatetic students. People who are by nature rootless hunters and gatherers cannot live and may not be able to be unified by such a rarefied tongue. Though the whole nature of Arab identity can seem foreign to democracy, commerce and urbanization, Macintosh-Smith still has hope for the people he fondly writes about.

The achievement here is one of quality as well as scale. He shows how a people skirted into the wrong pockets of history, and sometimes led by despot after despot (look at the developments in Sudan), can reach forward into unity and freedom, although their past was a torn canvas of poverty and dispersal. The book is a doorstop but reads with a breathtaking briskness. Its end notes are a luxuriant catalog of cultural and political materials from this intrepid people. They have found their historical champion at last, as this book has little chance of being surpassed.

Till Death Do Us Part

Late Life Love
Susan Gubar
Norton, 322 pages

Susan Gubar is a distinguished professor emerita at Indiana University, long a gem of their English and Women's Studies Departments. She is best known for authoring, along with Sandra Gilbert, the feminist gospel *The Madwoman in the Attic: The Woman Writer and the Nineteenth-Century Literary Imagination (1979)*. They literally revolutionized feminist literary theory in a work that is still standard fare in those departments. Gubar was diagnosed with advanced ovarian cancer in 2008. The bridge between cancer sufferers and their medical providers is another terrain of Gubar's. But the real theme of this memoir is finding someone as a true love late in life, spotting the *amour fou* over one's spectacles. It is written with a kind of measured verve, and extends the life of its writer and the romance that is its true subject is new and remarkable ways. It is in the end a testament of hope, of how autumns can be seen as springs all over again, the seasons containing one another inside of themselves like seeds.

Gubar is a columnist for the *New York Times*, writing a column called "Living With Cancer." She takes this winning, affable mixture of personal history and reflection and turns it on the romantic prize she found a short time before her diagnosis. He, too, was an Indiana University English professor. The two of them had to confront not just the issues of her treatment, but also the mundanities and awkwardness of aging. Her husband began to suffer age-related disabilities, and the way they maintain by learning to "catch" one another, trading off duties and discernments, is as engaging as a memoir of type gets. Their first challenge was moving out of a long-cherished but suddenly impractical home. They packed boxes and weaned the detritus with an energy of people half their age. (They *did* have help from their children, all from their two prior marriages.) Here's where the hope-lever, the fulcrum of positivity comes in: I am sick and old and he is old, but a fierce affection binds us to each other and to this country house, which we will have to leave. The chapter titles string together similar but different themes: 'Wrinkled in Time'; 'Recounting the Ways'; 'Enormous Changes At The Last Minute,' a title borrowed from another saint of septuagenarians, the fierce and undefeatable Grace Paley.

She speaks marvelously about the most extreme form of ageism, that suffered by her and her husband. She wants to be able to unspool an "imaginative account of the longevity of desire," but anger rears itself when they are belittled, condescended to, over-accomodated in restaurants and hotels, on the occasions when they are able to get out at all. People describe her late-life romance—or at least talking or writing about it—as "so-called senile-sexuality," something that should have been long abandoned before the time of their respective ages. (He is ten years older than she is, and seemingly ten years younger in his energy and physical stamina.) In quick ripostes, she assembles positive literary examples that "extol—amid the ordeals of ageing—the mutuality and reciprocity, the passion and compassion at the heart of tender relationships in later life.' Her insights all focus on newer, late-onset love rather than unions which were formed early and persevered for decades. She exhaustively examines Garcia-Marquez's *Love in the Time of Cholera,* balancing male lust and its straying with matriarchal fidelity, showing how Latin American couples seemingly weather all kinds of heartbreak that would cripple more self-regarding northern neighbors. One of the most delightful literary excursions and comparisons is of Beckett's 'Happy Days,' which, like all of Beckett, is after all a comedy. It is the play in which the heroine Winnie is trapped in a giant pyramid of goo, and whose husband Willie never leaves her side. She observes that "Winnie can't win and Willie cant tell himself to do much of anything," though the interdependence of the two is dynamic, an aspect of the life-force if there ever was one. She also explores aging love in works of I.B. Singer, John Updike, Louis Begley (good choice), and the Great Plains scribes Kent Haruf and Marilynne Robinson.

The pivotal year that is the book's center is her 71st and his 88th. He has been hobbled with multiple surgeries on his knee, when she was able to turn the tables, re-pay the favor of caregiving, and watch over him as his tendons strengthened and his ability to move improved miraculously before her eyes. Here is where the balloon of her literary observations gets caught in the shed of the mundane, the quotidian. The writing on this seems only half-intentional, but maybe the bubbling subconscious, that cauldron to which we must all submit, is another oar in the darkening, thickening water they need to navigate and row through together. They are determined to make the most of the time left in that journey, what Anne Sexton called the "awful rowing toward God."

She can take a simple notion such as second chances and develop the narrative of how her long professional friendship with Don deepened into love when she was grieving over the loss of her first husband. He, too, was a grief-stricken widower. She is excellent on how sexuality in old age requires not just patience but good humor and a taste for the unlikely, the farcical. Her consciousness of transience illuminates other late-love stories in addition to her own. She astutely notes the interchangeability of the terms "caregiver" and "caretaker", moving through famous unions that mirror hers, like that of John Bayley and Iris Murdoch (with her dementia thrown in), and Donald Hall and Jane Kenyon. One can have been young in sin, and have its glimmer stay with you, as celebrated by poets like Auden and John Betjeman, who gorgeously mourns the abilities and recklessness he had when a quarter of his age.

As Kingsley Amis told his son, the novelist Martin, the problem with age is that "it gives nothing back." In her borrowed time Gubar worries—for all her collaboration with the Muse—that so much of her life is simply hospital appointments, indefinite delays, biopsies, and the dreadful balancing of life-saving medicines that usually kill you in mismatched combinations. The physical awfulness of age is scrutinized anatomically. Things droop and sag, excretions drip out of one's orifices, sudden pains visit the slightest movements. But if we become gnarled trees, bending as we never used to against the wind, the book's message is that we still bend into one another. Like the Baucis and Philemon of Ovid intertwining their branches for an eternity they will never be conscious of, the persistence of love allows us to see the truth of things unseen *avant* the bending, things that were—in Pound's retelling of the myth—"rank folly to [our] heads before."

The Halt and the Blind

Unexampled Courage:
The Blinding of Sgt. Issac Woodard and the Awakening
of President Harry Truman and Judge J. Waties Waring
Richard Gergel
Sarah Crichton Books/FSG, 266 pages

Isaac Woodard was an Army sergeant in the Pacific Theater of WW II. An African-American, he served in the still-segregated, though post-Truman military. While unloading ships off Papua New Guinea, in the heat of Japanese fire, he showed bravery extraordinary enough to win a battle star. Wearing his uniforms after his discharge, the 26-year-old boarded a bus in Augusta, Georgia, on his way home to South Carolina. An hour or two into the journey, he asked the Greyhound driver to stop at a restroom at a state rest stop on the Interstate. The driver brushed him off, but Woodard talked back, saying that he was a man just like the driver, and he would appreciate the man pulling into the rest stop. The driver did halt the bus once they got across the state line in Batesburg, S.C., but it was so the driver could go to a pay phone and call the police. Two officers arrived, Woodward forgot to address them as "Sir," and they dragged him off the bus and onto the ground. One of them ground the handle of a blackjack or nightstick into Woodard's eyes, resecting his eyeballs and blinding him.

Gergel, a federal district court judge in South Carolina, paints what happened as one of two events that awakened racial sensitivity in the newfound atmospherics of cooperation after the War. First, Truman commissioned a civil rights study and immediately integrated the military. Simultaneously, Gergel's predecessor, Judge J. Waties Waring, issued a series of decisions undercutting South Carolina's particularly stringent Jim Crow laws. (Gergel now sits in the courthouse that bears Waring's name, and was most recently in the news for presiding over the trial and death sentence of Dylann Landis, who shot up a black Charleston church, showing no remorse for his actions.) The Truman administration influenced Carolina prosecutors to push hard on the prosecution of Batesburg Police Chief Lynwood Shull. But there were obstacles other than those one would most suspect, like getting blacks on the federal jury pool. The United States Attorneys there owed their jobs to segregationist U.S. senators. Additionally, local agents of the FBI, working up the case, had to maintain good relations with the officers serving under Shull. Accordingly, the Truman announcements of vigorous prosecution muted the public demand for justice and allowed the investigation to proceed at a snail's pace until after the 1946 elections, when it was thought the case could be swept under the rug of a dismissal.

But Judge Waring was not going to go along with the political subterfuge. Waring denied the U.S. Attorney's request for a continuance, but the prosecution was a sham and Waring quietly decried the Justice Department's politicization of the trial. Waring was from a prominent Charleston family but ironically had campaigned for one of the South's most notorious racist judges. Judge Gergel shows how the 'official story' unrolled that Waring and Truman underwent a fundamental political transformation in their view of civil rights, infused one another with strength and courage, and, with the help of the NAACP, began to roll back the travesty of racially rigged trials in the South. The truth is considerably more complex, especially with regard to Waring's personal life and choices of friends and associates.

This writer is not a criminal lawyer, but Gergel's account of the disastrously prepared prosecution of the police chief is meticulous and spellbinding. He works through the perspective of NAACP lawyer Franklin Williams to show the federal prosecutor's possibly purposeful incompetence. Shull's defense was that he never targeted Woodard's eyes. The story was anatomically unbelievable, given the time it took to gouge out the man's eye sockets. After the failed prosecution, Woodard began widening the message of his predicament from racism to veteran's affairs. Despite his advocacy for them, the Veteran's Administration itself filched on his pension because his disability had occurred, officially, after his discharge. (He unsuccessfully sued Greyhound Bus Lines for failure to provide security.) Peoples' memories during these precise years were weak, so his "veterans affairs" speaking tour was not well attended, and his struggle mainly influenced only the judiciary and civil rights organizations. Gergel writes that "Woodard's blinding would open the eyes of many Americans," but its influence continued only as a dripping seep into the chambers of Judge Waring, President Truman and Thurgood Marshall.

Woodard eventually bought a home, found itinerant work, and raised a family. He died in 1992. Police violence against blacks in the South continued, and was brought into sharper relief by state militias' reaction to racial protests in the following years. The most notable was the "Orangeburg Massacre" of 1968; the fact so few know about it is partly testament to all else that was happening in that epochal year. A demonstration was underway at the historically black South Carolina State University when a state highway patrolman and his deputies shot 27 people. At first, the federal civil rights prosecution against nine of the man's recruits drew an acquittal, and it seemed like the Woodard v. Batesburg Police case all over again. It was. Only recently, in the last ten or fifteen years, racial violence has come to the forefront of public attention, including acts by both public and private attackers. Again, it was the author Gergel who presided over Dylann Roof's shootings at the Emanuel AME Church in Charleston, and resulted in his death sentence by a state court jury.

Gergel ably lifts his looking glass to the incongruity of exactly *which* leaders would be influential in battling racially motivated police violence. Truman and Waring's backgrounds give no indication they would play a role—even as mere stepping stones—in the abatement of state sanctioned racial attacks. Their influence could be argued to be Zelig-like, bordering on the consequential and almost accidental. Truman was from a white farm family in the Midwest. He grew up in the part of Missouri that sided with the South, as did portions of other states like Kansas. Both his grandfathers had been slave owners. Truman used his civil rights commission as just enough fanfare to save votes for himself in mixed racial electoral regions. Waring could also be argued to have, if not shallow, opportunistic motives, at least ones that fitted his personal dilemmas. A year before

Shull's trial, the 64-year-old judge divorced his wife of 32 years and married a Connecticut heiress. For Charleston society, this was one step over the line—history and race relations be damned. It was then that Waring and his new wife moved to New York and came, understandably, under the spell of Thurgood Marshall.

Some might argue that the attack on Woodard is a thin reed upon which to string a history of racial violence and botched veteran's affairs. This reader sees each rung of the ladder of justice as necessary, however weak and nondescript one of the rungs might be. The book is a testament to the unlikeliness of influence, how certain struggles can progress on small and seemingly invisible stages, with effects taking years and diverted directions to come to any effect. The best parts of the book are ones where Gergel draws from his experience as a sitting judge, portraying the rigidity of racism in a jury pool, the nature of veniremens' decision processes, and the glaring agony of how it took a single incident to spotlight the darkness of a region's attitudes.

Prisons of the King

On Politics
Alan Ryan
Liveright, 1114 pages (Two Volumes)

For decades, political philosophy, both in the academy and in the history of ideas, has been the somewhat abstract discipline of ethical concepts and ideas of justice. Rawls's 'Theory of Justice' and Dworkin's 'Why Rights Matter' are probably the best and most justifiably influential examples. But Alan Ryan, an Oxford professor, takes an entirely different tack with his new, compendious 'On Politics.' Its 1100 page (wait, don't run) subject is Western democracies' search for and justification of their constitutive concepts, including controls on liberty and economic behavior, and their hegemony over punishment and the law enforcement functions, police-repressive apparatuses, etc.. Ryan's book is a portrait of European and American commitment to government's overall appeal, to making it appealing to the governed.

Ryan fleshes out the historical background of this enterprise by exploring politics as a branch of history, biography and philosophy. But, as he says, political theory is "not exactly history." It more appropriately ranges over centuries of "philosophies of government" to select the more attractive systems, or sometimes mere sympathies. He favors James Surowiecki's arguments in 'The Wisdom of Crowds' over Kierkegaard's '[T]he crowd is untruth." He blandishes Aristotle's collectivity-wisdom by quoting from 'The Politics': a multitude of citizens "thinking together" as an assembly is preferable to the propositions or actions of the smartest individuals among them.

Ryan sees us as political, which means uniquely "historical" creatures. What he means by this is that the political past infuses our explorations of what it means to be free and to be governed. We adorn our courts with the architectural styles of antiquity. We have jurists who believe that even as malleable a document as the constitution involves inhabiting the minds of its collective drafters, wandering the attic with interpretive lanterns that illuminate lost items of "intent."

Ryan sees us needing these ghosts in the modern machine of polity because we are self-conscious and nervous about the vagaries of political trends, and we want to anchor them to traditions and past practices. "Out of the crooked timber of humanity," Isaiah Berlin said, discounting systems, "no straight thing can be made." Still, its roots reach deeply, seeking viatic nourishment, because "[W]e share the ancient and medieval world's sense of fragility of the political order." We need structures and procedures in place to stem avarice, to dampen righteous indignation and keep it from being acted upon. We require the molds of institutional archetypes to shape and make useful our sometimes frightening (viz. Freud and Foucault) irruptions of instinct.

Nowhere is this trend—the insecurity, the grasp for past structures—more obvious than in democracy's conduct of punishment. Most European countries have abolished the death penalty, but abolitionists within the U.S. Supreme Court had only a small sliver of daylight in the early Seventies. Now arguments of "evolving standards of decency" cannot sway the majority. Complicating American punishment is also the "prison industry," which sustains many rural, under-industrialized communities, and which thrives on fresh inmate populations created by minimum sentencing guidelines.

Ryan focuses on how historically harsh sentences still infuse even abolitionist jurisdictions, stressing that there must still be some sense of an "ultimate" punishment—albeit less than death—for homicide, terrorism, treason. Allowing television into the courtrooms preserves the notion of the collectivity's demand for retribution and humiliation, even if elements of spectacle and sacrifice have faded away.

Elections are another venue in which the past, for all dusty remoteness, creeps into the modern political arena. Athenian courts were the result of balloting both legitimate and illegitimate, and resulting parricides were the precursors to our scandals and adulterous tell-alls. Congressional assemblies themselves wear the template of ancient days. Both Athens and Rome, like modern Britain, would be unimaginable without squabbling, bickering, the marshalling of leverage under the masquerade of "compromise." The health care and budget crises of the past four years allow extreme positions borne of the "exclusive importance" of such issues. Fears are ginned up with warnings of a return to the body carts of the plague eras, committees deciding life and death, the seizure of American lands and icons by our Chinese creditors.

Another question Ryan wrestles with is what political systems are eventually for. Ideas include the obvious safety and security issues, along with legal structures and the control of goods. A national character or identity seems also to be a political purpose, but at the same time, a true democracy must stress diversity. These are key concerns especially for emerging democracies trying to transition out of autocracies, and would include much of the turbulent Mideast. National identity concerns arise especially with countries trying to (politically) de-Islamicize, the best example being Atatürk's Turkey of the 1920s, and what people had hoped for in the North African "Spring"—Tunisia, Libya, and eventually Egypt—of 2010-11. Diversions can be allowed, but not deviance. The wiser regimes are defining almost any kind of violent extremism, appropriately, as deviant, unwelcome, geopolitically embarrassing.

Ryan's writing is vibrant, and bucks against the potential dullness of its subject matter. He adumbrates the driest descriptions of state processes with artistic and cultural shadings. He writes with passion and conviction, and she also writes with a musical sense of language, an artist's understanding of how politics and history, private and public events, overlap. And with respect to his discipline overall, there are few that can even approach him. If this broad a subject can hope for a definitive treatise, this is it.

Two Quiet Giants

Brave Genius
Sean B. Carroll
Crown, 473 pages

Vast numbers of the French kept their heads down all during the German occupation. They were *collabos,* or collaborators, and if they were writers, their "craft and sullen art," however compromised, was allowed—within the parameters of censorship—to flourish. If they did not cooperate, their creative efforts were vitalized, by cunning and subterfuge, while still keeping their essential character. Hiddenness let them hone whatever they did to a fine new sharpness.

Some figures, like (surprisingly) Samuel Beckett, involved themselves in dangerous, direct operations, like gun running, bombings, and highway ambushes. Others worked more subtly, but no less effectively. They supported the front line resisters whether it be with underground journalism, scientific assistance, or scattershot or pinpointed disruptions of the tentacular Nazi machinery.

Other figures operated with more secrecy. Two were Albert Camus and the molecular biologist Jacques Monod. Few had heard of both. Camus's books were nearly everywhere, and were quite influential. Monod's were more abstruse and specialized, reaching a wider audience later, though he was not a "popularizer" of science or of his subspecialty. One crucial thing Camus and Monod shared was the formative experience of Occupation. Both had what the British call "a good war." They were in the Resistance, and, while neither of them blew up any locomotives, shot any Germans or led any Jews to safety across the Alps, their courage was unquestionable. Monod, whose Jewish wife made it through the war with false identity papers, was a courier and an organizer; Camus was primarily a writer for the Resistance paper *Combat.* But these were dangerous things to do, and both had colleagues who were shot or taken off to the camps. Camus and Monod must have passed each other many times in the streets of occupied Paris, but there is no evidence that they met then. Their first meeting happened in September 1948, or, put another way, on page 290 of "Brave Genius." The thoughts and doings of Camus and Monod here are woven through masses of background information, but the protagonists sometimes disappear for many pages.

Caroll sets out the correspondence between the two in less than 50 pages. The connection between the them was sort of backwardly reified when Monod flirted with philosophy in his "Chance and Necessity" (1970), where he stated he was emerging as a new incarnation of "[m]y friend Camus, albeit in a lab coat." Monod had both artistic and philosophical tendencies and read his friend's books, but Camus knew little about science. Nevertheless, they soon found some common sensibilities, and Monod's personal copy of a book of Camus's essays was inscribed by the author: "Â Jacques Monod, sur la même chemin" ("on the same path"). It was a path partly marked out by anti-Communism. Monod had been in the Communist Party during the Occupation; Camus had a brief fling with it when he was a student in Algeria. They came out of the war despising both right- and left-wing totalitarianism. For Monod, the break finally came with Lysenkoist genetics–the same-mandated Soviet dogma that characteristics acquired by an organism during its lifetime were inherited by its offspring, and that the will of the proletariat somehow operated at the sub-molecular level. Some fellow travelling Western scientists felt obliged to defend Lysenko and criticize "bourgeois genetics," but Monod denounced Lysenkoism for the pathology it was, and he left the party. Monod's gesture impressed Camus. Revolutions, Camus wrote, tend to degenerate into repression; to be human was to rebel, if necessary to rebel even against a state wrapping itself in a revolutionary flag. Freedom was a human right, and the struggle to be free, to be authentic, and to oppose violence was a major basis of modern morality. There could never be a justification for barbarity and murder, or even for capital punishment. (See Camus's brilliant long essay "Reflections on the Guillotine" in *Lyrical and Critical Essays*.) His friend Sartre, trying to look on the bright side of Stalinism, arranged for Camus's *The Rebel* to be trashed in his magazine *Les temps modernes*, ending their long friendship in one of the great intellectual battles of post-war France.

In reality, how close was the Camus-Monod friendship? Though there were deep parallels in their work, Carroll does not foreground the precise encounters and communications other than through letters. There were letters and exchanges of inscribed books. There were never any speaking engagements, shared seminars, or mutual faculty tenures. Carroll, himself a scientist, deftly shows how close a tenuous and detached friendship can in fact be. And it *was* based on the overlap, the mutuality of their disciplines, which delighted the two men and many who worked with them. Monod's molecular biology, with its serendipitous, eruptive creations out of seemingly nothing, grew to resemble the causal circus of quantum mechanics. One thing did not necessarily follow from another. Events did not lend themselves to covering-law models or hard science explanations. Carroll puts it succinctly: "Molecular biology had brought Monod full circle to Camus's territory of the absurd condition—that contradiction between the human longing for meaning and the universe's silence."

The book is a fine testament to how two fine minds from very different disciplines, forged in the crucible of war, could come together in a fruitful if intermittent collaboration.

Sadness and Happiness

My Age of Anxiety
Scott Stossel
Knopf, 464 pages

Scott Stossel, a sufferer of acute anxiety for most of his life, has written an extraordinarily readable encyclopedia of mental disorders, their chemical and talk-therapy treatments, almost all of it funneled through the history of his family: his Harvard faculty father, his children, and his menagerie of health care providers. *My Age of Anxiety,* while violating perhaps J.C. Oates's prohibition on 'pathographies,' is memoir enough to acquit the author of voyeurism. And yet the lurid details (of emetephobia, for example) leave a bad taste in the mouth, rinsed only by the bracing tang of a beautiful reportorial style. Andrew Solomon's *Noonday Demon* comes to mind, as does William Styron's *Darkness Visible.* One assumes that Stossel, as editor in chief of *The Atlantic,* had no shortage of sub-editors to keep him on a steady course.

Stossel's fascinating angle here is the counterintuitive symbiosis of anxiety and depression, which seem to the lay reader and patient as distinct as a gallop and a trot. As psychiatrists, especially pharmaceutical-dispensers, would have it, depression is as common a reaction to threats and foreboding as is anxiety. They are different points along a modern stress sufferers gradient of psychic energy. I emphasize—Stossel emphasizes—"modern" here because it was only in the forties that anxiety became the sweeping, inclusive term it is today. Stossel notes that anxiety focus comes not so much from Freud, but from America and Europe's post-war obsession with Kierkegaard, an obsession this reviewer shares. For the Lowrie Dane, anxiety was not so much a foreboding dread as a 'dizziness of freedom,' the inability to wipe clean the glass of perspective given its prismatic, almost blinding angles of choice. Kierkegaard sought solutions in a recognition of human finitude, and devised probably the most unique and robust interpretation of Christianity in the history of ideas. Anxiety was dissipated by infinite faith in almost any object, an 'approximation-process,' he called it, of 'utmost inwardness.' This process *was* truth to Kierkegaard, and it provided to his followers a fragile membrane of tranquility, a 'bark,' he wrote in *Philosophical Fragments,* 'in which I row the fathomless sea.'

For all of this 'K Factor,' his concept of anxiety, as Freud's disciples came to England and the United States, got subsumed into that of the Vienna Circle: Fromm, Klein, Horney, Hoffman, Kohut and Fenichel. The main diagnostic manual of psychic disorders, the DSM, came into prominence in 1952, and it fastened on the still incipient, amorphous concept of anxiety as the *Grundrisse* of neurosis.

The central question after DSM was, of course, appropriate treatment—its genesis and its criteria of completion. Freud felt that talk therapy—his main treatment protocol—fastened on entirely internal mental phenomena created in early childhood. These neuroses could never be eradicated, but only identified by the patient, who then moved, in Freud's great phrase, from neurotic misery to 'ordinary unhappiness.' But this dolorous prospect was not good enough for America, whose formative document and endless optimism demanded happiness in exchange for its therapeutic dollar.

So along came the silver bullet of altered brain chemistry: psychotropics, pharmaceuticals, Mothers Little Helper. Stossel kicks in (sorry) to high gear here, with fascinating histories of the (often accidental) discoveries of muscle relaxants that became the first tranquilizers: Miltown, Librium, Valium and eventually Xanax. Psychology and psychiatry's hunger for the status of a hard science made talk therapy—however used in tandem with pills—take a back seat to Big Pharma's brain amine compounds. Medication was also easier, quicker as a stress reducer. Why add lateness to your shrink appointment (and having to pay if you cancel) to the jumble of worries he was supposed to help you work through?

Stossel surprises the reader with the sheer abundance (both courageous and pathetic) of his search for psychic peace. After 25 years with an orthodox Freudian talk therapist, he switches to a more humanist-existentialist follower of Rollo May's 'empathic' school, and one who patiently accommodates the growing trend of chemical cures. (Talk is still necessary, Stossel and his new guy have it, because anxiety grows 'from failed efforts to resolve basic existential dilemmas.')

But is there any modality—all of them spectacularly unsuccessful—that Stossel hasn't tried? Group therapy is here, as is rational emotive therapy, commitment therapy, interoceptive exposure therapy (say what?), meditation, supportive-expressive therapy, yoga, and the now blazingly trendy cognitive behavioral therapy.

In the end, Stossel seems to find harbor in the latter, a cerebral, methodical approach that seems the opposite of orthodoxy's 'free association' and notions of transference and counter-transference. His shrink asks him to imagine how he could have reached the heights of his success—keeping America's oldest literary magazine afloat in a constricting, possibly dying publishing industry—if his sheer will to achieve and self-confidence did not ultimately trump his debilitating, long-standing mental hurricanes. He cannot answer that question, which, coming in this marvelous book's final paragraphs, may be the closest thing to a cure that he could hope for.

Ethnology's Rivers & Tributaries

Gods of the Upper Air
Charles King
Nan A. Talese/Doubleday, 370 pages

It does not get much better than this in a profile of the history of ideas and disciplines. King traces the vast and quite positive influence of Franz Boas, the towering Prussian-Polish anthropologist who virtually invented anthropology's cultural branch when he fled Hitler to set up camp at Columbia and Barnard in the twenties. The man started out by being culturally embattled for his left-wing politics, shoved up to a remote section of the humanities building near Butler Library to keep him away from impressionable fellow faculty members. But his history of various civilizations had established him as the guru of early ethnology, an unlikely subject for a product of the "Prussian schoolmaster" (whose sternness and cruelty led Thomas Mann to lay Twentieth Century wars at the footstep of such a figure's influence), but who indeed (Boas) carried facial scars from fencing with swords on Berlin playgrounds in his grammar school days. Boas started penniless in the U.S., an outcast Jew who refused the professions and merchant mantles of his fellow co-religionists. But as King points out, by the 1930s, almost every cultural anthropology department in American (and foreign) colleges was chaired by one of Boas's Ph.D students. This writer worked in the library of Kroeber Hall as a Berkeley undergraduate, Arthur Kroeber being Boas's very first doctoral acolyte.

As Louis Menand has pointed out, Boas kept his creation—anthropology—in the solid corners of a hard science. He was an empiricist, who "collected facts, and was not inclined to theoretical speculation." "But he thought," Menand goes on, that "the basic fact about human beings is that the facts *about them change,* because circumstances and environments change. This is why field work was the *sine qua non* of his practice—to gauge the combinatory engine of genes, environment and culture, researchers had to be out in the muddle and muck of the primitive atmospherics of one's subjects. His student Ruth Benedict did very little field work among the Zuni, the Kwakiutl and the New Guineau highlanders she studied, and after only a few trips to Samoa Margaret Mead stopped visiting or even considering new data. The great Continental father of cultural anthropology, Claude Levi-Strauss, did hardly any field work after his study of West-Central Brazilian river natives. These brilliant, but somewhat armchair naifs of Boas's classrooms and influence, began to make ethnography resemble crypto-colonialism, the Western 'scientist' telling the native's own story without talking to or observing his subject.

Boas was blessed by acolytes of genius, four in particular. The first was Benedict, whose sometimes sloppily reasoned comparison of disparate cultures ('Appollonian' or group-identified Zunis as opposed to ecstatic, 'vision-quest' Plains Indians) in *Patterns of Culture* had a staggering influence—really a foundational one—in the discipline. His second prize student was Margaret Mead, whose Samoan studies of pre-marital sex among South sea island cultures ruffled the feathers of genteel, armchair academic ethnologists. Ellen Deloria was the third ("All my best students are women" said Boas). No anthropologist better understood and documented the languages and customs of upper Plains Indians, particularly her native Oglala Sioux, than did this dynamic, inexhaustible Teacher's College transplant. As soon as she was out of Oberlin, Boas heard tell of her language recordings, summoned her to N.Y. and his graduate programs, and the result was the classic 'Dakota Languages', a combination of essay studies and Smithsonian recordings that form the groundwork of Native American language investigations. She took the Boas mantle across the street to Barnard to spearhead his influence among female college students, who further branched out and carried the gospel to all corners of academia.

Boas's third prize student was the Harlem Renaissance author Zora Neale Hurston, who showed, as an African-American novelist, Northern readers a way of life somewhat at odds with the growing integrationist mentality which she did not entirely share. Hurston's work was—though not traditional 'anthropology'—was most representative of Boas's influence. The idea behind her novels was that we cannot see our way of life (our "culture") from the inside, just as we cannot see our own faces. The culture of the "other" serves as a looking glass, as Benedict put it in *Patterns of Culture*, "*The understanding we need of our* own cultural processes can . . . be arrived at by a detour." The outward focus was what we needed to understand the correspondences and similarities of a foreign culture with our own culture's qualities of mind. But in looking past the mirror we hold up to ourselves and directly at the others' lives, we grow our laboratory of specimens, deepen our grasp of what culture is.

And what is that most laden of terms? Benedict wrote of it as "coexisting and equally valid patterns of life which mankind has created for itself out of the raw materials of existence." The idea was to assess which practices were core and which were peripheral, isolating the ones that produce for a people the kind of society they want and are most adept at perpetuating. So the anthropological mirror described above has a moral purpose. Sometimes the unusual in another culture gives us a better idea of the flux of markers in our own. We see how repellant practices can become acceptable with a certain depth of understanding. Noting that Mead's first book jacket for *Coming of Age* featured a topless adolescent girl, she wanted us to see the tribal and arbitrary as possibly having a reasonableness we can come to take for granted. The seminal next-generation anthropologist Clifford Geertz, writing about Benedict, said this was "portraying the alien as the familiar with the signs changed."

These early explorations of how and what culture "is" gave rise to what it yielded as a true instrument of analysis of a people. If we see it as a lens through which we view a social group, then we are trapped in generalizations and making possibly unfounded conjectures about a 'Navajo consciousness' or a 'Kyrgyz consciousness." It will sometimes be hard to find differences among groups if this intersubjectivity, with all its commonness with other perspectives erasing distinctions, becomes the dominant metaphor. On the other hand, once one distinguishes a group's culture from its social structure—which positivists like Geertz attempt—then culture becomes tossed-off epiphenomena of tribal structures, something that only glosses off the underlying etiology of forms of life. Another potentially dangerous weakening of the term's usefulness—aimed often at Levi-Strauss with his rigid taxonomies of cooking and genital classifications—is that the ethnologist weakens her vision by seeing a culture as a frozen specimen, stuck in time's rictus for we students to study.

Boas's answer to this was to see cultural practices as existing in a constant flux, much as perception appeared to Whitehead in *Process and Reality*. Culture for Boas was "diffusion," or what he called "the spread of changing forms and practices across space and time." Deloria also rejected isolating her Sioux "talking boxes" in the time and place of their gathering. She thought that Sioux culture was nothing if not the way it was *presently* lived, with its combination of pre-white settler customs and 20th-Century ways of life, including the horribly diminished lives of Indians in the reservation system.

King of course does not miss the notion of "culture" now in our gender-exploratory and politically, culturally divided country. The differences between the Red and Blue state's views of things—from an outsider's perspective—goes back to Boas's first discoveries that cultural traits were plastic and not immutable, that they are not naturally predetermined, and that variations within groups are greater than variations between groups. (Note this concept's deft refusal to rigidify 'hard science' differences within a terribly divided 2019 American political climate, while at the same time rejecting all forms of racism and ethnic prejudice.) With these illusions of what culture is not (but has been claimed to be) out of the way, the old nature-nurture debate does not seem as acute as it was. Nature gives us the raw clay that caused Geertz to say that it is *human* nature to have culture, and for the collective consciousness of a people to identify with it. Lesser animals are presumed to learn to "know" how to live by adaptation. People are more world-creating; as the philosopher Dennett says, "the mind makes up the world." Our human consciousness progressed to where we are allowed to *choose how to respond* to our environment. To the Mayans, a pyramid-topped hill was a door into the house of the gods; to an Amazon land developer it is something to bulldoze out of the way, and both of them are 'correct.' "We can't rely on our instincts; we need an instruction manual, and culture is the manual" (Menand again). We discover it at the same time we are creating it. It is the pure product of our imagination, laid over the interconnected imagination of others; somehow it coheres into a fabric, a pattern hardened in the crucible of time.

Mean, Mean Streets

An American Summer:
Love and Death in Chicago
Alex Kotlowitz
Nan A. Talese/Doubleday, 304 pages

The language of this amazing book takes a lot of its chatter from police dispatches, detective calls, EMT recordings and logs, as well as the grim discourse in the ambulance bays of Chicago's giant, glimmering hospitals. Though the title hints at only a single summer, Kotlowitz spent four summers gathering his data, speaking to witnesses, assessing the entanglements that lay under the battlefield of homicides plaguing this city—the "most American of cities," as Norman Mailer described it—for the past decade. Like his earlier, equally fine work, 'There Are No Children Here,' about the infamous Cabrini-Greene housing project, Kotlowitz eschews complicated analysis and simply gives us the brute facts of what happens in the DMZs of this country's third largest city. When shots ring out on the street in the neighborhoods the author writes about, people do not seem to turn their heads. It is as natural as a honking line of calls or the outbreak of a rainstorm.

Kotlowitz returns to the neighborhood savant Pharoah, a man who had witnessed a cabbie shot before his eyes in 'There Are No Children Here.' As another writer has remarked, Pharoah's violence is "in his bones." The fear is augmented in a man named simply Thomas, who attended a South Side high school where, during his junior year, 21 students and recent graduates were wounded by gunfire. Between seven and ten were killed, and at the age of ten, he witnessed his 11-year-old friend and neighbor Nugget shot to death at her own birthday party. Earlier that month, Thomas's older brother Leon was shot out on the sidewalk in front of the projects and school. He became a paraplegic. Just as Thomas had helped Nugget by wiping away blood, brains and bone fragments from her braided hair, he stayed with Leon until the ambulance arrived. It is more likely than not, given Leon's blood loss, that Thomas saved his life. Thomas joined a gang called 7-0 for protection. Other gang members charged a porch on which he and a friend Shakiki were sitting, the gang member shooting her down in front of Thomas. Once again, he held a dying girl in his arms. She lived for another eight hours, lingering in the breezy summer night, in unimaginable pain.

The chronicle of Thomas becomes the grim narrative of his neighborhood, where muzzle flashes become as common as streetlights and the night stars. Often Thomas would simply refuse to go outside. Children still of short stature are taught to stay away from windows and get down under large items of furniture when the shooting commences. Thomas tried to get a non-gang street life of his own going—he ran dice games and peddled weed. He stayed away from harder drug sales and bartering in weapons, and never dreamed of committing robberies or burglaries himself. Among the more compelling passages in the book are Thomas's struggles with whether or not to cooperate as a witness for the prosecution, which he knew was his rightful duty at the same time as amounting to a death warrant. He declined to cooperate, putting himself in the police department's own crosshairs. He would get no further breaks on a stop and frisk. He had to have unloaded his day's wares.

Kotlowitz states the obvious—that Chicago's violence is overwhelmingly concentrated in its black and Hispanic neighborhoods. Oddly, he does not try to find out why Englewood—where all the above characters shoot and are shot at—is less safe that the majority of neighborhoods inhabited by people of color. All he can point to are studies in which weak community organizations, the atomism of violence, and distrust and noncooperation with the police are the most solid markers of the social structure. They are also the distorted gospel of youth growing up, watching their older siblings get out of the neighborhood, become kingpins within it, and if the latter is the case, eventually dying. Kotlowitz's deeper analysis stymies him. He simply finds no other causative forces except racism and poverty. "The problem of rising and falling crime is unanswerable; anyone who tells you they know [why it exists] is just lying."

Another oddity, an anomaly of statistics, is that other metropolises have enjoyed a drop in violent crime, sometimes dramatically. In New York City, for example, homicides are lower than they have been in 70 years. The same is true of L.A., Dallas and the notoriously unsafe 'District' heart of Washington, D.C. But Chicago occupies the unenviable place in the pantheon of murder cities: St. Louis, Memphis, Detroit and Baltimore. These pockets of poverty (St. Louis's main source of income now is waterfront gambling) send their children further and further up the sedentary plateaus of hopelessness. Even in neighborhoods with decent schools, the number of students laying low to avoid gunfire is startling. Access to computers is minimal; physical plane of middle and high schools is abysmal. The models for success—athletics, rap music—can be toxic and unreachable. There isn't a page in this work that does not stress the maze these children are caught in, and that doesn't give the clearest of pictures of the message of futility, of simply giving up.

The eerie omertà of the streets is what helps the crime rate stay steadily high. Only one in 10 shooters in Chicago gets caught, or is even reported. It is a "no-snitch-code-of-the-street," and ironically it is useful as a safety buffer for those—like young adolescent gun runners—who need protection against the bullets of their bosses' competitors. One photograph in another essay shows a heartbreaking scene out of the life of someone who should be at the advent of life, the threshold of his years ahead. It is a makeshift memorial, set up in 2015, for Alvin Randolph, shot while simply walking down one of the tougher streets of the notoriously tough South Side. There are flowers, weeds, signs on tiny posts stuck in the frost-hardened soil. There is something like a large dog or teddy bear looking out from the pile. This kind of bloodshed seems destined for no end. Kotlowitz is particularly astute in chronicling the residual effects of homicide, the aftershock of having high-caliber weapons going off through the night, like one reads about in Aleppo or other Mideastern hellholes. The PTSD is overwhelming. A subject like Thomas hits the ground at the sound of a motorcycle backfire. There is no end to it, and under the current administration, remedying the underlying causes is well down toward the bottom of its list of priorities.

Anat Crit

Better Living Through Criticism
A.O. Scott
Penguin Press, 310 pages

Is criticism an art? Can it be something like art, a creation that elevates and stuns us with beauty, like an urn or a well-wrought sonnet? Must it be an art to be effective, as though that were its ticket to legitimacy? If one rides alongside a stallion, does one have to track its path with the same sure-footedness, the same uniqueness of movement and grace? The essays of the best critics—Coleridge, Johnson, Carlyle—have filled all serious readers with wonder. But what about criticism generally, what is its purpose? One wonders what is left once the assessment function is taken away. Does it occupy the same high ground as its referent?

What is the role of a reviewer in an age when everyone reviews, everyone blogs, everyone assigns themselves this importance? A.O. Scott, the *Times* film critic, has written a book that explores the discipline's past, states its goals, makes a case for its being—when done right—the equivalent of its correlatives. He ranges through his argument freely, breezily, packing the hard points with syllogisms and anecdotes.

Orwell saw a dreariness in criticism, a down-and-outedness that exceeded the struggles of even primary source authors. "The prolonged, indiscriminate reviewing of books is a quite exceptionally thankless, irritating and exhausting job." He saw it as bottom feeding, wishful degradation, something that existed only out of necessity. Soon after writing *Animal Farm*, and with little inkling of its destined status, and still poor, he sketched out the reviewer as treading water above the eventuality of destitution:

> In a cold but stuffy bed-sitting room littered with cigarette ends and half empty cups of tea, a man in a moth-

eaten dressing-gown sits at a rickety table, trying to find room for his typewriter among the dusty papers that surround it. He cannot throw the paper away because the wastepaper basket is already overflowing, and besides, somewhere among the un-answered letters and unpaid bills it is possible that there is a cheque for two guineas which he is nearly certain he forgot to pay into the bank . . . . .

Half hidden among the pile of papers is a bulky parcel containing five volumes which his editor has sent with a note saying "they ought to go well together." They arrived 48 hours ago, but the reviewer was prevented by moral paralysis from opening the parcel. Yesterday in a resolute moment he ripped the string off and found the five volumes to be *Palestine at the Crossroads, Scientific Dairy Farming, A Short History of European Democracy* (this one is 680 pages and weighs four pounds), *Tribal Customs in Portuguese East Africa*, and a novel, *Its Nicer Lying Down*, probably included by mistake.

Orwell saw reviewing as something better than nothing, and reminded himself that all enterprises had something else to which they could cast a jaundiced eye. "Everyone else in the world has something else they can look down upon," he said, "and I must say, having experienced both trades, that the book reviewer is better off than the film critic, who cannot even do his work at home."

So what is it, the exemplary or simply worthwhile work of criticism? Scott warns that it cannot be too steeped in its time, citing masterpieces by Melville and Austen that were never appreciated and were often jeered at as they started their slide down into the canonical. He also argues that the critic must not be fearful of imperious judgments, assessments that stake their claim as a hill to die on. Clement Greenberg and Northrop Frye would agree, looking askance at critical work that invites a dialogue, that coddles the mediocre, that pre-judges an established giant's small products as belonging to a maturing granduer.

Scott forcefully endorses Harold Bloom's notions of works being usurpations of prior influences. He is very much enamored of the notion of "internal antagonism" in critical judgment, similar to Bloom's notion of an "agon." He is keenly aware of the tension between what must be sharply scolded, yet possibly credited for authenticity and sincerity. Tobias Wolff once told this writer how easy he goes on first authors because he knows "how hard it is to write a book." But he followed that by warning me against the flabbiness of endorsements, of glad-handing and reviewing the work of one's friends.

Scott is not a system builder. He has no grand outline like that of James Wood in *How Fiction Works,* or Wood's colossal, historical predecessor Northrop Frye. He reminds us that the critic can simply stand back and celebrate artifice, show the brilliant way "a thing can seem to know just what it is." One can swing freely between contradictions within a single work, walking carefully in the footsteps of moderation and responsibility, staying within standard deviations. Or one can "wave the bright flag of opposition," often instinctual and heedless, thrashing out a pattern while pushing against (as Bloom would have it) "the anxiety of influence." Scott welcomes the roller coaster of being "earnest or flippant, plainspoken or baroque, blunt or coy, dilettante or geek." When he says that one can follow the precepts of theory "or just go on your nerve," how much he reminds us he is of the latter school. Or anti-school.

The first half of this book illustrates, in a passage from Teju Cole's *Open City,* the sort of self-revelation of a superior work's majesty, the quick, unfolding beauty of the *quidditas.* Julius, the protagonist, ruminates as he wanders a bewildering Manhattan, a place so different from the squalid Nigeria he hails from. He stands before a painting in the American Folk Art Museum. He is purely a lens at the point of rapture he reaches before a picture of a young bather. "I lost all track of time before these images, fell deep into their world, as if all the time between them and me had vanished, so that when the guard came up to me to say the museum was closing, I forgot how to speak and simply looked at him. When I eventually walked down the stairs and out of the museum, it was with the feeling of someone who had returned to the earth from a great distance."

Scott finishes this passage with a sigh: "That's what," he says, "we are looking for."

Rose of Mississippi

Varina
Charles Frazier
Ecco/Harper Collins, 353 pages

Charles Frazier has written an astonishing novel centered around the illustrious wife of Jefferson Davis, as it were the First Lady of the Confederacy. As with much of Frazier's writing, it is difficult to find an awkward sentence or phrase here. He continues to be one of the great poetic chroniclers of the Upper South. The Clinch Mountains, the Blue Ridge and the Great Smokies belong to him and fellow denizens thereof like the Virginia poet Charles Wright, and the always surprising Ron Rash. But the historical content in *Varina* is what enriches those of us for whom the Confederacy remains a blur, a moral stain on the nation, a vacuum—or all of the above. Frazier sets us in the boat, fixes the tiller well, and keeps going straight ahead until the remarkable woman's life is justly told, however culpable she is regardless of intentions. Frazier is like a symphony conductor, his flourishing hand extracting the notes and the spaces between the notes with equal elegance.

Varina Howell Davis was neither arrogant nor obnoxious. She was a spirited and accomplished woman, tempering her husband's prejudices with the graciousness of a well-bred planter's daughter. Her husband Jefferson Davis was the tenth son of an impoverished Kentucky farmer; Varina was a Mississippi aristocrat. She chafed under his sway, but her loyalty to his ambitions seldom wavered throughout their long marriage. She was eminently fitted by both education and outlook to be more than a First Lady, and would arguably have made a better leader than her stubborn and sometimes tactless husband.

Varina was only seventeen when she met Davis, then a widower of 35. She had come fresh from the Briers, a Natchez plantation surrounded by rafts of magnolia, oak and pine. She was intrigued by Jefferson's wit and erudition, as he was impressed by her knowledge of Latin and the classics. After their first meeting, she admitted she found much to praise in him, despite her family's Whiggish politics. "Would you believe it," she told her mother, "He is refined and cultivated and yet . . . a Democrat."

They married in 1845, before her twentieth birthday. With her wedding gifts came her "civil death," forfeiting all her civil rights as well as her property to her husband. Eschewing her entreaties to return to Natchez, they set up housekeeping at Davis Bend, Louisiana. Throughout the South, ancient Athenian democracy—a system also built on the forced labor of slaves and war captives—was esteemed as a model of cultural achievement. Also as in antiquity, women played few major roles outside the household. Varina knew how to feign a feminine weakness, and would have agreed with her contemporary Lucy Holcombe Pickens of South Carolina, that "submission is not my role, but certain platitudes on certain occasions are the innocent deceits of the sex." She rejected submission and subservience while appearing loyal to the Southern code.

Varina accepted slavery as a way of life. A slave woman held her at her christening; her family's slaves bestowed the traditional yams at marriage and offered their condolences upon the death of her firstborn. But she could be the punishing goddess, the Latin *dia boias*, and could relegate underperforming house slaves to field labor. One aspect of slavery that repelled her was the promiscuous relations of plantation owners with their female slaves, and she could detect husbands' features in the faces of mulatto children: "We live surrounded by prostitutes," her contemporary Mary Chesnut declared, "and like the patriarchs of old our men live in all of one house with their wives and concubines." She followed her husband to Washington several years after their marriage, when he was appointed to the Senate in 1847. And when Lincoln and the "Black republicans" won the presidency in 1860, her husband lost all hope of reconciliation with the North. He returned with Varina to Natchez, and the delegates to the Confederacy's founding convention rewarded his decision by making him the chief of their breakaway republic.

Davis suffered from ill health during his presidency, and Varina was never convinced of the South's readiness for war. She even maintained a correspondence with the daughter of a Union general, Edwin Sumner, who escorted Lincoln to Washington in 1861. A woman of lesser status may have been imprisoned as a spy for such disloyalty, but her position as First Lady protected her. One of Frazier's sources, Joan Cashin, wrote of Varina's ambivalence to her role: "She was a conscript, not a volunteer." Her detractors, ever aware of her olive complexion, called her a "squaw." But at the same time the Confederacy was being undermined by the "internal secession" of its women, and within two years of the war's outbreak the new republic was threatened by the disaffection of the wives who had cheered and urged their men to the recruiting booths in 1861. This internal secession of the Confederate women deepened as the war neared its end. Varina's Natchez had fallen at last, and Jefferson's plantation at Davis Bend was soon in Union hands. Richmond was to fall soon. Surprised by Union cavalry in Georgia, Davis escaped death when Varina threw her arms around him when he tried to flee a Union platoon.

Davis was manacled in a cell at Virginia's Fortress Monroe, and though he was indicted for treason was never brought to trial in his two years of detention. Varina's request for lodging with her husband was declined, and she never forgave the insult. While she remained loyal to him, she was unable to forgive his apparent unfaithfulness with wives of wealthy Alabama landowners like Sarah Dorsey and Virginia Clay. Frazier shows how she drew great consolation from her children, including the five of six who predeceased her. Her last child, the daughter Winnie, was celebrated as the "Daughter of the Confederacy," and her early death in 1898 plunged Varina into an "utter loneliness," a grief without mitigation. When her husband died in 1889, Varina moved to New York, and became a memoirist, book critic, and etiquette advisor to Joseph Pulitzer's *New York World*.

Though her journalism allowed her to meet other giants of the age like Booker T. Washington and Russia'a Prince Peter Kropotkin, Varina was still filling her role as the reverent widow of the Confederacy, excusing the evils of slavery and racial prejudice. Her views enjoyed some advancement under the spell of Unionist, liberal New

York City, but her core held fast to the notion of the South as a lost, brimming kingdom, albeit built on the backs of captive Africans and traitorous commerce with Britain. The book ends marvelously with scenes from her husband's funeral, but she is still blinking with surprising apologist naivete, only moderately moved by the tide of Emancipation, while sitting at her typewriter above enlightened untapped late century Manhattan. Varina herself died in 1906 at the age of eighty. Her own Richmond funeral was the occasion for a somewhat forgiving praise for the Davis couple. As the newspapermen, including her own bosses, declared, the North and South had finally joined hands, a part of reconciliation, *complete* reconciliation, was forgiveness of the still deluded.

But was she of that mind till the very end? In the year of her death, when resistance to Reconstruction included lynchings and rogue mutinies of Southern state militias, it had been five years since she penned the most astonishing of diary entries. As Cashin notes and as Frazier's ellisions suggest, her intelligence led her to write vividly of her doubts about the subjugation and cruelty that had nourished her "brimming Kingdom." The diary notation was brief. It was isolated in its own one-sentence paragraph. It could not be misunderstood or mediated. It said simply that "the right side won the Civil War."

Nature and Verse: Robert Hass

Summer Snow
Robert Hass
Ecco/Harper Collins, 178 Pages

The vivid, prismatic poetry of Robert Hass suggests that the contents of the mind, or more explicitly the concept of personhood, does not belong to us entirely. He believes, at least to the extent that some of his short poems suggest a "message," that the mental structure of any knowing subject—especially one reading or writing *poesia*—is little more than a collection of ephemeral instants or a pure side-effect of language. The chatter that drifts through the mind, more than anything we feel we are accomplishing, has more to do with our ontology, our "whatness," than we can ever realize (except, of course, through reading him). The growth of this mind-as-identity increases exponentially with age. As Hass's early poems broke across descriptive frontiers in describing nature with his fellow poet and friend Gary Snyder, his resignation to late middle age shows us how much more the mental life is (involuntarily) foregrounded by the ageing process. The very language that provided the tools for trimming his beauteous arbors, in books like 'Praise' and 'Human Wishes,' now seems like a sometimes irritant, an audiographic flow chart that prickles with our insecurities, our regret at our errors, and the fear of the oblivion that he suspects is the only thing lying beyond death. This is illustrated brilliantly in the poem on the book's back cover, 'Stanzas For a Sierra Morning':

> You couldn't have bought the sky's blue.
> Not in the silk markets of Samarkand. Not
> In any market between Xi'an and Venice.
>
> Which doesn't mean that it doesn't exist.
> Isn't that, after all, what a stanza is for,

So that after a night of listening, unwillingly.

To yourself think . . . . .

The key word here is "unwillingly." In our youth, what impressed us more about ourselves than "[L]istening to [oneself] think"? We would drift off full of newly-hatched plans and projections, the form we wanted to impose on the world. Now, as we age, it is a static, a chatter that keeps us from the meditative states we imagine our last period of life entitles us to.

Hass asks the questions of how we create poetry, but also why: desire to change the world for the better; to be able to create complex figures for utopian possibility within a realistic world that we recognize as essentially our own (whether we want to hear ourselves think or not). Hass has always described situations, whether ordinary or extraordinary, that suddenly—like the Zen poets he translates—shift his sense of the world, like a change of angle or complexion of falling light. Sometimes he just accepts raw material with no application of metaphor or meaning-seeking. As someone who just lost his father, the present writer appreciates the lines "No metaphors yet/For my father-in-law/He still in my head belongs to being." So this is, if anything, a reification of William Carlos Williams's "No ideas but in things." Here Hass, like the Paterson doctor, evokes a sense of being—emotional, surely, but also physical, in which abstraction has an unfortunate way of detaching us too quickly from the substance of experience.

"It is very good to be walking," Hass writes in "Abbot's Lagoon: October," "Because you can almost hear the earth sigh/As it sucks up the rain." Both the poem and its image are as explicit (yet not mundane) as the guidebook itself that he references. (He won the Yale Series of Younger Poets Award in 1973 for his aptly titled first effort, 'Field Guide.') But we shift back to the changes in light, the glancing columns and cascades, the way perspective threads itself between illuminations like the landscapes of Chinese scroll painters:

Towns on the Northern California Coast are foggy in

August
With shafts of startled sunlight sometimes in the
afternoon.

This begins "Christmas in August," an almost Woody Allen-like ('Annie Hall's "Jingle Bells" on Rodeo drive) diptych of the west Coast's climatological contradictions: "[I]t was August," he concludes the poem, "the planet just turning toward the dark,/ A long way and not a long way from the short, dark days/ We gather to celebrate the light surviving through." The light of the imagination throws its beams out, at first uncertain and wobbling, then into a "surviving" settlement into form and meaning, or at least the sense of a meaning. We can have—to satisfy Williams—both a world of ideas and things intermixed. There is no former without the latter, but that latter is the human element, the cerebral paintbrush that hues up the flatness of unprocessed terrain.

Hass relates the interplay of fancy and clear observation in another poem largely concentrated on his struggles translating the great East European poet Czeslaw Milosz in "An Argument About Poetics Imagined at Squaw Valley After A Night Walk Under A Mountain." It starts out:

My friend Czeslaw Milosz disapproved of surrealism.
Not hard to construct, in imagination, the reasons why.
Late night and late winter in Warsaw: two friends
Are stopped by the police of the General Government
Who speak atrocious Polish.

This summons up Milosz's famous WW II poem "Campo dei Fiori," which contains eerie comparisons of a carousel while SS "[g]unfire crackles on the other side of the ghetto wall." Hass's language is similar to both Milosz's Polish and Hass and Milosz's English. Hass writes "The bright melody drowned/ the salvos from the ghetto wall." He takes Milosz's long digressions on what an SS arrest conjures in the Polish streetwalker, but Hass wants the verse juxtaposition to be sharper and more concrete, less contemplative and stylized. In these specifics he can capture a kind of literary transference.

And death is here in abundance, under every rock. 'Patches of Snow in July' is a series of short pieces with titles like 'Death In Infancy,' 'Death In Childhood,' 'Those Who Die in Their Twenties,' 'Planh or Dirge for the Ones Who Die In Their Thirties,' and, finally, 'Harvest: Those Who Die Early in Their Middle Years.' ('Planh' comes from Pound's 'Planh For The Young English King,' really about the Crucifixion.) Representative stanzas here are breathtaking summaries of the developing artistic consciousness, in this particular poem a reflection on the mystery of suicide which, like that of his friend, plagues "makers and unmakers," artists and revolutionaries, in the years after adolescence in which we construct our personalities.

> If you leave the world you grew up in,
> Which, if it happens, happens to most Americans at that age,
> There's something in that eros of the other that gives to the desirer
> Or admirer another pair of eyes, sophisticates the world
> Just when our appetite for glamor in its various forms
> Is sharpest. And so, terrible as it is in a way to say it, the world
> We lose when we lose the ones who die in their twenties
> . . .doesn't lose the brilliance of its luster.

The lustered brilliance of the world is taken by the dying one as her final vision, drenched with despair but lived with a fiery, intrepid effort at understanding. The luster of we survivors persists in our vision of that person delivered just as his life has crested, preserved in amber, not having to endure the ravages of decline, of talk in our head that we suddenly stop wishing to hear.

And death, for Hass, is a welcome conclusion and return to the earth he so worships and whose stewardship is the task of so much of his poetry. He describes, in 'To Be Accompanied By Flute and

Zither,' an anniversary poem for his wife, the poet Brenda Hillman, how death might be something like the high vistas we reach on life's quotidian hike. Verse is both a merry accompanying chronicle and then a doxology: "A medicine bundle for/the hard stretches when we carry what we've glimpsed into the grinding/ days down the trail which we'll be walking, muscles a little sore, as/a breeze comes up and gives its lightness to the summer air." The lightness is something like an afterlife, a celebration, after long peregrinations, of that second "P" of paradise.

The Shimmer's End

The Town
Shaun Prescott
Fararr, Straus & Giroux, 190 Pages

This astonishing debut novel operates on both a literal and an absurdist/allegorical level, sometimes simultaneously. The realist musings center on a writer entering an unnamed town, renting a room, finding a pub with an echoing radio DJ named Ciara, and settling down to write something, non-fiction, about "[T]he disappearing towns of the Central West of New South Wales." Not much disappears on this level, except the horizon, one or two characters, weather patterns that confuse and amuse the reader, and endless skies that lay above the last, lost continent. It seems that the town is certainly vanishing literally. No one moves in. No one leaves. No one traverses the canvas of the painting, and its edges and borders never expand. Still there is the character and voice of the writer. The literal plane lies very much under the influence of Australia's great stylist Patrick White. But the style is not as ornate. There are no multiple voices, no single voice speaking in several registers.

This literal level also resembles the work of Peter Carey and Tim Winton. It contains meticulous physical descriptions of the entropy the writer is attempting to capture. The plot slides forward nicely on Prescott's spot-on, imagistic scene building. The town seems to have had a purpose at one time, a monochromatic stretch of mini-malls and shopping plazas, fast food chains, parks where people seem neither to come and go so much as stay stationary, their shadows, cone-like, stretching and receding, and seeming to be as alive as the shapes that cast them. The writer gets to know numerous people around town, and they take on the character of the landscape, both here and not here, both stationary and moving.

Tom is a musician with sufficient chops to have been in several bands. But it all seems to have led to his present lassitude, where he simply drives the town transit bus. But of course there is no one who is working, no one who seems to want to go anywhere, no one to get onto the bus or off of it. One looks down the row of seats and does not even see clown masks, deformed riders, not even transparency. There is a pesky number named Jenny, who actually owns the pub the narrator drinks in, but only occasionally materializes in order to wipe the counter or serve the double-dose of boilermakers that is called by some odd, Central Australian name. One particularly bellicose character—almost a stereotype of the Australian philistine—is named Steve Sanders. He carries a chip on his shoulder and for unknown reasons seems to be wanting it knocked off by the narrator. There is Rick, whose aspirations elevate only to bagging groceries at a supermarket. Vaping and rapping teens run in and out of the picture, attempting, along with the reader, to make sense of why they appear and disappear.

The one person who ripens into a character's ripeness is Ciara. But the station she broadcasts has no listeners, seemingly no physical plant or towers, and has nothing but dreams of a richer existence, perhaps offering her music as a bridge to somewhere more substantial and interesting. The writer strikes up a friendship with her, but it is undefined. Could it be romance or a companionship with benefits? She does not seem to know and neither does the narrator. It seems that only the narrator cares or wishes to care.

Still on the realist level, houses appear abandoned or vanish altogether. They are like the subdivisions of Albuquerque that dissolve and reappear on 'Breaking Bad.' An 'aggressive sadness' overtakes those who get stoned or 'juiced' enough to rise to that level of consciousness. At one point the polis, slight as it is, seems to resemble "a depressed country [music] festival in a 2 a.m. lull." When is someone going to start something? When will the people show enough intrinsic character interest to begin interacting with one another. The métier here seems surrealist as well as absurdist. People attempt to leave, and it is here that the absurdist line of the drama kicks into full steam. There is a train station like the scores we have seen in Peter Weir movies or imagine from our plane windows as we fly over the Outback. But of course there are no tickets, no conductor, no locomotive. The roads that might lead out of the place turn back on themselves. Everyone seems too stuck with 'misfortune humping his leg' that they neither board nor disembark. People seem unable to muster the energy to escape or to even talk about improvements or criticism.

The absurdist-allegorical element of the novel spans time as well as space. The town may once have been a place people would come to, but no one seems to remember why, or when that was. They continue to be numbed by the dry, blasted landscape that causes character to remember and misremember, speak circularly about themselves, building scenes and characters that sometimes remind this reader of the meta-landscapes of the writer's fellow Australian Gerald Murnane. The narrator himself seems to forget where he came from. He muses, looking out into the shimmer: "I tried to trace the highways east and west of the town in my mind, but my memory faltered at the shimmer." The stillness and frozen inaction seem to stretch as far back as anyone's memory, and to encompass any eternity that the narrator and his 'friends' might be able to imagine stretching out into the future.

The metaphor and the trope of vacuity ramps up when holes begin appearing on the landscape. Everyone seems to be sitting back and enjoying the possibility of solidity, infused with some kind of narcotic drip, when emptiness comes with its unassailable and invisible power. Holes begin to appear. Some of the holes are craterlike, some very tiny. The narrator's reality seems to break into fragments whenever one of them appears. People remark that it is not "your typical hole" and that it could "well be an environmental disaster." But of course no one is able to gauge what kind, what its nature or duration might be. Municipal workers put up poles, barricades and tape, but everything continues to dissolve as the workers' deadpan comments attempt to latch on to something.

But the emptiness brings out the best in speculative, ephemeral fiction, especially that coming from Down Under. The novel is one of possibility rendered by device and the minds of characters determined to stay where they are long enough to figure out the dissolution solution. It sometimes seems thin on character, but why would it not be if vanishing is the principal trope? Both the reader and her narrator are impressed by how increment—only small steps, in both mind and action—appears to be holding the world together. Whether it ultimately succeeds is less important than watching the poetic, mirage-making dissolution process.

Lured By the Wolf

My War Criminal
Jessica Stern
Ecco/Harper Collins, 435 Pages

Jessica Stern was part of Obama's NSA staff, and had a role in interrogating Radovan Karadzic, the powerful Serbian nationalist who many trace to the mass killings at Srebenica, during the Bosnian Wars and adjunct ethnic cleansing of the Balkan Muslim populations. His professional training was as a psychiatrist, and he always claimed his true calling was as a poet. His "Wolf Poems," translated into English before his trial in the Hague began, contain valuable material for psychological profiles of the man and specifically prosecutorial evidence. An added twist here is an involution of the journalist-subject relationship. Stern takes Janet Malcolm's maxim, that journalists are intrinsically dishonest and lull their subjects, and flips it around. She thereby marvels at the intoxicating attraction of talking to a subject who's become like a Svengali, and tries to dictate the truth of the story. It makes for spellbinding reading and a journey into the Balkans' eerie history of 25-30 years ago, when the "Tito-wall" fell and internecine score-keeping kept the Carpathian streams flowing with the blood of an entire Muslim population.

In 1995 Karadzic was indicted by the Hague and the next year arrest warrants were issued against him following a Rule 61 hearing. In 1993 the American Psychiatric Association's Board of Trustees stated that "Dr. Karadzic's actions as a political leader constitute a deeply profound betrayal of the human values of medicine and psychiatry." It specifically cited his brutal and inhumane role as Bosnian Serb spearhead and front man. The APA cited him as "accountable for the policy of ethnic cleansing, organized rape, mass murder, and the establishment of concentration camps." He was alleged to have deliberately used his psychiatric training to create military and political policies that would create fear, terror, and extensive post-traumatic stress disorder in civilian populations.

Where Stern comes in is with legal doctrines relevant to command responsibility and superior orders, and she was an expert in the notion that "[A] person who gives the order to commit a war crime or crime against humanity is equally guilty of the offense with the person actually committing it. This principle . . . .to both the military superiors, whether of regular or irregular armed forces, and to civilian authorities." Stern is astute on Srebrenica in particular, focusing on the forensic evidence of its mass graves which corroborated eyewitness accounts, intelligence data from satellite reconnaissance photography, and Karadzic's boastful, sometimes clownishly poetic statements to his generals and to the media. All of this command authority was vested in him as President of the Bosnian Serb Republic and Commander-in-chief of the Bosnian Serb Army. Stern appears immune from bamboozlement when she states that "Dr. K" was adept at adopting Bosnian Serb military and political tactics to external political circumstances, suggesting elements of rationality and calculation in his political thinking and actions, rather than a pure destructiveness that may speak to grandiose delusions of suicide and apocalypse. Karadzic made tactical blunders at times, but showed the ability to compromise, making him appear at times reasonable and clear-headed.

Stern stresses that his career represented age-old Serb nationalistic dreams. His political voice echoes with Serb nationalist themes espoused particularly by Serbian academic "Orientalists" and Orthodox Church figures and leaders in the Serbian Academy of Arts and Sciences. His language is riddled with a grandiose sense of destiny, imbued with a 600 year old sense of blood-and-soil tragedy and sacrifice. He rediscovered a mythical, primordial language, identifying with Peter Petrovich Njegos, Montenegro's 19th century prince-bishop-poet. Group therapist to his wounded nation, Karadzic claims to have "plumbed the depths of the Serbian soul and set to himself the task of throwing off the memory of the Ottoman yoke on behalf of his people." So Stern has her plate full here. She suggests that part of his unique importance—and his interest as an interview subject—lies in the coalescence of a genocide perpetrator with a charismatic narcissistic political figurehead. The themes of his poetry are exile, death, destruction, and a nostalgic return to a forsaken homeland, all suggesting a self-fulfilling prophecy in which the poet-physician turned political leader inscribes his inner conflicts onto the pages of Bosnia's tormented history.

Stern herself admits an attraction to at least *the notion of* the man's deluded, mythical message. It is a mandate to revenge his people for the massacres on The Field of Blackbirds in 1387, when Ottoman armies crushed a phalanx of Serbian Christian troops in a decisive battle of their own "forever war." She remarks how striking his presence is, how tall he was, and how well-spoken he sometimes seemed. She appears sometimes dazzled by his guiltlessness and absolute lack of remorse, showing the fascination of many crime writers with their subjects who live above and beyond the strictures of morality. Retribution for a crime that enslaved a people for many generations can carry on its own face a patina of legitimacy. "The Turk," i.e. the Ottomans, bled their own culture into what Stern sees as the fulcrum of her subject's outrage. His resentment lies in the tincture of Asian "barbarity" into European civilization. It is not unlike Russian nationalists today who resent the "Muslimification" emanating from Asiatic centers like Kazan and Birobizhan. Grudges, Stern seems to say, can unleash volumes of stored-up power, and can result in cultural reifications as well as political and ethnic realignments.

One of the problems Stern notices in herself here is the inability, when under his spell, to challenge him in any way. And is not this type of challenge the very anodyne that Malcolm tells us the journalist must deliver, even if by deception? Stern's profile here is as much one of herself as interlocutor as of Karadzic as glam mass terrorist. She feels anxiety at undercutting anything he says, even considering so giving her spasms of anxiety. "I utter it [a blandishment?] before having a chance to worry if he'll turn against me, tell me never to return," she writes, and is placated when "he didn't kick me out, which would have made it harder for me to finish my book."

It sometimes strains credulity to hear Stern say, of her boorishly non-apologetic, conscienceless subject, that she was hoping he would express some regrets. He never does. So she has her book. The incisive history and psychological profiling of this profile of a madman far outweighs these self-revelatory contradictions in the author. Recent behavior by our own President brings to mind Mencken's maxim that "The American boob loves a bully." No normal human and no normal author could possibly love the Butcher of Srebrenica. But at the same time Stern can get a little too fascinated by him. After awhile, with all due respect to Hannah Arendt, evil rises above the merely banal and shows the full, destructive results of its brutality. In these moments we return to our own values, steady ourselves, and are forced to turn our nonetheless fascinated faces away.

Fathers and Writing Sons

Mad, Bad & Dangerous to Know
Colm Toibin
Scribner: 267 Pages

The title of this remarkable triptych of essays comes, of course, from Lord Byron's description of himself, I believe when someone asked why he took such delight in being around young, naked Greek soldiers in the Greco-Turkish War. But it is a book about fathers, patriarchs, progenitors, those units of our parenthood whose accomplishments began with the seduction—on at least one occasion—of our mothers, be they Irish, American, or deistic in their own origins. Toibin turns his fiction-honed microscope on the meaning of fatherhood, a concept that has had a lot of rough going these past few decades. If there is as little influence from the father as, say, one sees in an O'Neill play, then the role could be said to be greatly diminished. Then along came IVF, sperm donors, lesbian couples searching sperm bank albums for appearance, IQ, net worth. The male parent can be seen as having his best presentation in a moment of selfish ecstasy, in a test tube or the coursing stillness of a frozen embryo. What is a father, anyway? And how about those fathers of literary figures?

Irish literature is full of attempts to kill one's parents. So much so that Oedipus and Electra may seem to have slumbered for millennia, only to pop up on the gritty pavement or pub floorboards of 1920s Dublin. Toibin here starts with the wider fictional world of orphans, heroes and heroines in the novels of Henry James and Jane Austin. The patriarchal concept was always connected to money, which is to say, in the Anglo-Irish world, to class, to that rigid demarcation that fastens to and follows every soul just as surely as the castes of the Hindus. But Irish literature, in particular, is best described—much money or none—as a laboratory of the notion of parenthood, and the enormity of its absence. As Toibin says at one point,

"The novel is a form ripe for orphans." Here, he focuses on palm-of-the-hand biographies of Sir William Wilde, John B. Yeats and John Stanislaus Joyce, sires of the three greatest Irish writers of the early years of the 20th century. All were the fathers of geniuses, clearly. But what were each of them like themselves?

In Ulysses, Stephen Dedalus says "[A] father is a necessary evil; what links them [to offspring] in nature? An instant of blind rut." But dads can also be at center stage, possessing the sharp intellect and grace of their sons but in a thwarted, mangled kind of vessel. Toibin attempts to capture the three fathers' social milieu that enables readers—who can be presumed to know the sons' works—to make the father-son connections, both social and imaginative, on their own. The first of three had the most promise. Oscar Wilde's father William was an opthalmological surgeon of great note, and was eventually knighted for the seemingly mundane accomplishment of the 1900 Irish census. Though from the subjugated island, he could, like his contemporaries Lady Gregory and others, navigate the heights of British society. Toibin notes how, for all his accomplishments, the man was inherently unreliable and distant as a father, as much from the climate of his times as from anything organic or genetic. "Irony and inconsistency," he writes, "derive considerable strength from the ambiguity of [the father's] position. . . . their ability to draw power from two opposite sides without having to fully obey a set of rules to which either of these two sides adhered." "In the soirees of his parents," Toibin goes on, "the idea of loyalty, whether to the crown or to Victorian mores, was never stable." The old man had a gifted surgeon's hand, but had several children out of wedlock and was accused of raping a female patient while under anesthesia. #MeToo, one must not forget, was unfortunately a hundred and twenty-five years away.

W.B. Yeats's father John was an equally interesting character study. He was a painter, a craftsman in the plastic arts. One of his engravings hung above my twins' cradle along with a nighttime lullaby written by his son. But he had what Kierkegaard called "the incompleteness complex," a maddening inability to finish what he had begun. For an artist, this was almost certainly a form of financial doom, one which built upon itself and became a self-fulfilling prophecy. He soon decamped from Western Ireland and lived in London, and then New York, writing long, endearing letters to a love interst (he was a widower) and his gaggle of brilliant, Fenian children. What was arid in the father was fecund in the offspring, in a way that causes Toibin to draw parallels with the amazing James family in America: "I was alert to the similarities between the two families—the Jameses and the Yeatses—and the similar ways in which two famous sons had been influenced by their father." The issue, especially Henry James, made a point of being their father's opposite, meticulously finishing everything they ever started."

The father known best is, of course, John S. Joyce, or his fictional equivalent, Simon Joyce—"as fine a little man as ever wore a hat," as he says of his drinking friend Paddy Dignam in the Hades episode of Ulysses. Simon Dedalus, like John Joyce, was "always a little bit drunk," making himself a character crying out for slapstick and unintended antics. Toibin points out that much of Joyce's Homeresque masterpiece can be seen as an effort to empathize and understand his father. "Joyce," he writes, "allowed a complex imagination to shine its pale, unsettled light on what had already passed into shade so that he could coax it back into substance, courtesy of style." Here and elsewhere, Toibin's book invites comparison between the three father-son bonds, only to depart from the analysis in sometimes incomplete examples. Granted, the three men were so different that it is difficult to arrive at conclusions about their similarities. The uniting factor needs, somehow, to be something more than historical inevitability. A link is required over and above the fact that their three sons literally and almost solely formed a national literature for Ireland in the half-century from 1880 to 1939, the dark year (Werhmacht, Luftwaffe) when both young Yeats and Joyce died. (As Auden's encomium to Yeats refrains, "The day he died was a dark, cold day.") All three of them had taken their patrician chaos and made from it immortal poetry, material that will be read as long as people read English.

But in the end, and with subtle nuances and historical referents, Toibin seems to link the three men in a circle of agonizing influence, something that would give Harold Bloom enough gossamer to spin into a similar study. Toibin is understated here, as almost shaded as he is in his elegant fiction. Though he lets the reader find depths and complications in his well-described portraits, he shines the lamp we need on the perilous biographical trail of the sons. Toibin says of his fellow Irish artists, including these three, that "[E]very writer had to invent a world as though from the very beginning." That "beginning" includes not just the father's "blind rut" that was perhaps their own greatest creation, but the world that surrounded the old men, making the young they left behind into something majestic, something forever unequalled.

Big Brother, 2020 and 2.0

The Resisters
Gish Jen
Knopf: 301 Pages

Gish Jen has written a novel that grows naturally out of our current political and intelligence imbroglios, and it is a command performance. This writer has watched her work carefully since the novel *Typical American,* where a fantastically zany Chinese family puts the cast of 'Parasite' to shame with the extended cons and counter-cons afoot among a group of immigrant families. In an excerpt in the New York Times Sunday Review, she treated us to passages of *The Resisters*—ingenious inventions that had a more definite real-time, actual existence than the digital grid through which they were re-imagined. These included "Enforcebots" (police robots); "One Chance Policy" (surplus families permitted only one pregnancy, whether or not it produces a child); "PermaDerms" (permanent skin whitening); "SmartGuns" (just what they sound like); "ThoughtCommand" (next-level voice commands), and, lest we forget the resonances of the Orange One, "Ship'Em Back" (mass deportation of immigrants). Of course, this gives you an idea about how much here is real and how much needs to be imagined. As the writer Frank Bruni has written, "Satire is hard when your subject has already beat you to it."

Income equality, almost medieval as it is in this country, does not need to be calibrated much to make plausible the divide Jen has here with the privileged class being the "Netted," with their "angelfair" skin sunning on balconies of skyscrapers that remain the only thing above water in flooded coastal cities. Everyone else, far, far down the ladder of economic security, are the "Surplus." Their skin is copper-colored, and reminds you of Shakespeare's 'Tempest' islanders: "Dark they were/And golden-eyed." They live in stilted houses in the rancid swamps and ravines of the non-flooded lowlands. Many "Surplus" people have had their jobs replaced by automation and when that is the case and they cannot be occupationally re-tooled, they become "Unretrainable" and live on a (guaranteed!) income that barely keeps them from out-and-out destitution. And there is plenty of the surrepticiously sinister here, something on the order of eugenics. The Surplus and Unretrainables both are forced to survive on drek simply deemed "mall-truck food," some of which contains winnowing agents of several poisons which may or may not spearhead a vast attempt at slow genocide. The divisions and stratifications seem more sinister from the mere fact of their being algorithmic. Orwell wouldn't be able to follow the tech-talk, but would recognize the basic scaffoldings of his landscape.

The Internet exists, and does not have to be so elaborately imagined. It is called the "Autonet" and is made up of surveillance technology, the Internet, and "spooky action at a distance," such as voices emanating from walls and instant transmission of facial recognition photographs and captured telephonic dialaogue. There is an "Aunt Nettie," who reminds us of Margaret Atwood's *The Handmaid's Tale*. She has an unseen, matriarchal and omniscient authority. The problem is whether she *is just* a voice in the wall, a voice in the ether, or the bigger question of humanness and personalty. Is there a body behind the voice. Or is there an algorithm behind the body behind the voice? Everybody still with me?

Set in the mix of all this is a Surplus family of resisters who engage in all manner of quaint, marginally useful, and possibly illegal activities such as knitting, gardening, reading literature and, of course, the Great American Pastime. They are a dystopian Bad News Bears, and they play for high stakes and long odds. The daughter, Gwen, is a pitching prodigy, playing in family- and neighbor-organized underground baseball leagues tucked into underground sites and Brownfields locations unlikely to be policed, even by drones (Even drones can have bigger fish to fry). Why is baseball illegal? It detracts from the endless pressure on the Surplus to consume. They must stay hidden nevertheless. This entails hacking the implanted microchips that are used to track their movements. Gwen is waiting for her big break. She uses the old names for her pitches: curves and sliders, fastballs and knuckleball pitches. She looks to make a jump somewhere, to accomplish something akin to caste climbing. (Indeed, there is little downward movement left; the Unretraianble are dying in droves after being fed from the toxic roach coaches).

Gwen's break comes when she "crosses over" into the world of the Netted, as a freshman on the team at Net U. Pressure rises on her almost immediately when it is learned that ChinRussia, America's superpower rival, begins training its own team for something like an Autonet-guided but actually real, flesh-and-blood Olympics. Baseball becomes something like demonstrations, marches, acts of civil disobedience. It is a foil to the artificial intelligence and bland homogeneity of existence. What, really, would be the point of automating something like two sets of nine players running the bases and defending against one another? It had, in fact, already been done in previous, less digital and automated ages. One coach explains it as follows: "We are here because we believe anything can happen in a ballgame . . . you can get a guy and all his stats but give him a stick to swing, and you still don't know what will happen." This is, indeed, the essential attraction of all sports. But it has special meaning within an otherwise completely planned reality, an existence that really seems to be more and more dominated by algorithms.

So the Resisters soldier on while more and more of the population surrenders itself to gene improvement and planning the whole next generation of disciples for Aunt Nettie. There is an eerie moment in the book when a character's mind is surgically merged to Aunt Nettie, so the line between human and automation becomes more blurred than ever. But it is people who carry out these heinous acts—even in a world dominated by technology and soulless automation, humans are crueler than machines. This was the prophetic subtext of Kafka's 'In The Penal Colony.' Jen treats it all with her customary lightness of diction (she is one of our best stylists), but the whole enterprise, like something out of a novel written a hundred years previously, send the hair on the back of your neck straight up.

Gish Jen has given us a novel that is utterly clever but never gets too full of itself. The AI and Internet inventions and their effects never get gimmicky. This is an old-fashioned struggle of diversity and imagination against a world that machines have turned into something quotidian. Nine players, nine candles are lifted in a dark, cheerless Babylon. And from the stands we hear what resisters need to hear—we hear the cheering, the unsuppressibly human, the desire to knock it out of the dreary, high-walled park.

Robert Stone's Fiery America

Three Novels: Dog Soldiers; A Flag for Sunrise; Outerbridge Reach
Robert Stone
(Edited By Madison Smartt Bell)
Library Of America: 721 Pages

For Nancy Gottesman

There are writers who appear, possibly once in a generation, who seem to galvanize time's eerie striations and craft novels that are vortices, focusing the chaos of public life into a pattern, a self-identifying "direction". In the Thirties, artists like Dreiser and James T. Farrell painted with tawny brushes, forming a sort of ashcan school of the poor and dispossessed in the eastern cities. By mid-Century, Irwin Shaw, John Updike and Saul Bellow breathed adulterous sparkle and angst into the Eisenhower years' long, flat monotone.

In the Sixties, for all its literary menagerie, one man alone took the hues of war, uprisings, generational divides and espionage and painted brilliant canvases that thrilled and terrified at the same time they were congealing into indispensable time capsules. His name was Robert Stone, and three of his early novels have been gathered together by his friend and acolyte Madison Smartt Bell, resulting in the latest gem from Max Rudin's amazing editorship at the Library of America.

Stone had a Melvillian, seafaring pedigree. He got out of the Navy in the late Fifties and kept his sea legs for the remainder of his turbulent life. He fiddled in odd nautical jobs in Key West and San Francisco, and on the strength of a single novel chapter became a Stegner Fellow at Stanford's Graduate English Department, where he met Larry McMurtry and Ken Kesey. Kesey brought him to La Honda, to the early acid tests and Golden Gate Park Be-Ins. His ingestion of drugs was as legendary as his memorization of whole short stories of Chekhov. He formed friendships with Vietnam and Sandinista figures, which gave him his material for the National Book Award-winning *Dog Soldiers*, first of the three here, a "Sixties" novel if there ever was one.

By the early part of that decade, the U.S. had reached its apogee in terms of world dominance, success, and political hegemony. 'Dog Soldiers' turned that log over to trace the dark, incipient underlife of paranoia and delusion, the intoxications of crowds and power. "The paranoid," as William Burroughs' said, "is simply the one with all the information."

Dog Soldiers is one of the best Vietnam novels, with almost none of its scenes set in that country. What Stone gives us, with bright, acidic irony, is a smuggler's story featuring a small-time journalist, John Converse, who got out of Saigon just as the choppers were landing on the embassy roof. He ships heroin from Burma to the States, where everything immediately goes wrong. Government agents and competitive dealers are hellhounds on his trail. It is a book about the effect that Vietnam had on America. When you unleash carpet bombing on a soon decimated but valiant agrarian culture, and do it for shadowy reasons, your moral compass wobbles and sometimes breaks. The message then becomes get what you want, do what you please to people, and forgot the consequences. In other words, it sets the stage for and becomes the story of the 70s in the United States.

Stone's masterpiece was the sinister, turbulent *A Flag For Sunrise*, published in 1981 and again a National Book Award and Pulitzer nominee. Here are all the components of an intelligent, seamless thriller: betrayal, blood, ambivalence, duplicity, sex and courage and "the dream life of the race," the way so many events flowed into the subsoncious of the time, only to surface again in later decades. Set in the fictionalized Central American Tecan (obviously Nicaragua, in the "waist" of the Western hemisphere) the mineral-mining oligarchs have overstepped their bounds and are backing the 'White Hand' rightist militias who are slaughtering insurgents throughout the countryside. The rebellion against the U.S.-backed government will be led by indigenous Atapa Indians; by a highly sexed American nun, "the Queen of Swords"; by a psychopath who has deserted the

U.S. Coast Guard, and by gunrunners and hangers-on who seem lifted from Todd Browning's classic circus tragedy, "Freaks." Opposing the revolution are a half-baked CIA agent, a remittance man for Wall St. capital, and an American journalist coupled with a "capon Priest" who is the nun's parish Father. The CIA man, Holliwell, covers as an academic anthropologist. He falls in love with the Queen of Swords, and caps the cross-narratives with quips like "It would be strange to see people who believed in things, and acted in the world according to what they believed." (Send organized religion to the trash compactor.)

Holliwell is the easiest character to get to know and side with. He genuinely *is* a cultural anthropologist, "forever inquiring of helpful strangers the nature of their bonds with one another," and for whom "regret" is "second nature, the very fluid in his veins." Holliwell, too, like the 'Dog Soldiers' characters, cannot get rid of "the saffron taste" of the Vietnam failure, where he too had been stationed: "Cooking oil, excrement, incense, death; the smell of the world turning." Holliwell cannot, despite the foregoing, get just why America is so implacably hated in revolutionary movements, especially Central America's. He gets trapped between the revolutionaries and the agency that sent him to undercut them.

As *A Flag For Sunrise* moves toward its freewheeling, ultra-violent climax (the greatest street firefights since Hemingway's 'To Have and Have Not') we are on each of the patrol skiffs and landing craft, working their way up the torrid river, not knowing which beachhead is controlled by whom. (Stone certainly knew his Bay of Pigs invasion history.) The jungle night is filled with crimson flares, anti-aircraft searchlights, radical Catholic activists digging foxholes and loading the clips of their M-16s. As the battle rages, Holliwell's beliefs are cut down to skeletal epiphanies: "Yankees are the blue eye. . . . the blue eye is blind, sacrificed." The Church yields to and advances the populist uprising. It yields to the insurgents' homeland, slowly growing back to what V.S. Naipaul called 'the bush.' Spider monkeys are climbing on Toltec stelae, hints of Olmec and Mayan culture with their human sacrifice. We are suddenly, through the ancient rites of battle, thrown down through "the brain coral" that grows around "the skull of the earth," hiding the core truth of Darwinian violence as the only true path to power.

Outerbridge Reach, the first book this writer ever reviewed, takes its historical departure from an incident in which a yacht company hires a PR firm to have one of its head men, Marty Hyland, advertise their boats by having him win a race around the earth with a champion yachtsman. A documentary filmmaker, Strickland, comes along for the ride, to experience "the swamp spray and the suck." Stone here reaches his stylistic apogee. Hyland's Porsche has "rusty rings, but its engine reported like a Prussian soldier on the first turn of the key." At the publicity party launching the race, Hyland wears a "brick-red blood pressure mask around his eyes, which resembled those of a raptor." Nearly every page sprouts up such lyrical, metaphorical fireweeds. The result is nearly perfect artistry, with the suspense building the same way is does whenever Stone's characters get on a boat with a daring, dangerous agenda.

The company's goal is that the yacht has to win, so when Hyland bows out and a Capt. Owen Browne takes over, starts to meddle with coordinates, cuts corners on his routing, changes canal paths and suddenly reappears at points the ship would have had to sprout wings to get to. The denouement (remember Rosy Ruiz winning the N.Y. Marathon? Something like that) would amount to a terrible spoiler, but suffice it to say we move back and forth between the tumultuous (and deceptive) course of Browne's voyage and his wife's below-decks affair with Strickland. The book forwarded Stone's reputation solidly into the early 90s, with critics and publishers chasing him across the globe with commissions. And with passages like these, sizing up New Jersey's Outerbridge Reach (that would eventually become a steel and human graveyard for 9/11 victims), what material *doesn't* become rhapsodic magic in Stone's hands:

> On Browne's left, the hulks lay scattered in a geometry of shadows. The busy sheer and curve of their shapes and the perfect stillness of the water made them appear held fast in some phantom disaster. Across the Kill, bulbous storage tanks, generators and floodlit power lines stretched to the

end of darkness. The place was marked on the charts as Outerbridge Reach.

As with all LOA editions, Stone's childhood, career and publishing history are set forth in an excellent chronology assembled by Bell. If, during this time of quarantine, you feel like getting out of the house, strap yourself to the rocket-sled of these three books and let its cannon shoot you through mid-20th Century's most hidden and harrowing battles.

Break Time

On the Clock
Emily Guendelsberger
Little, Brown, 321 Pages

This author has captured the work atmospherics of a significant plurality of America's work force. Low level service jobs take up more than a third of the supposedly marvelous jobs reports, and Guendelsberger should simply put Dante's 'Abandon Hope' Hell-gate above the remaining 300-odd pages we endure with her. First she was at a call center. Then she went to McDonalds. She ends up in an Amazon warehouse, where hours ran to 10 a day, people could be locked in on a night shift. Boxes would often fall—probably not just books as Amazon had become Everythingstore—from pallets stacked as high as sixty feet. What was the last book you couldn't stand? I mean really threw across the room? Imagine getting hit by an 80 pound box with forty copies inside.

Emily G. has a great gift for anecdote, for capturing days of atmospherics in a simple break signal horn, or in the robotic voices and echoes of voices that mute other sounds in the product tower canyons. Sometimes, Amazon keeps the scholarly identity, and offers shelves of serious oak for serious classicists. But you look downward and see a squat man wearing a Rapture T-shirt and chewing tobacco. Minimum wage jobs look upward to where the stepping stone can be forgotten. But it also looks downward, digging up the blue collar past. The smells, the noise, the fumes of things that start to block the sun and sink into your skin. At least she is free of the splatter grease, which seemed like an aery kind of colored, mercury fire, guided out of a gun barrel by a muted blast.

Many of the ills of these jobs amount to pushing people far beyond their limit. She is terrified that the driving customers at McDonalds will boil in their cars or charge her, or both. She realizes that management has rigged the number of personnel to have every second person performing the job of a third. "Understaffing is the new staffing," she writes, watching out over the endless sea of cars. The resulting stress thwarts logic, patience, paying attention, resisting temptation, long-term thinking, remembering things, empathy." One starts to deaden as the pace increases. People cannot take bathroom breaks. One woman was dismissed in a Sunbelt Wal-Mart for "menstruationg on herself." Her colleague, who brought her fresh (and paid for) pants and sanitary napkins, was also later fired.

Much of this amazing book follows the form of daunting texts like Lucy lberts's *Squeezed*. Vast segments of the population work hour sthat exceed what the law permits. Vast numbers of them work without benefits. Vast numbers get no monitored meal and rest breaks, and have no safeguards in place for timely payment and after-payments in the event of termination or resignation. Though labor and employment codes of most states—especially New York and California, to which others follow suit—contain elaborate protections in the form of pay data information, little of it is followed, and employers sneak in to commit sabotage which, when added up, consolidate from small acts into massive savings. Though Private Attorney General Act functions add juice to the penalties, the volume of compliance actions cannot keep up with that of violations.

Much of this comes from the decline of trade unionism in America. The statistic on their decline is dreadful. For decades there hasn't even been one significant piece of pro-Union legislation. On the contrary the tide has been in the other direction. In 2011, Wisconsin's Scott Walker, generally a lapdog to Trump, stripped public-sector unions of much of their bargaining power. Throughout the last years of this past decade, Indiana, Michigan, Wisconsin, West Virginia and Kentucky have passed notorious so-called "right to work" laws, which make union dues optional and were once common only in slave states. Since 1961, and especially in service jobs like the author's McDonalds and the hellish Amazon factory, the Supreme Court has ruled that workers cannot even be required to pay for a union's negotiations on their own behalf.

So we now have what in India is called "caste slippage." More and more people are shoved downward into occupations which have little more protections than did the workers at the Triangle Shirtwaist Factory Fire in 1911, when scores jumped to their deaths due to lack of fire extinguishers, blocked doorways to prevent rest breaks, and faulty infrastructure. The American service industry workforce appalls Europeans, the Japanese, and most labor regulators of western industrial democracies. Mothers cannot find affordable child care to even *get* to work, and when a second spouse works the price of housing and child care is bid upward to where the 'Two-Income Trap' authored by Elizabeth Warren and her daughter opens its vices and takes away what had been gained by the promise of an additional salary.

So we are a nation of fast food workers, or at least a lot of us. It is more emblematic of income inequality than any other phenomena, including education levels, socio-economic backgrounds, and the view that these jobs are transition points when in fact they are circular mazes that explain the gray in the hair of your barrista or burger window worker. Guendelsberger gives this menacing world what Henry James called its "felt life"—the overwhelming fatigue, distraction, confusion and supervisory scolding that has set labor policy back to levels unseen since before the middle of the last century. She weaves exemplary, illustrative anecdotes in with just enough statistics to give the world they describe a logistical structure. Corporate profits go up, the overworked poor worker, in a circular paradox, works even harder and can only afford or have time for the very fast food being discussed, which in turn sends these low-paying industries' profits soaring. It will not get better soon, especially with the currently emasculated Labor Department.

Interconnections

The Man Who Saw Everthing
Deborah Levy
Bloomsbury, 212 Pages

Deborah Levy writes amazing novels of sexual and political intrigue, one never far from the other, one lending its delight and menace to the other in a sort of catch-playing of narrative structures and atmospherics. Her imagistic scene-building is here in abundance, as well as her bullet-fast, bulletproof dialogue. Clipped speech makes for shuttle diplomacy and truncated decisions, and very little escapes the attention of her narrators, her characters, and the sort of Proustian, omniscient overlord that hovers over the entire panoply. Levy has amassed a body of work which rivals that of her fellow countrymen Tessa Hadly and Anne Enright, and reaches back to the influences of Penelope Fitzgerald and Doris Lessing. In terms of substantial, intelligent creation it will stand second to none in our time. It is recognized—this new novel is her third Booker nominated volume (spanning several genres) in the last seven years.

The Man Who Saw Everything switches between the present (well, London, 2016) and the past, specifically Communist East Germany in 1988. Almost on a twin set of tracks in the same trainyard, it goes from the hardscrabble realism of Montebello Road pubs to the phantasms of hallucinations and dreams, and the speech that belongs to that particular, often hidden, level of being.

Meet Saul Adler. He's dashing, well-spoken, floats through the room with womens' eyes magnetized upon him. He is a historian of, for lack of a better term, male white supremacy: the long, dreary wreckage of totalitarianism and testicular tyranny. Nothing seems to stick to him except shimmers of admiration. The novel opens with him about to leave London for East Germany in 1988. His research topic will be cultural resistance to Nazism. Appropriately, it was the title of his Ph.d thesis. Through the use of flash forwards and the literary equivalent of cinematic jump-cuts, we slowly come to realize that his professional pursuits are strangely intertwined with personal relationships. And what relationships those are!

Adler's personal life was *penetrated* by history—there is no other term for it. Adler's Jewish mother had used herself to protect against the counter-intuitively bad father—a Bolshevik seemingly on the right side of history at the time, but boorish, loud, poisonously overbearing. (He was worse than the Partisan Review old guard—he continued to believe in communism even as Soviet tanks were rolling through the streets of Prague.) But his mother was killed in a car wreck when Adler was 12, and his beauty drew in plotters and prevaricators, with their harm not just limited to the political. This past has irreparably harmed him in ways he has never realized. His girlfriend, a photographer, sets a disastrous chain of events in motion. He is her favorite subject—she loves photographing him. Adler resents that he may be loved by her for his beauty alone. At the same time, the girlfriend accuses him of a deep, paranoid detachment.

The novel is filled with specters and ghosts, inhabiting both the political and personal climates. The girlfriend's camera has Adler under constant surveillance, not a good thing east of what used to be the Wall. He falls in love with a man and then with a woman. The narrative flashes forward, and Levy has a reckoning for Adler that hovers between real and dream lives. He is in the hospital recovering from being hit by a car. He'd been walking across Abbey Road, on the famous crosswalk, for a picture commissioned to satisfy a Beatles fanatic and *eminence gris*.

This novel's suspenseful progress builds slowly, efficiently, making your skin crawl and your blood chill. It follows the pattern of two earlier books in which layers of psychic turmoil are peeled back like onion skins, with a bracing tang that goes way beyond tears. A noted playwright for the BBC, Levy was riding a train in 1988 where she met a theater director who advised her thusly on finding a voice: "To speak up is not about speaking louder, it is about feeling entitled to voice a wish." He went on and she noted everything he said. "We always hesitate when we wish for something, but in my theater I like to show the hesitation and not conceal it" she later diaried his words, verbatim, a beacon for a young playwright. . "A hesitation is not the same thing as a pause." "It's an attempt," the director went on, "to defeat the wish. But when you are ready to catch this wish and put it into language, then you can whisper and the audience will always hear you."

Levy transposes what she learned from him to the business of writing prose. "For myself," she writes in one of her many essays, "it is the story of this hesitation that is the point of writing." Levy has taken this point of hesitation, its grooming and leavening toward fulfillment, in marvelously exploratory directions in work after work, in a wide variety of genres. Her rich, obsessional body of work is consumed by questions of formulated narratives following those of actual, felt life. One might call them scripts. They are scripts of identity, gender, ethnicity, nationality. They are the stories of crossing borders between nations as well as states of consciousness.

Overall, her prose is sprightly and rapid. The characters gather themselves and just as quickly unravel, unspool, all in locations that have the glamor of the Corniche or a Cotswold estate cribbed from Fitzgerald's Great Egg, Long Island. "Another airport, another country. Another hotel" one character sums up from the story collection *Black Vodka*. There are no grand reveals in this type of subtle, highly evocative fiction. There is only the evocation of states of mind and qualities of heart. It is the subconscious, "background knowledge" she calls it. It is in fact unsought-for and unwanted knowledge. It is a body of once conscious slippages that characters want neither to remember, confront or resolve. In this new novel, she reminds us that what we most want to know from others, or ourselves, is something we may in fact want to slip away, to forget. In another essay she gives us the road map for the whole mess of consciousness: "The things we don't want to know are the things that are known to us anyway, but we do not wish to look at them too closely."

Everything Levy writes is hard-earned, softly processed, and opens and shuts with the melodious precision of a music box. Read Levy, and read the paragraphs like those eerie thoughts she countenances. Look at them closely. You cannot look at them *too* closely.

The Pandemic's Cassandra

Station Eleven
Emily St. John Mandel
Vintage: 338 Pages

A book is about to be reissued—and I mean *really* reissued, 100,000 print copies—by the young Toronto writer Emily St John Mandel. Her newest novel, *The Glass Hotel*, is no sneeze, dealing as it does with Bernard Madoff's Ponzi scheme and other post-2018 financial mega-scams. But this short tome she wrote in 2014 has an eerier and much broader subject. Its narrative posits a global pandemic, an animal-to-human transferred respiratory virus that shuts down her country, then the country below it, then Europe, and then the whole world.

The virus is called the Georgia Flu, named after the Georgia Straight that lies between British Columbia and Vancouver Island, where the first North American patients presented with it. It arrived from China, and for a certain patient population that contracts it, the result is a rapid, terribly painful kind of "drowning in the open air."

Politics and cronyism push aside science in certain bumbling leaders' attempts to remedy the ensuing disaster. Medical professionals across every corner of the earth become an army of sacrificial warriors, working with inadequate supplies, inadequate protection, funding battles and recriminations that could not come at a more absurdly inappropriate time. Millions of service and hospitality workers lose their jobs, and the notion of going out to dinner with friends seems as long ago a memory as square dancing or circling around a Maypole. Of course, the book begins with the usual fiction disclaimer that it is "A work of the imagination, with any resemblance to actual events and people, living or dead," being "entirely coincidental."

The opening scenes involve the death, on-stage, of a famous Shakespearian, Arthur Leander, filling the rafters with one of the lesser known Lear speeches. He's been a cad, left several families, and is pursuing a Cordelia (our narrator Kristin) who may be some thirty-five years his junior. She is part of a group of Renaissance faire-style wandering tragedians, The Traveling Symphony, which fastens onto audiences of stranded travelers with high art and foreboding predictions. But nothing predicted itself is tragic: the seers and composers provide only the normal supply of sadness and happiness. Every dip in fortunes eventually balances out with something like a double rainbow.

Then, as one character in the acting company hears on the radio on a plane into New York, a shadowy, invisible infection has begun to blanket the continents. The captain announces that flights have diminished; a "disease of some sort is spreading," and passengers are advised to talk to ground personnel about something called PPE (Personal Protective Equipment) once they have landed and gathered their bags.

> The story of the pandemic's arrival in North America had broken while he was in the air. This was another thing that was hard to explain years later, but up until that morning the Georgia Flu had seemed quite distant especially if one happened not to be on social media.... [I]t was a mysterious outbreak of some virus in Paris, and it hadn't been at all clear that it was developing into a pandemic. But now he watched the too-late evacuation of cities, the riots outside hospitals on three continents, the slow-moving exodus clogging every road, and wished he'd been paying more attention. The gridlocked roads were puzzling, because where were all these people going? If these reports were to be believed, not only had the Georgia Flu arrived, but it was already everywhere. There were clips of officials from various governments, epidemiologists with their sleeves rolled up, everyone wan and bloodshot and warning of catastrophe, blue-black circles under bloodshot eyes.

Since Leander's death, Kristin's wanderings with the Travelling

Symphony allow her to sharpen her acting and dancing skills, and she dips into memoir, trying to bring to terms her mentor/lover's very public end via ruminations on art's relation to reality. She is driven somewhat by her memory loss—she cannot remember the year of his demise—but is fascinated too that the dead, at least the *famous* dead, can hold whole traditions within themselves, becoming wonderfully sealed time capsules. Her memory loss seems traceable to the advent of the virus, going off "like a neutron bomb over the surface of the earth." The pandemic has killed ninety-nine percent of the world's population, but there are still pocketed clusters, shards of cities, settlements that are all too hungry for the Symphony to remind them of what the world was like before: iPhones, television, automobiles, department stores. Survivors live in airports, masked and gloved, and when victims die they are buried in trenches along the taxiway, with planes' tray tables serving as tombstones. One empty airliner itself is retrofitted as a hospital:

> The maintenance of safety required some calibrations having to do with memory and sight. There were things Clark trained himself not to think about. Everyone he'd ever known outside the airport, for instance. And here at the airport, Air Gradia 452, silent in the distance near the perimeter fence, by unspoken agreement never discussed …. Don't think of that unspoken decision, to keep the jet sealed rather than expose a packed airport to a fatal contagion. Don't think about what enforcing that decision may have required.

For a book about the world's collapse, *Station Eleven* is remarkably calm, quietly calibrated. There are no exploiters of the disease's afterlife, no road warriors or warlords exploiting those still in need. There is, however, a self-proclaimed Prophet who reminds the female narrator Kristin of the Lear actor Leander. The Prophet is a David Koresh type, reciting snippets of scripture, "marrying" underage girls and populating their settlement, also travelling, with "Sisters of the Light." When the Prophet threatens the Symphony, instruments become weapons, intelligence outmaneuvers might, and the Pentecostal aberration goes the way of most things lost by the spread of the "invisible granules." The vivid life of the Travelling Symphony is vibrantly told, though some of the artistic shop talk—barres and shoes, hair knots and second positions—can get a little monochromatic. (The author was a dancer with the acclaimed Toronto Ballet.)

Kristin's best friend is Miranda (everyone here has Shakespearian names), a line artist who draws a story of post-dystopic travel which is itself called *Station Eleven*. The comic traces the Symphony's travels though it was begun before the illness spread and miraculously survived. It is a totem of the former world, much as the Symphony itself is a reminder of prelapsarian culture, a fabric woven of what is missed, what was remembered, and what has a chance of surviving. Mandel's style here is chiseled but also lyrical, paradoxically abundant within its spareness. The pages range like a video camera across the tableaux of the camping symphony: moonlit snow falling on spruce forests; the papyrus-like flat explosions of color in Miranda's *Station Eleven*; Miranda on Lake Ontario's night beaches gazing out at drifting structures battleshipped with lights—Charon-boats going either nowhere or to another world.

Mandel is not so interested in how an apocalypse may affect art and culture writ large. Rather, it is individual rather than collective destinies that are explored. The calm, deep and even atmospherics of her prose keep doom at bay—we feel only the pleasantness of a good dream following a nightmare. The moral weight, the urgency and fear of a global disaster are mediated. We never feel its full effects. What belongs to the troop of artisans is a kind of zany optimism, the notion that the way down is the way up, and that they had pretty much captured all that was required of the abyss. *Station Eleven* is much more about memory and loss, yearning and nostalgia—the materials of art rather than the metrics of a catastrophe. Both are here, but the disease is no longer foregrounded after it has done its work of wiping the earth clean again.

If reality, as Wittgenstein said, is merely the "shadow of grammar," then our reality today is a shadow, a *something,* captured by the brain of a tiny Canadian ballerina with a dystopian instinct, a lapidary style, and a gift of prophecy seldom seen in someone so young. If you can get out of the house now, skip the toilet paper stop and get at the end of the line of the first bookstore that reopens. The shelves will soon be bare.

The Bow Tie Justice

The Making of a Justice: My First 94 Years
John Paul Stevens
Little, Brown: 525 Pages

John Paul Stevens does not have the panache of a glamorous justice. He lacks the towering height and baritone with which Thurgood Marshall moved mountains. If you are looking for sarcasm, the witty *bon mots* and jousting with counsel that Scalia made his métier, J.P. will not provide. He doesn't have the look of the white boys' club of the chief justice, Neil Gorsuch, and the near-adolescent newby Brett Kavanaugh. There is none of the fire and obscure origins of a Sotomayor or Clarence Thomas. He never had the scholarly, grave demeanor of a Stephen Breyer. Nor was he possessed of the impish, brilliant sparkle and ongoing fame machinery of the Notorious RBG. He is short of stature, understated, careful in his choice of words, and Midwestern enough to call himself a Chicagoan "right down to the atoms."

He was even appointed by a sort of accidental President, Gerald Ford, in the Spring of 1975. He was swiftly, unanimously confirmed, a near impossibility in our current political climate. But he was the third-longest-serving justice in American history. He had a flair for organizing clerks and other justices into cadres on certain issues. Before retiring in 2010, he had seen issues as diverse as the obscenity allegations against rap lyrics, the reinstitution (over his dissent) of capital punishment after its four year hiatus beginning in 1972, and constant, incessant attempts by conservative state legislatures to thwart, at nearly every turn, women's control of their bodies and reproductive health. He presided over busing and integration decisions, many of which had tapered off in their intensity. He seemed able to get interested in anything, which is exactly what you want in a jurist of any kind. When asked how he would act when confronted with certain hot button issues, he would say, as the great Thomas Coke intoned centuries before, "I will act as a judge should act."

His early life was freighted with fascinating misadventures and a determination to avoid the obscure destinies he saw in store for many of his schoolmates. He grew up in Chicago's Hyde Park, home of both fearsome ghettos and the illustrious University of Chicago. He was a true believer in the Cubs, which makes his innate hopefulness brush up against the borders of delusion. His family's hotel business flourished in the late nineteenth century and into the period following WW I. But it failed miserably with the Depression and post-Depression cons by failed business's "revitalizers." (He kept his sharp, cynical eye out for one of its richest magnets, Chicago ward politics.) There was a bizarre early robbery of the Stevens home when all this was going on, performed either by gangsters or suspicious police officers, which can sometimes occupy the same human form on Chicago's South Side. His special fascination (and brilliant command) of the criminal law got its start by watching his father's criminal trial for embezzlement, growing out of the hotel failure backwash. The man was acquitted, but young John Paul got a taste of how zealous prosecution can ruin a man, his family and his legacy.

After a University of Chicago B.A. and law degree from Northwestern, he enlisted in the Navy, was elevated to officer rank, and served on perilous intelligence assignments leading up to the cross-channel invasion FDR was pulling Churchill's teeth to approve. He won a Supreme Court clerkship. He worked in Washington, feathering his nest with the power elite, and acquired a particular interest in antitrust law, the play between monopoly power, its exercise, and the grip that unregulated conglomerates had on the commerce of his native city. But public life seemed to call him, seemed to be the ultimate ticket out of his hometown, and he dropped an antitrust partnership at a silk-stocking D.C. firm to serve as counsel to the House Judiciary Committee. Back in Chicago, he investigated political corruption on the Illinois Supreme Court. When plucked by Ford for the court in the tumultuous mid-70s, he was ready to go, and after 35 years he has tales to tell that can surprise and astonish. His views of fellow justices are unpredictable. He had great disdain for Nixon's Chief Justice Burger, and a surprising—given their divergent political orientations—admiration for Clarence Thomas, extolling his "incredible life story," "strong work ethic," and "equally strong intellect."

His clerks tell stories of his legendary accessibility, much like that of William Rehnquist. When my law review editor and I were groveling in the 80s for reviews and case notes from the likes of Michael Tyger and Richard "Racehorse" Haynes, our assistant simply called Stevens's offices and ask if he would do a piece on the life span of a judge-made law (that was its eventual title.) He did not put any of the usual time or editing qualifications on his agreement to do so. It was a three word acceptance; "Be happy to." It took a few years, but the piece was well worth waiting for and broke splendidly out of the law review article mode.

His article for us on juridical origins of certain bodies of law reflected his long-running fascination with constitutional and statutory interpretation. He looked at discerning the intent of the legislature as a sort of clumsy spelunking, stumbling along dark caves with weak lanterns. But legislative research was for him the true path, the "measuring up" of the lawmakers' efforts against the broader canvas of the Constitution. He truly saw the latter as a living, evolving document. His distaste for Scalia's 'Originalism' kept him from even dignifying it with the label of jurisprudence. Originalism was then blanketed in the more palatable, marketable label of "textualism." He pointed out that selecting meanings for Constitutional words based on their understanding by the men of that time was itself a choice, as much a subjective decision as other approaches to the document. And he regarded that selection as one "[U]nfaithful to the expansive principle Americans laid down when they ratified the [Constitution]; it countenances the most revolting injustices in the name of continuity, for we must never forget that not only slavery but also the subjugation of women and other rank forms of discrimination are part of our history." He went on to write that "textualism" was nothing more than a sort of hermeneutic cowardice. This doctrine could work well and be pulled out of a hat with some ease, but he saw it as "judicial abdication in the guise of judicial modesty."

Stevens began to take over Earl Warren's penchant for protecting the rights of the accused, and became the Court's most visible and influential master of criminal law and procedure. He had a long memory of his father's humiliating trial. His solid position in the Court's liberal block led him to author landmark decisions on Fourth Amendment searches and seizures, complexity exceptions for juries and the right to speedy trials for the accused, expansion of Miranda rights, and, finally, a believer that the Eighth Amendment's bar on cruel and unusual punishment made the death penalty abhorrent. He joined with his friend and fellow justice Harry Blackmun in stating that he would no longer have anything to do with "the machinery of death."

There are only two real flaws in this doorstop of personal reminiscence and court history. There is very little about his personal life, and neither of his wives garner much more than a sentence each. It is as if he were the Souter-like bachelor living in a farmhouse with his mother. No detail is provided about the end of his first marriage; his second, Maryan Mulholland Simon, died in 2015. He keeps with the habit of justices muting their personal lives with the exception of formative career relationships (Marshall's NAACP leadership comes to mind, as does Sandra Day O'Connor's truly beautiful memories of her childhood horse ranches). The other obstacle in the book is the perennial lapsing into legal jargon such as "colorable," "justiciable" and "facial validity." Still, his first 94 years shed great light on a judicial life well lived, sweeping in its effect, and unassailable in its role in 20th Century legal history.

Razor and Silk

Unfinished Business:
Notes of A Chronic Re-Reader
Vivian Gornick
Farrar, Straus & Giroux; 161 Pages

When Sonny Mehta died last month, he said he wanted to be remembered not so much as a publisher, writer or critic, but "as a reader." Vivian Gornick, master non-fiction stylist and *New Yorker* staffer, seems to have the same sentiment. The book begins with a dedication to Randall Jarrell, of which she says "[H]e was the man who believed we are devoted to the act of making literature because it leads us to the act of reading." She dealt with many literary peregrinations in her last, marvelous *The Odd Woman In The City: A Memoir*, a version of Alfred Kazin's *Walker in the City*, but with less biographical (of authors) dead weight and with the zest and verve of her usual style. These dues-paying anecdotes of encounters with life-changing writers give us all we can ask for in a memoirist and critic—the time and place of the life-changing book; the utter uniqueness of the subject's style; a straightening of the reputation of some (particularly Colette) who have suffered some unwise, glib, diminishing effects of time.

With Colette, Gornick says "[W]hen I was in my twenties, my friends and I read Colette as others read the Bible. She was our book of wisdom; we read her for solace and for moral instruction." "We read her to learn better," she goes on, "who we were, and how, given the constraints of our condition, we were to live." As a woman, she felt that society's prejudices could be flipped to her advantage. Her condition of being female made for the following paradox: "[W]e imagined for ourselves lives of worldly independence and we understood that Love (as we had known all along) was the territory upon which our battle with Life has to be pitched." (This brings to mind the Yeats 'Crazy Jane' poem that states "Love hath pitched his mansion/In the place of excrement.' Gornick's view was that no one understood this better than Colette—show girl, call girl, mistress to literary giants, and indefatigable writer of the best memoirs in the French language. Her work, to Gornick, sounded depths of understanding that were like "nothing we had ever encountered." To Gornick, being swamped by sexual attraction had the power of metaphor—the intelligence riveted your eyes to the page, gathered up you scattered, racing attention, and made of the subject of a woman in love as lofty a subject as religion, war, catastrophe. The rigidity of male-female perceptions strikes her as best put in 'The Vagabond,' and in the following passage:

> How is it that the man who is in love with me is not in the least disturbed that he knows me so little? He clearly never gives that a thought...[never] does he show any eagerness to find out what I am like, to question me or read my character, and I notice that he pays more attention to the play of light on my hair than to what I am saying... How strange that all is! There he sits next to me...[but] he is not there, he is a thousand leagues away!

She notes how Colette grieves, via the character Renée, some deep dishonesty and animal crudity in the sexual transaction: "The next time [our bodies] touch our souls will withdraw again behind the barrier of the same dishonest but disobedient silence...we had learned already that embracing gives us the illusion of being united and silence makes us believe we are at peace." There can be deep deceptions in the act of love, but there is a mutuality about it. Someone blames the other for some superficiality afterward, but both know the game when they are having at it.

Gornick is at her best in the opening essay on Lawrence's *Sons And Lovers*, and only through her examination of it do I now understand a professor's pronouncement that it was the first 'Modernist' novel. Her Oedipal deconstruction of Lawrence's text is masterful, overpowering earlier analyses by Joyce Carol Oates and Geoff Dyer. The sons all loathe the collier father who Paul Morel's mother seems to mold into the gritty man's opposite. At the same time, no one can shake off the fact that they all *are* him, a vessel of his philistine, immoderate anchor to the upward aspirations of their lives. Paul Morel, who the Mother pedestalizes into an object of sensitive and erotic transcendence, also realizes he would be passionless and obtuse without his father's drinking and dancing with which he follows a day down the Nottinghamshire bucket-cave. Paul contains the multitudes of the rube and the intellectual, which makes for the dissonance that give the narrative its magic velocity: "But if he had let himself think about the split within himself, it would have made him ill; so Lawrence doesn't make him think about it, but allows the reader to do so." If Fitzgerald's maxim that genius is the ability to hold contrary ideas in the mind without breaking down, without being forced to choose between them, then our hero Morel is at an incipient stage of that balancing. When it fully ripens, he can make his escape to London; he contains a great deal of Lawrence himself, without the author's didacticism that so repelled salon society.

All this illustrates the experimentation contained in the novel, and what my early prof was getting at. Much of modernism—Hemingway, Dos Passos—had the author plunking character development externally into an obedient character who takes it gratis, develops it a little, but can sometimes have very little cognizance of its origin or self-creation and, ultimately, his awareness of it. But with Paul, and his vacillation between erotic love and the life of the mind, Lawrence has his vibrant, living laboratory. As Gornick says, "It is through [Paul] that Lawrence will investigate how much devotion either to the flesh or the spirit is required to address what I now saw as the underlying concern of *Sons and Lovers*: how to construct a self from the inside out." In other words, the turbulent, unbalancing, but ultimately competent construction of the artistic personality.

Gornick is particularly good on the vacillation—the vagaries and vicissitudes—of the animal/spirit divide in the artist, and the ability to switch perspectives instantly and incisively and to undergo the pain of being at home with one's confusions. "This habit of Lawrence's of making the character suffer two or even three reversals of judgment in the space of a single paragraph, is a vivid presence in the book." "It not only signifies," she goes on, "the routine instability of one's actual moods, it nails the torment at the heart of any decision rooted in mixed emotions... I feel viscerally the shock of Lawrence's acuity in tracing the staccato nature of emotional confusion." Most importantly, Gornick recognizes Lawrence's mastery (F.R. Leavis placed him in 'The Great Tradition' of British novelists) of a writer becoming comfortable within his or her confusions, that negative capability in not grasping after an escape from a confused but insightful state.

Gornick is simply unbeatable as an all-purpose critic. Reading her is bracing, exhilarating, and always foregrounds what the artist purely presents through the text, and eschews the windows of theories and social contexts that detract, dissipate, and send so much criticism into ideological ruts.

Strout, Again

Olive, Again
Elizabeth Strout
Random House: 235 Pages

Strout's first novel, *Amy & Isabelle* (1998) received widespread critical acclaim. It was one of those rare works of literary fiction that climbed the best-seller lists in all media, and gave Elizabeth Shue an excellent film debut. Strout overcame the second novel curse with *Abide With Me* (2006). The reception was tepid but it was by no means ignored. Within two years she wrote a modern classic, *Olive Kittridge (2008)*, garnering not just critical and commercial success, but sales of $25 million by May 2017. It also won the 2009 Pulitzer for fiction. Within the next decade saw *The Burgess Boys* (2013), also a national bestseller and a darling of the critics. She seemed to be—with her mastery of family nuances—turning into the new Anne Tyler or Meg Wolitzer. Then came *My Name Is Lucy Barton* (2016). Lucy Barton next became the compelling main character in Strout's 2017 *Anything Is Possible,* and now we have its marvelous sequel, *Olive, Again.*

At one time (a very short time) she hedged her bets with a law degree [a very dear subject to this writer], commenting to Terry Gross on the experience as follows:

> I wanted to be a writer so bad that the possibility of failing at it became almost unbearable to me. [Law school was more of an operation for me, I think.] I really didn't tell people as I grew older that I wanted to be a writer—you know, because they look at you with such looks of pity. I just couldn't stand that.

You do not have to read *Olive Kittredge* (or see its amazing HBO series with Kate Winslet) to enjoy *Olive, Again*. But you will certainly want to. New layers of the woman's life are laid on like paint or wallpaper, making her even more vivid and mischeviously likeable. Explaining the genesis of her sequel she has written: "That Olive! She continues to surprise me, continues to enrage me, continues to sadden me, and continues to make me love her." Strout continues to plumb the heartaches of her characters, to give you what Yeats called her "moments of glad grace." She continues to set her story-linked novels in a sort of *Winesburg, Ohio* milieu, with her cumulative, time-lapse portrait of the people of the citizens, the broken-hearted citizens, of Crosby, Maine.

This novel starts shortly after the death of her husband Henry, and when she strikes up a friendship with Jack Kennison, a Harvard professor whom she and Henry had blown off as an entitled nothing, never moving his discipline, or the department of the school, in any sense forward. She re-assesses her sharp judgment of Kennison after learning that he had collapsed on a hiking path, and Olive learned that he, too, was lonely following the recent death of his wife, and suffered regrettable alienation from his own first child. It takes the edge of everything in her that is bossy, cranky and brave. But it leaves the compassion that was discernible by deft members of her first book's treatment.

Olive is not, bear in mind, without her curmudgeonly misanthropy. In one of the 13 linked stories, she recalls a "stupid baby shower, its inane chatter about preschools, outfits, fussiness in infants and in detached, wandering husbands." But things start to get happy with violent speed, and Olive has to abandon her cynicism about "talk of varieties of booties" to actually assist in the birth of the baby in question. "Labor brilliantly sets the tone of love-hate with humanity that animates the entire book.

Olive begins to see the truth of Martin Amis's maxim that the problem with old age is that "it gives nothing back." "Olive did not understand why age had brought with it a kind of hard-heartedness toward her husband…something she had seemed unable to help… as her heart became more constricted, Henry's heart became needier; What crime had he been committing, except to ask for her love?"

Another compelling story is "The End of the Civil War Days."

Here a couple lives in vicious detachment in a house divided by yellow police tape, necessary to secure her loss of dignity after she catches her husband in one of his affairs. It is enforced even though the affair was long ago: "Back then there was no forgiveness and no divorce." Their uneasy equilibrium is fractured when the one, true and common success of this union—before the affair—is the return of a beloved daughter who has also been tainted by the world's benighted graininess. The girl suddenly announces that she wants to become a dominatrix. Just when gleams of hope come through the clouds, the vagaries of these characters' lives roll over the sunny spot with the force of an angry thunderhead.

More than in her previous novels, this second Olive is conveyed in more precise, clear, clean and unaffected prose. An argument can be made that Strout is one of our better stylists, the sheen and effortless virtuosity of her diction and rhythms can be intoxicating. The polish of her sentences can almost blind you—but clarity and tranquility are the after-effects, so matter how strenuous the etiology. One of her great talents is ranging over an incredible variety of minds: the young with their insecure wonder; adults with their striving and envy and eventual compromise; and the old with their social failures and belated epiphanies. A gem of this genre is "Helped," where a woman has lost both her husband and her house in a terrible conflagration. Picking through the burned lumber and tainted ashes is heartbreaking to the narrator; it is almost unbearably painful and insightful for the reader.

Strout belongs to the indispensable canon of Alice Munro, Ann Beattie, Anne Tyler, the indefatigable Kate Walbert, and Hilary Mantel. She has the great mixture of urban and rural, she has the half-retired Northeast of Penobscot Bay down cold, and she shows a promise that restores our faith in the novel, the short novel, the linked-stories novel. Her Crosby, Maine is a shimmering, edgier adjunct to Anderson's Winesburg. She has staked out a territory all her own, a landscape that is pure beauty and enlightenment—not always pleasant—to find oneself walking through. It is a primordial forest of Freudian complications, set in a 21st century milieu that is dead accurate and shiveringly entertaining.

A Gay Rights Prophet

The Deviant's War
Eric Cervini
Farrar, Straus: 494 Pages

When you drive down Seventh Avenue in New York City, just before Sheridan Square and the Christopher Street Cigar Store, you can see the Stonewall Building on the left. One might expect a monument of some sort there, but there is only the glossy, nondescript building, its sides shining above the river of cars, its bottom floor no more than a utility space now. In 1969, a gay bar by the same name inhabited this space, and one night, in response to police harassment, gay male patrons fought back with pitchers, chairs, and their fists and boots, and the provisional army branch of the gay rights movement was born overnight. It was the place where gay liberation would show itself to the world at the exact moment it took the world's violence into itself—the commitment to fight back, keep battling and eventually prevail. In the fickle whims of history, it was a long time coming. It was the acme of a movement that by its very nature had to be secret, whose members practiced a reluctant but necessary secrecy, and whose explosion had been foretold by a handful of courageous foreseers—people who gestured and wrote and spoke in a code that allowed them to be who they must be, beneath a forced mask of society's disguises.

Long before that night, a gay Jewish scientist named Frank Kameny challenged the anti-gay orthodoxy of nearly every kind of workplace, specifically the academic scientific establishment, which by all accounts and common sense should certainly have known better. His sheer determination began to chip away at homosexual barriers to tenure and college administration, and laid the groundwork for gay people to work in an environment similar to the one in which they were beginning to finally, openly conduct their lives. He was an unstoppable dynamo, a valiant writer and speaker whose politics would seem accepted and almost commonplace now, but who had to raise the weapons of his insight against the sightless, powerful barriers of the Other, the straight world that wanted to keep homosexuals, to the extent they would be acknowledged at all, out of sight and out of mind.

Kameny was born in Queens in 1925, to a middle-class family in Forest Hills. Soon enough he displayed a Kripke prodigiousness, the ability to master mathematical and spacial models and calculations, and carry them around in his head like a Mozart overture, all before he entered primary school. When he started first grade, he had been reading for three years, books strewn throughout his tiny attic room where he had assembled a telescope. Within a year or two he settled on a career as a scientist, and chose astronomy, fascinated as he was by the blanket of stars he watched arc over the waters of Long Island Sound. He showed bravery in WWII combat, and on the GI Bill took a Ph.D in astrophysics from Harvard, beginning an academic career by teaching astronomy at Georgetown. Soon after he returned to the military and became a topographer for the Army Map Service. Sputnik had shaken the U.S. government out of its late 50s torpor, and he was pegged as an expert mapper of both terrestrial and extraterrestrial spaces.

Government policies, especially in areas like his that had espionage uses, had long barred homosexuals from military work or work at private companies with government contracts. It was part of a larger system begun in the 30's that forbade queer characters in films, forbade bartenders from serving gay clientele and banned them from teaching in most schools. They were surveilled extensively by local police and the FBI, and if the pink triangle went into your 'file,' those arrest records were forwarded to federal agencies that held a monopoly on employee background checks. By 1957 this policy had taken its toll on Kameny. He was terminated from the AMS when their HR department discovered he had been arrested in California for cruising a public toilet in a beach town. Though many tried to move on, Kameny discovered, during his long unemployment, that almost any federal astronomy job required a security clearance. His choices were few. He had to fight it. His administrative remedies seemed to deepen the hole he had found himself in. He took his plea upward to the secretary of the Army, the head of the Civil Service Commission, and to congressional leaders, including the president himself.

He was befriended by like-inclined attorneys, and began litigation that would be the first on record for sex-choice equality. His legal team took things all the way to the U.S. Supreme Court, already inundated with racial equality appeals. They denied cert to his wrongful termination petition. He was barely existing, working odd jobs to pay rent and feed himself. Kameny came to believe that a more effective platform than litigation would be an organization, watching the formation of identity groups like the NAACP and the Student Nonviolent Coordinating Committee. In 1961, he founded the Mattachine Society of Washington. While prior gay organizations had concentrated on finding jobs and sustenance for those fired over their sexual preference, Kameny, again looking to direct-action tactics of the civil rights movement, decided that platforms, manifestos and polemic would further the cause faster and more effectively. Through the Mattachine organization, he at first only helped fired gay civil servants regain their jobs. But soon he became more public, battling against irritated congressional committees and organizing the first gay picket of the White House. (Congressional Savonarolas were at their high tide, and ironically, the most hostile and famous of all, Joe McCarthy, is rumored in Robert Tye's new biography to have been gay, as was his assistant Roy Cohn, who in turn was lovers with an alleged "spy" his boss had in his crosshairs.) Finally, in 1971, he became the first openly gay candidate for Congress. But he never gave up on litigation, realizing the judicial branch of government would be the most receptive as standards of tolerance were evolving as the result of Sixties social movements. He set out at that point to find L.G.B.T.Q. activists willing to become plaintiffs in employment discrimination cases. It was still two years before Stonewall when he convened a homophile convention, and had it adopt the Mattachine platform of encouraging in gay people "feelings of pride, self-esteem, self-confidence and self-worth . . . . these feelings being essential to true human dignity."

Kameny has been profiled before, most notably in John D'Emilio's "Sexual Politics, Sexual Communities" and David K. Johnson's "The Lavender Scare." What Cervini adds to the scholarship is a perspective on Kameny's initial reluctance to go public as a political crusader, and his problematic relationship with the police-repressive apparatus that patrolled the Manhattan streets by night. It was almost as if the offshore tsunami of Stonewall was waiting for its incipient prophet. Kameny both was and was not that figure. The zeal that gave fuel to his cause also made him a difficult manager of organizations, given to what seemed to many to be petty squabbling and an obsession with hierarchy and titles. Perhaps what he never enjoyed in the military chain of command found expression in these later turf wars in the ever-evolving organizations.

Cervini is a fine writer, one of our foremost chroniclers of L.G.B.T.Q. history and a meticulous and exacting scholar. Fearful of bogging down in too much analysis, he writes at a clip that allows history to unfold before your eyes, but leaves gaps in the meaning and significance of key events. Allowing political action to speak for itself would be more appropriate for a novel. We yearn for more exegesis in biographies, especially those of political and identity-politics leaders. Cervini's position seems to be that Stonewall speaks for itself, and that his subject's work leading up to it gave the gay rights movement its indelible stamp and forward momentum. Kameny was there every step of the way. Without him there would have been no Harvey Milk, no Larry Kramer or Tony Kushner, no pre-enabled warriors to carry the rainbow banner through subsequent decades. It is a pity he did not live to see the two giant and recent Supreme Court decisions—on gay marriage and Title VII discrimination—that were exactly the judicial recognition he fought so hard for.

Out on the High Wires

Instructions for a Funeral
David Means
Farrar, Straus & Giroux: 190 pages

Not much happens in a David Means story. But then suddenly everything does, especially the violent wounding of the male psyche, its turning into itself to form the harsh outlines—and sometimes the soft corners—of that battered, constantly turning wheel of effects that fog up out of the Great Lakes. These are Means's signature venues. Returning to this form, his new book starts with a quote from William Carlos Williams: "To refine, to clarify, to intensify that eternal moment in which we alone live there is its single force—the imagination." Williams's great friend Wallace Stevens also thought that "God and the Imagination are one." ("The Final Soliloquy of the Interior Paramour"). When this aesthetic and ethic are poured into the vessels of Michigan's Upper Peninsula or Cleveland's waterfront flatlands, the result can be artifacts that don't quite fit into Stevens's "sublime"; their effects are more like a gritty authenticity, the sparks that come from flint and steel waiting to combust a nest of riven string.

The first piece in this book, "Confessions," floored me when a version of it came out in Harpers, disguised as a sort of essay about the perils and vagaries of patrimony. In exploring the older man and the version of him that has descended into the author, Means investigates extensively, and would not dream of coming up with something as tidy as an "answer." His stories cohere, and are among the stylistic majesties of our literature now. But he is as fascinated by ephemera as he is of solid earth and steel, all of which populate his stories with a rusty, dilapidated vengeance. "Of course, part of any job is to look like you're doing the job, and to pretend to be exact even when in truth you're never going to get close to the ideal point of precision." Precision within rumination, within reverie—this is

Means's powerful and utterly unique terrain. He navigates it like nobody else, and is amassing a body of work that honors and exalts the short story.

Means sees all of us as facing eternity, and the varieties of confrontation follow the past that has been injected into each knowing subject. Means's profound recognition is that we are all facing, before that (blissful or damning) oblivion, a common set of quotidian concerns. Most of the people facing them are Midwestern mental patients, down-and-outers, broken down into fragments and their respective attempts to reassemble. Two of the stories borrow themes from Cheever, most notably that of the homeless, feckless brother. Each of the brothers is named Frank, or Frankie, and the one that takes its name from Cheever involves a group of men sitting around on the steps of a halfway house, smoking and jabbing at one another. The narrator steps into the scene like something out of the New Journalism. Means destabilizes things by introducing a first-person narrator who says "I'd like to pause at this point." He goes on: "If I put Frankie's story in here, flashing forward, it would seem forced and ill-suited to the actual situation at hand, which included me at the top of the stairs." This reifies the narrator's involvement, but stresses he must remain a spectator, unable to step in and change anything about the sibling who holds forth at the stoop's gritty bottom step. One can be either the artist or the liver of life, but not both. And the viewpoint of the former makes living, especially as a caregiver, an influencer of a family member, seemingly impossible.

The second male sibling story is "Two Ruminations on a Homeless Brother." Here too we see the dreadful necessity and at the same time the pain of detachment. Like a sax solo, Means's prose meanders around the brothers' relationship, their interface with other siblings and their father (the father of "Confessions"?), and most importantly the world. The story opens with a life-slice of a homeless man going about his existence, and there is no indication, other than in the title, of any dance between observer and observed. The voice then shifts into the second person, with phrases like "It's not just that ..." The narrative devolves into a kind of deposition, with this line beginning as the topic sentence of every paragraph. There is no resolution in the resolution, where the narrating brother is realizing that a second barrier—concrete and barbed wire—also keeps the brothers apart, something other than estrangement. One brother is in the joint and the other isn't—"It's not just that in the car before going up on the third visit you'd granted yourself a bitter kind of solace, because you were not locked up there and he was." There is resignation, acceptance here. It may be, in its single dimensionality, the only kind of caregiving the reluctant observing brother can satisfy.

One thing that becomes clear in Means is that for every impulse of violence, that violence we saw in the beginning as being a male's métier in America, there is a redemptive potential waiting to be mined, a kind of earthly grace that could be a counterpoint to Flannery O'Connor's Thomist balm. In the story "The Ice Committee," a Vietnam vet recalls how he and a buddy were in the Tet Offensive firefights of Hue, where the U.S. Army fought off the Viet Cong at tremendous cost. They call in air support, a signal of both their fear and humiliating inadequacy:

> We hated them the way you'd hate any savior. They saved your life and took it at the same time, if you know what I mean.

The drifters hanging with the narrator don't have any idea of what he means here, not even the Hue buddy. But the reader picks up on it, seeing the fearful child frozen in the man tipping his machine gun over the Citadel wall. The frightened kid is both saved and broken, the inbound fighters marking him as someone who couldn't quite chisel out his own and his platoon's salvation. The same kind of weak inner hero populates both "Fistfight, Sacramento, 1950," and "The Tree Line, Kansas, 1934." The American male seeks self-definition in violent conflict. It is easier to lash out in self-formation than to exhibit the vulnerability which love can pierce. For O'Connor, the love came from God. For Means, it comes from his iron detachment, his ability to see the narrator's limits, his realization that a moral education is not so much a firm arc as an amorphous, foggy reverie. It is something where answers swim away but self knowledge gives a kind of peace, a species of living with what is and with the limits of what obtains. Means has made this his literary terrain, and holds fast to it, seemingly startled by its variety and abundance.

Means's world is not one of clear reflective surfaces. Rather, he works in the shards and fragments of broken bottles and tossed windowpanes, the kind of litter thrown from the bridges and city tenements of his Michigan childhood. But the flash-back, the illumination, is just as bright as what we think of as clarity. It is more feeling than thought, more atmosphere than venue, more quandary than resolution. It is a fictional world we cannot do without.

The Traveling Chair

The Mercy Seat
Elizabeth Winthrop
Grove Press

Two weeks ago, Justice Sonia Sotomayor dissented from a Supreme Court denial of an emergency stay of execution for a condemned inmate in Tennessee. It was a straight-up Eighth Amendment argument, with Sotomayor positing that the three-stage death cocktail's first step—completely anesthetizing the condemned with the tranquilizer Versed—was sometimes unsuccessful, proven to be so in other identical executions. This left open the strong possibility that the prisoner would remain conscious to feel both the stage-two respiratory suppressant, and then the final-stage circulation blocker potassium chloride, which Sotomayor described as the equivalent of being "suffocated, and then burned alive." "If we let his execution go forward," she concluded, "we lapse back into accepting barbarism."

Keeping the discussion in an unforgiving, Old Testament vein for a moment, the Mercy Seat was, according to the Hebrew Bible, a golden lid on the Ark of the Covenant that two cherubim beat into a rounded shape so that God would have a place to sit in the peripatetic first and second Temples. Artists' renderings of it look like something out of the Liberace Museum, but there you have it. The Big Guy had big work to get to. He wasn't picky about the furniture.

The history of capital punishment in the U.S. goes to the very core of the country's "judicial character" (J. Blackmun, 1992), and could and indeed has filled entire libraries. A young novelist named Elizabeth Winthrop has given us, in her own "Mercy Seat," the slightest glimpse of that history, but one which concentrates execution's pros and cons amazingly in the space of a few months in post-war 1945 Louisiana.

The Mercy Seat focuses on the pre-midnight execution of a young black man, Willie Jones, for rape. The framing details are taken from the execution of Willie Francis, a 16-year-old convicted of killing a white pharmacist several years before. Willie Jones, the first of nine voices narrating the novel, takes a stab at calming detachment by marveling at the fact that he will be one of the first victims to be given a seat in the travelling electric chair. That's right, a travelling electric chair. As the high summer midnight approaches, a crowd gathers around the penitentiary wing where Willie and his father—the only other black voice—appear respectfully for the boy's head to be shaved. "You got to be clean to see the Lord" says the prison barber, dipping his razor in an old tin pail. The warden sneers that the current cannot travel through hair: "You gotta be bald, boy, so [it] can pass right through that thick skull. Ain't got nothing to do with the Lord."

This is an author who has read and internalized her Faulkner (*As I Lay Dying*), as there are few if any mis-steps in the increasingly sharpening, deeply insightful characters' ruminations. The most salient voice is Willie's, resonating with *To Kill A Mockingbird*'s Tom Robinson in seeing an overarching, sourceless guilt in simply being who he is in the Gothic Jim Crow vice of injustice. If his impending death is at all comprehensible, it springs from the guilt he feels for his lover's suicide once her father discovered their affair. (Of course, her voice is the one we miss most, and lives only in echoes of the thwarted town's nervous, unprepared "rememberers.") The only thing the book could use more of is additional black voices, Willie's community, whether they be startled or furious or numbed into resignation.

Given the gravity of what is looming, and of the uniqueness of the new, macabrously mobile device that will take Willie's life, it is the executioning forces that suffer the worst pains of indecision. No one has yet to see the travelling chair, inching down the two-lane blacktop from Angola in an ominous, tarp-covered truck. The district attorney is surprised and ashamed at how easy the prosecution went, and examines his motives in light of exculpatory witnesses and documents. Among the best, most believable and historically informative voices is that of his wife Nell. A stranger to the South, she feels lost in what she sees as its backwardness and cruelty, and views her husband's agenda as repellant enough to undercut her love for him, and for humanity as a whole. Much of the dreadful power of the place is self-made or imagined, especially for the stranger. Its forces appear infinitely strong, Satanically dark and sudden, but then just as quickly vanish, fragmenting into oblivion:

> The women in line behind her [at the Gulf fishmonger's] were talking about the boy, how it was sad that even the young ones couldn't keep their trousers zipped. She'd stared hard at the glassy round eye of a snapper on ice.
> Behind her, a moth thumps madly against the screen, and when she reaches out to brush the moth away, she is surprised by the power of its beating wings against her palm, less butterfly than beast, a ball of flapping fury that turns into dust against her hand.

The parish priest is tortured by what approaches, wondering at the hubris of men who take upon themselves the task of God, the task of death. He is driven back to the alcohol that nearly wrecked his seminary days: "He runs his finger around the wax seal … and thinks: he should pray, he should pray; it was prayer, at first, that saved him from the stuff. But when he shuts his eyes to speak to God, he finds he has nothing to say." His calling cannot protect him from the inferno in which he lives; like Pascal, the motions of grace, the goodness of the heart—these things cannot equip him to push back against external circumstances. Like Nell, he feels the sting of the South's utter strangeness: "[H]e feels he hasn't found his footing yet, a way of wading through blind hate; the South feels more foreign to him than his mission in Madagascar ever did."

Midnight approaches as the wall clocks tick the seconds away, into the brimming void. Willie's father burdens the back of his mule with his son's incipient headstone, and even gets it set up in the cemetery. Breezes blow across the marshy Atchafalaya flatland as the chair makes its journey south to the special unit. The thing is finally unloaded. The workers note that the wood is not smooth and uniformly colored as was reported, but shows marks of singed flesh, shadows of gripping hands, and rips and tears in its canvas harnesses. The wires are checked, the auxiliary loads on the wall are set for the prison captain to throw the switch. His guards are glib and jocular—it's just another black boy going "to take the juice." Like a piece of ironing, the dust is shaken from the hood that will go on Willie's head.

In an unexpected ending that can only be conveyed in voices, the chaplain's questions of hubris are answered with irony, hope, and the foibles of man's best-laid plans. This writer is not a spoiler and will say only that Winthrop pulls off a staggering, bravura conclusion. The hood comes off and we turn around, blinking at where we are. Have heaven and hell changed places? Who is dead and who is truly alive? We recover ourselves, recover our composure and our hope, and ready our suspenseful thirst for Winthrop's next journey for us, into her next new land of unlikeness.

Photo: Amelia Wirick

Richard Wirick is the author of four books that have been translated into more than ten languages. *One Hundred Siberian Postcards* (2006), short memoir-fiction pieces, was a *London Times* Notable Book and nominated for the PEN/Bingham Award for best first work by an American writer. It was followed by another story collection, *Kicking In* (2010). The novel *The Devil's Water* was published in 2014, and a new novel, *Volta: Chapters Of The Ghost Year,* is forthcoming in 2022, as well as a third story collection. He writes for a wide variety of periodicals in the U.S. and U.K., and is a senior voting member of the National Book Critics Circle. Originally from the Midwest, he practices law in Los Angeles, where he lives with his family.